BLACK MEN
and
BUSINESSMEN

Kennikat Press
National University Publications
Series in American Studies

General Editor
James P. Shenton
Professor of History, Columbia University

Steven M. Gelber

BLACK MEN
and
BUSINESSMEN

The Growing Awareness of a
Social Responsibility

National University Publications
KENNIKAT PRESS • 1974
Port Washington, N.Y. • London

Library of Congress Catalog Card No. 74-77654
ISBN: 0-8046-9062-6

Manufactured in the United States of America

Published by
Kennikat Press Corp.
Port Washington, N.Y./London

TO MY MOTHER AND FATHER

Contents

Acknowledgments

Irvin G. Wyllie, Chancellor of the University of Wisconsin—Parkside, was instrumental in getting me the grant for my initial research in the area of business employment policies toward blacks. The Johnson Foundation of Racine, Wisconsin, supported the preliminary study.

I owe a special thanks to E. David Cronon of the University of Wisconsin—Madison for his helpful assistance throughout the development of this study. Edward Coffman and Ralph L. Andreano of the University of Wisconsin—Madison read the text and made many valuable suggestions. My wife Hester was especially helpful in her gentle but unyielding criticism of both organization and style.

While I used many libraries and received great assistance from librarians, I am particularly grateful to Hester Grover, Archivist, and Mercy Johnston, of the American Friends Service Committee archives at Haverford and Philadelphia.

BLACK MEN
and
BUSINESSMEN

Introduction

The civil rights revolution of the 1960's produced a fundamental change in the attitudes of American businessmen toward Negro employment. Prior to the racial unrest of the sixties employers at their worst had practiced blatant racial discrimination against blacks. At their best, businessmen had been color blind, requiring that blacks conform to all the qualifications traditionally demanded of whites. However, after the civil rights revolution elements of the business community embraced the idea of "affirmative action," which meant that employers not only gave blacks equal opportunity but took positive steps to see that blacks were recruited, hired, and promoted. The affirmative action programs did not significantly reduce the level of black unemployment and underemployment. But whatever its lack of impact on black economic problems, business acceptance of affirmative action marked a radical departure from traditional employment practice. Affirmative action was the result of a long and complex process in which businessmen altered their personnel policies in order to maintain the most satisfactory relationship with their changing socioeconomic environment.

Through their protests, American Negroes were able to bring about increased government pressure for black employment. The combination of black and government demands changed the attitudes of the white public, which in turn created the setting in which the business community could alter its traditional discriminatory practices. As a result of black activism society as a whole came to accept employment discrimination as a social problem, and therefore business attempts to eliminate unfair employment practices became socially responsible activity. A thread of corporate social responsibility runs throughout American business history, but it was not until the late 1960's that the business community could count employment integration in its census of good deeds.

While it took a social revolution to get employers to accept their responsibility to hire blacks, that acceptance did not permit the business community to rest easily on its laurels. Black employment after the late sixties frequently embodied affirmative action which required the employer to extend more of an effort to employ blacks than he did to employ whites. Affirmative action meant additional costs for hiring sometimes less qualified blacks and ran counter to the two most fundamental values of the American businessman. The extra expense violated the Capitalist Ethic, which mandated minimizing costs to maximize profits, and the selecting of less qualified blacks over more qualified whites violated the American Creed of equal opportunity. Although affirmative action was the most socially responsible course of action in the lates sixties, it left the business community confused and divided because such social responsibility flew in the face of society's most cherished traditional values.

Thus, in the twenty-five years after World War II businessmen went through three major stages of personnel policy in order to conform to changing social forces. Initially in the forties and early fifties, they refused to apply the American Creed to blacks because they feared the costs of white opposition to black workers. During the late fifties and early sixties, employers hired qualified blacks for production jobs and token blacks for white-collar work. In this way they could exploit the manpower pool while conforming to both the American Creed and the Capitalist Ethic. Most employers refused to move beyond this state of ideological equilibrium, but some of the nation's most important firms adopted policies of affirmative action in the postriot period of the late sixties. These firms once more violated the American Creed, but this time for, not against blacks. They justified their action on the basis of the need for a calm and stable society. Although they were willing to accept some of the short-run costs of affirmative action, it quickly became apparent that voluntary business action was not going to solve the black employment problem, and the business community began to call for increased government assistance either to make affirmative action profitable or to relieve the business community of the responsibility of solving black unemployment.

The fact that businessmen were followers rather than leaders in the process of changing attitudes toward Negro employment in no way reduces the importance of these changes to the economic status of blacks. After a detailed exploration of the relationship between economic growth and employment opportunities for minorities, Dale L. Hiestand concluded that changes in employment patterns were "primarily determined by what are usually called noneconomic variables. These would include the impact of social changes, such as the decrease in racial prejudice and discrimination. . . ."[1] Altered business attitudes led, in turn, to changes in the Negro's economic situation. After 1945, income (whether in terms of real, money, wage-earner, or family income) increased more or less steadily. However, relative to white income, Negroes made little, if any, measurable gain.[2] In occupations, as in income, Negroes steadily moved upward after 1945. Unlike relative income, however, the relative occupational position of blacks did improve, particularly in the skilled trades and lower level white-collar work.[3] No analyst has explained why Negroes improved their relative occupational positions but did not also improve their relative incomes. The answer may lie in the fact that most of the breakthroughs into new jobs after 1945 were of much greater symbolic than numerical value. Employers placed blacks on jobs they had never held before, but the shortage of qualified black applicants plus the inability or unwillingness of industry to train Negro applicants minimized the economic impact of the changes in hiring policy.

Critics often labeled postwar Negro employment breakthroughs as "tokenism." One or two isolated Negroes in a firm may have been tokens in the eyes of the black community, but to the employer they frequently appeared bigger than life, and more numerous. The introduction of blacks into an all-white work force usually marked a major turning point in an employer's attitude toward minority hiring. The success of even a token Negro robbed the employer of his basic arguments against employing blacks. His work force did not walk out at the sight of a black face. His customers did not take their business elsewhere. Successful integration in one department set the stage for integration in other departments. Successful integration in one firm provided a model for other companies to follow. Although second steps and third steps frequently had to wait for some form of external pressure, "tokenism" was a necessary first step in the integration of business.

This study explores the reasons businessmen took steps toward equal employment, how their changing attitudes affected their employment practices, and how their changing personnel policies affected their attitudes toward Negro employment. To some extent I treat the "business community" as a single entity and in doing so I lump together big business and small business, privately owned and publicly owned firms, retail, manufacturing and service industries, unionized and unorganized companies, and firms in diverse geographic locations. Where data permit I try to distinguish differences among the various kinds of business organizations, but where such distinctions are not possible I believe that generalizing to the "business community" is still both useful and legitimate. Despite the important differences among companies there is a "business community" whose general attitudes toward employing blacks can be examined. Obviously at any one point in history there were companies, even large numbers of companies, which did not agree with what I term the business attitude of that particular time. Nevertheless, broad reading in the general and business press, as well as investigation in private sources, does indicate that there is a mood, or spirit, which reflects business thinking at a given time. I will examine how and why that mood has changed since World War II.

The question then arises, did the public expressions of businessmen accurately reflect their real attitudes? Public expressions of belief are voluntary. Businessmen had little reason to lie except if they believed that public profession of a particular set of values would enhance their positions. Unless we assume that all businessmen were chronic and compulsive liars, their printed comments reflected either their own views or the views they felt the public expected. My confidence in the legitimacy of public sources has been bolstered by the lack of conflict between public statements and their comments in private conversations. I have found no major discrepancies between the thousands of confidential interviews which the American Friends Service Committee held with businessmen over the last twenty-five years and the public remarks which many of the same individuals made. Further, in my own experience with businessmen, both in private interviews and at several conferences (where I was not known as a research interviewer) I discovered businessmen generally said the same thing in private as in public, although in more picturesque language.

If we accept the proposition that public expression accurately reflected the attitudes of the business community, the question remains, did business attitudes reflect actual business practice? From the businessman's point of view the answer was yes. From the black community's point of view the answer was no. When employing his first black worker the businessman frequently labored mightily and brought forth a token. He was proud of his action, and to the businessman it represented meaningful implementation of his new racial policy. To the black community which expected solutions to broad economic problems tokenism was a "shuck." But whether they had hired one black worker or a hundred, by the late 1960's most businessmen would probably have professed agreement with Arjay Miller, the president of the Ford Motor Company, who said in 1965, "In today's society the advancement of brotherhood is part of the business of business." Miller went on to claim that American business "had entered an era of entirely new dimensions in its relationships and responsibilities toward communities, the society, and government."[4] I will attempt to explain why and how the business community came to accept Negro employment as a legitimate manifestation of social responsibility in the twenty-five years after World War II.

1

The Concept of Social Responsibility

Two distinct but intertwined forces shaped businessmen's attitudes toward employing Negroes after the end of World War II. First, employers viewed Negro workers from an economic perspective. As a source of manpower, blacks offered employers a large pool of workers willing to labor for artificially low wages. However, black wages were low, at least in part, because businessmen feared Negro employees would be an economic liability. The business community believed blacks in nontraditional jobs would produce unrest among white employees and a drop in sales to white customers. Thus the businessman had to weigh the benefits of cheap labor against the potential costs from white opposition. According to classical economic theory the businessman would make the decision designed to bring maximum profit. To the extent that he made decisions rationally based on profit maximization, the businessman was adhering to the *Capitalist Ethic*.

The *American Creed* is the second force which influenced employer decisions to hire blacks. The creed is best summed up in the words of the Declaration of Independence, "all men are created equal" and have the unalienable rights of "life, liberty, and the pursuit of happiness." Although, as Gunnar Myrdal has noted, Americans have consistently slighted the ideal of equal opportunity in practice, they have nevertheless institutionalized it as part of the capitalist mythology of rags to riches.[1]

Despite the eighteenth century origins of the American Creed, it was not until after World War II that it was widely applied to Negro employment. The postwar period was one of transition in which public demands for equal employment began to compete seriously with public objections to black employment. The shift in broad social attitudes reduced the potential cost of employing blacks and meant that businessmen could adhere to both the Capitalist Ethic and the American Creed. The favorable public reaction to equal employment opportunity for blacks marked the transformation of Negro employment into a form of social responsibility.

Like many such catch-phrases the hotly debated and somewhat amorphous words "social responsibility" had no precise definition. Most users of the term agreed that socially responsible action by a firm included a concern for the good of society rather than an exclusive concentration on profit maximization. While socially responsible action might, in fact, benefit the company, immediate monetary gain was not its prime purpose. One corporate president said he made socially responsible decisions "not with expediency alone in mind, but with a real effort to judge rightness and wrongness. . . ."[2]

Although the employment of blacks did not become a common manifestation of corporate public interest until the post-World War II period, the idea that businessmen had a responsibility to society has deep historical roots. Until the end of the nineteenth century, religious laws theoretically took precedence over economic laws. The church in the middle ages limited the prices and profits of businessmen with the concept of the "just price."[3] In preindustrial America the Protestant businessman was no less obliged to temper his search for profits with moderation and concern for the commonweal. In 1639 the city of Boston fined merchant Robert Keayne eighty pounds and admonished him "in the name of the Church for selling his wares at excessive rates, to the dishonor of God's name, the offense of the General Court, and the public scandal of the country."[4] The growth of American cities decreased the control of the church over the activities of businessmen, while at the same time the development of capitalist economic theory gave business a philosophical rationale for its new freedom. The rise of industrialism not only freed businessmen from governmental interference in pricing, but also gave them a freer hand to deal with their employees. As the factory system replaced earlier methods of manufacture, the traditional protection of the apprentice codes ceased to have any real meaning. Members of the white working class joined black slaves as victims of unbridled economic exploitation.

In the early days of American industrialization employers made some attempts to control the damaging effects of the factory system. Businessmen had successfully thrown off the restraining medieval yoke of the just price, but not all employers were yet willing to treat labor as a commodity subject to the vicissitudes of the open market and the dubious protection of Mr. Smith's invisible hand. The textile mill operators of Massachusetts were among the earliest business practitioners of social responsibility toward employees. The "Waltham System," in which mill owners erected dormitories and kept close watch on the manners and morals of their female operatives, is frequently cited as an early example of socially responsible employers' concern for the well-being of their employees,[5] although even here there is some question as to whether the boarding school environments at Waltham and Lowell were not due more to the manpower needs of the companies and the cultural background of the workers than to the charity of the owners.[6] This concern for employee welfare did not last long. The fierce competition of the postbellum period combined with social Darwinism to produce an age of industrialists who were less concerned with a fair return to consumers and employees, and more concerned with maximum return to investors.

The concept of social responsibility, which had its sources in the religious domination of preindustrial society, virtually disappeared from business thought during the Gilded Age. Late nineteenth-century industrialists used the laissez-faire theories developed a hundred years before by Adam Smith to free themselves from any obligations to society. Instead they developed the rationale that unhampered capitalists operating in a free market would create the most perfect possible world. Inherent in this philosophy was the belief that businessmen could solve all of society's ills. Although in its purest form the laissez-faire philosophy did not require the businessman to do anything but single-mindedly pursue profit, it contained the germ of the belief that when social problems arose, business, rather than government, should solve them. These closely related, if somewhat contradictory, philosophical solutions to social problems would reappear regularly during the twentieth century. On the one hand they prompted the business community to oppose any intervention into social problems, and on the other they led businessmen to claim that only they, and not the government, could alleviate social ills.

By the end of the nineteenth century most industrial leaders accepted the idea that competition would ultimately produce the best society, and they completely disassociated their businesses from the specific problems of the country. With social controls on business lessened, and in the absence of effective legal or voluntary restraint, businessmen felt free to administer their enterprises as they saw fit. William H. Vanderbilt exemplified the divorce of business from society when he informed a newsman that the New York Central Railroad was run not "for the benefit of the dear public," but for the profit of the stockholders.[7] Andrew Carnegie took a similarly isolated view of his business when he told the Stanley Investigating Committee, "I was in business to make money. I was not a philanthropist at all."[8] Of course, like other Gilded Age moguls, Carnegie *was* a philanthropist. However, the captains of industry fulfilled their social responsibility with charity and considered their business affairs to be personal matters beyond either the concern or control of society.

Had more Gilded Age employers shared Andrew Carnegie's "gospel of wealth" and returned their personal fortunes to the people from whom the money had come, perhaps businessmen could have forestalled the anti-big-business aspects of the Progressive Movement. However, the brash statements of contempt for the public welfare and the brasher actions of the robber barons contributed to the rise of Progressivism. During the Progressive Era pressure from the consuming public, from organized labor, and from industrial leaders who wanted to rationalize the economic order forced the business community to become more concerned with the needs of the public.[9] It was a long step from the "public be damned" attitude of the Gilded Age moguls to the placating observation during the Progressive Era of Theodore N. Vail, president of the American Telephone and Telegraph Company, that "we feel our obligations to the general public as strongly as to our investing public, or to our own personal interests."[10] Vail's willingness to concede that business had to judge its actions according to their impact on society as well as to their effects on profits was not a repudiation of the Capitalist Ethic. The antibusiness attitude of the Progressive Era had impressed upon business the necessity of recognizing that long-run profit depended upon public acceptance of business actions and that public acceptance would come only when the people believed business was acting in the public interest. Consequently businessmen began to emphasize the supposed social benefits of capitalism and social concern of capitalists.

Business participation in World War I removed any lingering doubts in the mind of most of the public about the benign nature of American enterprise. For a decade, from the end of World War I until the crash, businessmen retained their positive public image. The 1920's were no less a period of business dominance than the 1890's. Taking their cue from the Progressive period, businessmen in the 1920's integrated their economic philosophy with a positive attitude toward the general welfare. As business historian Morrell Heald has pointed out, "The spirit of boosterism and 'service' which Sinclair Lewis satirized in *Babbitt* filled innumerable business speeches and articles. It was seen, by men who took it seriously, as evidence of a growing sense of responsibility on the part of those best qualified to provide leadership for a permanently prosperous America."[11] Business paternalism toward employees and toward the community depended upon substantial profits and widespread public acceptance of business good intentions. The depression brought an end to both profits and good will. Despite the pressures of the depression, which tended to focus all business energy on mere survival, some corporate leaders retained a callous remnant of their sense of social responsibility. John B. Nicholes of the Oklahoma Gas Utilities Company devised a plan which would have provided the unemployed with five-gallon cans of restaurant table scraps in return for chopping wood.[12]

As World War I had rescued business from the bad press of the Progressive Era, so World War II refurbished the depression-tarnished business image.[13] With the war came recovery. War contracts once more allowed business to earn high profits *and* praise for acting in a socially responsible manner. National mobilization created a unity of purpose which tended to obscure the profound changes the New Deal had caused in the relationship of business with the government and with the consuming public. Under Franklin D. Roosevelt, the government had usurped the role of industry as protector of the American way of life. During the twenties the business community had shouldered the responsibility of taking care of the unfortunate. Through welfare capitalism and widespread support of private charity efforts such as the community chest movement, private enterprise kept the wolves of want from the citizen's door. When, during the depression, businessmen were unable to keep the wolves from the factory gates, employers were forced to concede the protection of the public welfare to federal legislation.[14]

While the war dominated the scene businessmen could work toward the common goal of victory and recoup some prestige they had lost during the 1930's. However, with the end of World War II the business community had to come to grips with the legacy of the New Deal. The people had come to look toward governmental leaders, not business leaders, when they wanted something done. The business community had suffered a sharp, and apparently permanent, drop in status. During the thirties business had made a feeble attempt to counter its weakened image through a campaign to inform the people both of its good deeds and of the benefits of the American economic system.[15] Yet, despite their favorable war experience, businessmen continued to feel unappreciated in the postwar period, and the business community launched a second propaganda drive to convince the public that business had the nation's best interest at heart. The "sell-America" campaign of the early 1950's used magazine advertisements, movies, car cards, and flyers to inform the American people that the economic system of free market capitalism was the solution to all the country's problems. This quixotic crusade in public indoctrination was partly a response to the Cold War, but it was also an attempt by businessmen to assure the people (and perhaps each other) that capitalism was a socially responsible economic system.[16]

The sell-America campaign went through two phases. During the first phase the business community reverted to Gilded Age arguments and tried to deny that it had any specific obligations to the general welfare while at the same time insisting that capitalism would benefit both workers and consumers. The business community explained, through the use of textbook homilies on the merits of the free market, that everybody would profit if each sector of the economy stuck strictly to its own proper sphere of activity. However, the first phase failed to persuade the public that selfishness was good for the country, and it failed to persuade the first Republican administration in twenty years to roll back the economic reforms instituted by the New Deal.

Unsuccessful at convincing the public that the invisible hand of the free market kept a sufficient check on the reins of free enterprise, businessmen tried to demonstrate that the visible hand of business was doing something besides lifting the consumer's wallet. The second phase of the sell-America campaign soft-peddled strict laissez faire and emphasized the business community's commitment to improving the quality of American life. When they discovered the country would not accept a return to the unfettered days of the Gilded Age, a small but articulate number of businessmen and business commentators joined with the Eisenhower administration to try to recreate the climate of the 1920's by espousing increased business social responsibility.[17] The pressure for business to adopt the new approach grew slowly but steadily until the mid-1960's, when employers faced constant and unrelenting demands from the popular and business press to conform to the new norm.

Although opposition voices in the business community continued to make themselves heard well into the 1960's, the concept of the socially concerned businessman became so acceptable that even the Chamber of Commerce of the United States, a conservative organization of small and medium-sized companies, financed major studies of social problems.[18] By 1968 *Esquire* magazine believed so many businessmen wished to be known as socially responsible that it began to cash in on the social concern movement. *Esquire* sent the nation's top five hundred corporations an advertising prospectus which asked, "Can you answer these questions? What is the purpose of your business besides making money? How is your company involved in making this a better world? Of course you can!" answered the magazine to its own rhetorical questions. "Your corporation is probably very much involved in the solution of social problems."[19]

There is no way of ascertaining either the depth or the quality of the business community's acceptance of the concept of social responsibility. The response to *Esquire*'s advertising prospectus was not overwhelming, but the vast majority of the firms that did answer the magazine's appeal expressed agreement with its assumptions. Yet, two surveys conducted in the late 1960's discovered that while businessmen did feel a concern for the problems of society, they were more worried about business problems and less worried about social issues than the population at large. A 1967 National Industrial Conference Board survey asked executives what national problems they felt were urgent enough to warrant company time and money to solve. Very few of the more than one thousand businessmen who replied listed social problems. Businessmen worried most about economic problems directly related to their firms.[20] The fact that this spontaneous listing of national problems placed business difficulties ahead of social concerns was perhaps indicative of the understandably dominant role of the Capitalist Ethic in business thought. However, when faced with a list of fourteen specific social problems, well over half of the same businessmen said their companies would take the initiative to correct the problems.[21]

PERCENTAGE OF BUSINESSMEN WHO SAID THEIR COMPANIES
WOULD ACT TO SOLVE SOCIAL PROBLEMS

Issue	All Respondents
Improvement and expansion of local school facilities	55.6
Improvement of local school curriculum	48.5
Problems associated with school drop-outs	53.9
Improvement of work/career opportunities for minority groups	69.2
Retraining of workers rendered unemployed by automation	72.6
Construction or improvement of medical facilities	62.1
Medical care for the aged	35.9
Provision for or improvement of low income housing	31.3
More and better cultural facilities and activities	59.1
Purification and improvement of water supply	68.3
Reduction and control of air pollution	73.5
Improvement of urban and interurban transportation	60.4
Development of community recreational facilities	55.6
Improvement of law enforcement at local levels	61.4

While most businessmen, in 1967, did not consider social problems high on their list of priorities, 95 percent of them did indicate a willingness to become involved in solving such problems. Even if the businessmen's support for action in the socioeconomic sphere was only public posturing for a national survey, it indicated that businessmen assumed that society expected them to be concerned with the common good.

The following year, in 1968, another survey, done for the National Advisory Commission on Civil Disorders, found that 86 percent of a national cross section of employers felt an obligation to make a strong effort to provide employment for minorities. Nevertheless, when asked to rate the seriousness of a long list of social problems, in 90 percent of the cases the businessmen rated them as less serious than did a general sample of the population.[22]

PROBLEMS IN THEIR CITIES RATED "VERY SERIOUS" BY
EMPLOYERS AND BY THE GENERAL SAMPLE

Problems Rated	Employers	General
Control of crime	64	71
Unemployment	21	36
Air pollution	26	33
Race relations	46	52
Providing quality education	35	45
Finding tax funds for municipal services	41	42
Traffic and highways	31	27
Preventing violence and other civil disorder	50	55
Lack of recreation facilities	11	31
Corruption of public officials	9	19
100 percent equals	434	1,953

Both studies indicate awareness and concern on the part of the business community, although the second survey supports the proposition that businessmen were followers rather than leaders in sensitivity to social problems. Together, the two surveys indicate that by the late 1960's both management and the public expected business to be active in the field of social responsibility, although the studies are certainly no measure of how many businessmen actually were.

Growing public demand for business social involvement in the 1960's conflicted with the traditional view that businessmen should be hard-headed realists who did not confuse the needs of society with the rights of the stockholders. Thus businessmen were faced with what business scholar Thomas A. Petit has called "a moral crisis."[23] On the one hand their business ideology told them they should ignore extraneous demands on their time, effort, and money. On the other hand, the real demands of law, customs, and morals pressured them to act in a publicly beneficial manner, even at the expense of profit maximization. Petit argues that because businessmen found it "easier to accommodate ideology to the operational ethic of social responsibility than to remake the world to fit the ideology of the profit ethic," they changed their ideology rather than their operational ethics.[24] In other words, employers preferred to alter their practices and reinterpret their values rather than maintain socially unacceptable traditional practices merely to conform to ideological orthodoxy.

What Petit calls a moral crisis is merely another name for the tension between the laissez-faire belief that social problems should not even exist in a perfect capitalist state and the business community's belief that it could best solve those problems. Businessmen were thus torn between wanting to do nothing about social problems and wanting to make sure that *they* did whatever was done. This ideological paradox gave rise to several conflicting schools of business thought on social responsibility during the 1960's. The most conservative employers were those who defended the values of what Richard Eells has called "the traditional corporation."[25] Managers of traditional corporations emulated the corporate leaders of the Gilded Age. They divorced philanthropy from business, pursuing the former as private citizens and the latter as pragmatic capitalists concerned primarily with maximizing profits. The traditional businessman was morally certain that the "corporation has no moral obligation nor social responsibility for any kind of joint management of a nation's resources."[26] Or, as *Business Week* editorially noted in 1967, "It is not the business of any corporate management to run a public welfare establishment. Efficient production of goods and services is the name of the business game."[27] The extent of traditional management's social concern was succinctly stated by H. L. Hunt, the Texas oil tycoon and patron of right-wing thinkers, when he said, "The most philanthropic thing a man can do is to provide gainful employment to as many people as possible."[28]

The laissez-faire philosophy of traditional businessmen precluded not only business social responsibility but also governmental action to alleviate social misery. Traditionalists viewed "intellectuals, 'do-gooders,' and reformers" as "naive about human nature and many of the reforms they propose are doomed as impractical by the self-interest of individuals."[29] Although opposition to welfare legislation was particularly strong in the immediate postwar period, it continued to appear in the writings of extremely conservative businessmen and right-wing ideologues well into the 1960's. However, by the time of the civil rights revolution even many traditional executives had begun to take a more conciliatory attitude toward governmental action. For example, in 1968 the president of a major midwestern company which manufactured heavy equipment took the traditional position when he explained that his primary obligation was to use company resources so as to insure maximum profits for shareholders. While he declined to accept business responsibility for social welfare, he did point out that high profits meant high taxes and taxes enabled the government to attend to the welfare of its citizens.[30]

Theodore Levitt has been the most articulate spokesman of the "neotraditionalist" doctrine that the business of government is welfare. The neotraditionalists continued to reject business social responsibility but broke with pure laissez-faire by conceding the right of governments to intervene in social problems. In a widely discussed article that appeared in the *Harvard Business Review,* Levitt vigorously opposed any eleemosynary activities by business. He warned against the potential fascism that might arise from powerful corporations controlling programs outside of their traditional areas of competence. However, Levitt argued that there were social problems which existed despite the benefits of free market capitalism, and he called upon businessmen "to accept the fact that the state can be a powerful auxiliary to the attainment of the good life."[31]

The acceptance by neotraditionalist businessmen of government welfare activity may have been an attempt to reconcile their moral dilemma. If it is true, as one scholar has said, that the business "role sets certain norms which tell the businessman it is wrong to assume diffuse moral responsibilities," and at the same time society demands that "individuals should be guided by 'social conscience' as well as by private conscience," then businessmen could assuage their consciences by shifting the burden of welfare activity from the private to the public sector.[32]

A few large corporations claimed they simply ignored the short-run demands of the Capitalist Ethic and acted in the public interest with virtually no thought of corporate gain. When IBM announced it would build a cable manufacturing plant in the New York City slum of Bedford-Stuyvesant, president Thomas Watson said he did not think the operation would realize a profit in the near future. IBM built the plant, said Watson, because, "a very large company has a responsibility to society as well as to its employees and stockholders."[33] Most corporations, however, were not willing to disassociate themselves so completely from the traditional entrepreneurial goal of profits, and some companies sought to solve the dilemma by pursuing socially responsible goals while at the same time turning a profit. Even the severest critics of business involvement in public welfare conceded the propriety of action which showed immediate economic return. In his otherwise all-out attack on social responsibility, Theodore Levitt hedged by saying, "Corporate welfare makes good sense *if* it makes good economic sense—and not infrequently it does."[34] Showing a profit resolved the moral crisis because it was the perfect laissez-faire solution—solving social problems through profit-making activity.

Although at least one prominent businessman claimed that the self-interest argument was a mailed glove over the velvet fist of humanitarianism, most businessmen seemed unaware of their basically unselfish motivation.[35] For example, Herbert D. Doan, president of Dow Chemical Company, told a group of college newspaper editors that Dow was concerned with "how we can make a buck at social change."[36] Doan's mercenary approach to social problems was echoed by other leading corporate heads. R. V. Hansberger, president of Boise-Cascade, told a meeting that government had failed "utterly with the monstrous problems of our new urban society and is turning to business for help. . . . There need be no compromise of the profit incentive when business turns its attention to the rifts its technology has provided in society," said Hansberger. Even though he admitted that many social problems were the result of business, Hansberger promised "leadership responsible to a new image, to the total needs of society, and *in the enormous and profitable markets represented by those needs*. Society has no other place to go."[37]

Statements about the profitability of social responsibility led some critics to accuse American businessmen of attempting to exploit social problems for corporate gain.[38] Indeed businessmen were trying to do precisely that. While the critics objected to corporations profiting from curing the ills they had caused, businessmen and politicians believed only industry could cure the problems and only profits could tempt them to do so.[39] As one public administrator put it, "Frankly, we must bribe business into the slums."[40]

Businessmen whose firms could not take direct economic advantage of the growing demand for business involvement, or who did not wish to appear exploitative, used the philosophy of Charles E. Wilson, president of General Motors, to justify their acts of public concern. Wilson found it difficult to distinguish between his own company and the nation as a whole and in 1953 told a Senate committee, "for years I thought what was good for our country was good for General Motors and vice versa."[41] The idea that a firm would benefit from improvements to society at large was valid, but as *Fortune* pointed out in 1968 socially responsible acts by business "will presumably benefit not only the corporation that originally shelled out for those good works, but other corporations too, including competitors that poured all their resources into mere profit maximization."[42] Businessmen recognized the obvious validity of *Fortune*'s observation and frequently felt compelled to demonstrate that their corporate good deeds would have some kind of immediate benefit for the company. John D. Harper, president of the Aluminum Company of America, believed that acting in the public interest would result in both monetary and nonmonetary gain. Harper told the National Association of Manufacturers, "If you reduce delinquency, crime and illiteracy you reduce your own corporate tax load, and you convert welfare cases into productive workers. You may even pick up some new customers in the bargain!" He went on to explain that a company could not only make more money but also gain prestige from taking the needs of the community into account. Harper claimed that business support for an orchestra or theater group would help in recruiting professional employees, and could "result in enhancing our reputation as advertising can never do."[43]

However, many business proponents of corporate concern contended that it was enough that social responsibility made for a better society. In the long run a better society would mean better business for everyone.

Henry Ford II told Ford Motor Company shareholders that company executives participated in welfare activities partly for citizenship reasons— "business and industry have an obligation to serve the nation in times of crisis"—but more importantly because "whatever seriously threatens the stability or progress of the country and its cities, also threatens the growth of its economy and your company. Prudent and constructive company efforts to help overcome the urban crisis are demanded not only by your company's obligation as a corporate citizen but by your management's duty to safeguard your investment."[44] Donald J. Gaudion, president of Ritter-Pfaudler, told his stockholders much the same thing, but in somewhat more explicit terms: "I have long been convinced that whether we like it or not, corporate management can no longer remain uninvolved. If we do we will find that extremists are taking over and we will be trying to do business either with fascism on the right or anarchy on the left."[45]

Firms which engaged in public interest activities, whether for profits, for prestige, or for the long-run good of society, usually had one thing in common—high visibility. The companies which acted first were those in the public eye, either because of their size or because of the nature of their product or service. "Immature" corporations with fewer than one hundred employees were not active in "public service," presumably because they were still trying to obtain a minimum level of profit and growth. However, once a firm had grown to one hundred employees, other goals began to play a more important role in the corporate teleology, and the company was much more likely to become involved with the public interest.[46] Not all mature corporations were concerned with the needs of the public nor did all immature businesses ignore social responsibility, but the mature corporation was more frequently the pioneer in social welfare action.[47]

In firms with more than one hundred employees social responsibility was not correlated to sheer size. Large and highly visible firms felt the winds of change earlier and more strongly than their smaller colleagues, but whether a company moved with first breezes or held fast in the teeth of a hurricane depended less on size than on the temperament of the firm's chief executive. Men who owned the companies they managed found it easier to take a strong stand on matters of corporate involvement than professional managers. Social activism, however, was not limited to companies run by their owners. A dedicated and powerful executive, whether he were an owner or a hired manager, set and enforced policy according to his own values. Ultimately the chief executive's beliefs about the proper role of business in society determined how the firm expressed its concern for the common good.

Richard Eells has proposed four goals beyond profit maximization which influence business decisions. First, most businessmen want to be leaders. That is, they want to be recognized by their colleagues as pace setters in all areas of corporate activity. They want to dominate not by power or by influence, but by reputation. Second, Eells says businessmen seek integrity, that is, an honest, ethical, and responsible business career. Although many business critics would claim that this goal is most widely honored in the breach, businessmen frequently use moral arguments to explain company policy. Third, businessmen seek amity. They want to be loved—or at least liked. Businessmen want the same kind of acceptance and approval for their firms that they seek in their personal lives. More-over, businessmen recognize that community acceptance is essential for a favorable relationship with the local government and work force. Finally, Eells lists power and influence as a real, if unstated, goal of corporate executives.[48]

Businessmen who took socially responsible action during the years after World War II almost invariably justified their activity with one of the four goals discussed by Eells. The most important goal appears to have been power and influence. When the capitalist system did not automatically correct its own failings, businessmen wanted to be sure they, not govern-ment, were in charge of the remedial activity. The top-level managers who made company policy enjoyed positions of leadership and power within the firm. Most of them quite naturally believed that businessmen should have power, not only in the firm, but in society as well. Business-men's sense of personal and corporate power led many of them to oppose legislative solutions to social problems. After 1945 most businessmen opposed legislation because they believed business could initiate voluntary action to solve social problems and at the same time prevent the drift of power from the private to the public sector.[49]

Although the public did not always agree, businessmen widely as-sumed that they had the ability to lead the nation in the attack on social ills.[50] At the same time the business community feared that its power to lead the crusade against social problems was being usurped by the govern-ment. In 1960 Keith Davis, a spokesman for the business point of view, said that business had the power to solve social problems[51] and warned that unless businessmen exercised their power they would lose it.[52] The business community widely accepted the logic behind this "iron law of responsibil-ity." Time and time again businessmen called upon each other to exercise their natural leadership and power. In 1967, Arjay Miller, the president of the Ford Motor Company, told a University of Illinois audience that the "efforts to meet the society's most pressing needs will move ahead regard-less of what business does." Thus he noted, "Business has only two choices, to become an unwilling participant in policies and programs it had no hand in developing, or join sensibly and purposefully in helping to map out sound courses of action."[53]

The belief among businessmen that they were the natural leaders of society led easily to a "gospel of wealth" mentality.[54] After World War II the gospel of wealth, or as it has been called more recently, the "public trustee theory," was practically never propounded in its unadulterated classical form. No businessmen claimed they had a God-given right (as did George F. Baer) or a special obligation (as did Andrew Carnegie) to decide what was best for society. Businessmen no longer relied on their monetary success to prove the religious worth of their ideas—at least not explicitly—although Meade Johnson, president of the firm bearing his name, came very close when in 1959 he said, "A free society rewards socially desirable institutions by permitting them to survive and grow."[55] The feelings of paternalism that were almost inevitably associated with wealth and power were reborn into the postwar world in a much milder form. During the 1950's and 1960's businessmen acted more from a sense of personal commitment than from a belief in the divinely inspired obligations of the wealthy.

The morality which inspired some businessmen to pioneer in areas of social responsibility in postwar America was more than the code of business which Eells referred to as integrity.[56] Standard business ethics require fair and honest dealing with competitors, suppliers, and customers. Morality demands adherence to a set of usually religious values stricter than simple honesty. Morality is a code of conduct accepted by a businessman as a guide to total conduct, not just to his actions as a corporation executive.[57] Thus the morally motivated businessman is concerned not only with his corporate dealings, but also with the impact of corporate policy on society and is looking back to the preindustrial society when religious laws governed business practice. In 1968 George Champion, chairman of Chase Manhattan Bank, asked, "Isn't it time somebody stood up and said business should participate because it's the right thing to do—the humanitarian, the moral, the Christian-like thing to do?"[58] Champion was not alone in wanting to keep Christ in commerce. In an emotional response to Theodore Levitt's call for a return to classical capitalist ideology, F. S. Connell, executive vice president of A. O. Smith Corporation, accused businessmen who operated exclusively for profit of being "bloodsuckers." "I believe," continued Connell, "that we must have responsible, God-fearing, hard-headed businessmanship. . . . The fact—not theorem—that faces us now is that we have too much forgotten God, and our responsibilities as His people."[59]

Businessmen who engaged in social welfare activity out of religious scruples placed themselves outside of the accepted capitalist frame of reference. Traditionalist business critics of the Christian theory of public concern called it "startlingly naive" and said it "ignores some of the basic and fundamental realities of historical development and of the contemporary institutional setting in which business enterprise operates."[60] Most businessmen shrugged off religiously based pleas for action, but those few reached by religious considerations were frequently pioneers in initiating socially responsible programs.

Religiously motivated employers frequently led the business community in demonstrating concern for social responsibility because they found it more difficult to reconcile the contradictions between the economic demands of the Capitalist Ethic and the moral appeal of social responsibility. Like all men, businessmen sought to achieve a condition in which their actions were consistent with their values. Faced with a situation in which their expressed values were in conflict with their business policies, employers had a choice of three methods by which to bring their value-action systems into harmony. They could change their actions, they could change their values, or they could rationalize the discrepancy. Whenever circumstances allowed, businessmen almost invariably chose to rationalize. Rationalization permitted them to keep their traditional ideals and to maintain their established methods of operation, while at the same time explaining away any incongruity. However, where a businessman suffered from an acute case of cognitive dissonance, that is, where the inconsistency between values and actions was too strong to be explained away by sophistical excuses, he had to adopt the more extreme solution of changing either his actions or his values. Businessmen with a powerful commitment to personal values would tend to change their actions even in the face of opposition from their colleagues, customers, or employees. Employers who placed less importance on ideology than on minimizing friction with their cultural environment would change their values to conform to the actions society forced on them.

The healthy economic climate of the 1950's and 1960's encouraged businessmen to respond positively to the growing public demand for corporate involvement. As Eli Goldston, chairman of the board of Eastern Gas Associates, told a corporate audience at the Harvard Business School, "Almost anybody can show a reasonable profit in today's growing economy; the challenge is to combine the second ingredient, social benefit to society, and to achieve these while making a profit."[61] The Eisenhower, Kennedy, and Johnson years were good ones for business, and management could afford to conform to the public's new expectations. The importance of the social mood in determining business social responsibility was illustrated by the comments of ALCOA president John D. Harper when he observed, "Business is involved right up to the neckline in hundreds of public problems, and the public—that is to say, our customers, our neighbors, our employees and our stockholders [and he might have added, our colleagues] —expect us to accept the responsibility of helping to solve these problems."[62]

In the final analysis, businessmen became more socially responsible after World War II in direct response to the demands of government and the public. Legally businessmen had to become more responsible, particularly in the field of fair employment, but, equally important, businessmen sought what Eells called "amity," that is, respect from the community. The vice president of the Federal Reserve Bank of Philadelphia, Robert N. Hilkert, put it frankly when he said, "social responsibility is 'in' and business 'in-groups' are composed of men who are deeply concerned about social responsibility. . . . Modern business knows that society *expects* business to be socially responsible and business today recognizes the importance, yes, the necessity, of being responsible to society's expectations."[63]

2

Integration and Legislation: FEPC

The business community's first postwar encounter with the problem of employing Negroes came as a result of the drive to permanently legalize the wartime ban on discrimination in employment during the years 1945 to 1948. While a few businessmen supported permanent fair employment practice legislation, most opposed it. Apart from hard-core conservatives who suspected FEPC was part of a communist plot, most businessmen recognized the inconsistency of their position and attempted to rationalize their opposition to a law that had proven successful in practice and with whose aims they agreed. Thus, right from the start of the postwar period, businessmen experienced the problem of reconciling the Capitalist Ethic and the American Creed.

Since an FEPC law would apply equally to all and therefore eliminate employment policy differences based upon personal values, anti-FEPC employers could not hide behind the Capitalist Ethic by claiming that they would be punished in the market place for integrating their work forces. Instead, while giving lip service to the American Creed, businessmen rose above the relatively mundane argument that fair employment practice would give an advantage to competitors who did not employ Negroes, to more rarefied discussions of freedom of association and freedom from government coercion.

Business aversion to a permanent fair employment practice act probably stemmed in part from a desire to roll back the regulatory encroachments made by government during the depression and the war. Employers saw the battle over FEPC as a symbol of postwar power. If they could stop equal employment legislation, then perhaps they could recoup other elements of their erstwhile status. The business community had made some concessions to the unusual demands of the war, but for the most part they had limited blacks to semiskilled positions. The end of the war meant the end of emergency conditions, and the business community hoped to be

23

able to stop the momentum fair employment forces had generated during the war.

Blacks, even more than most Americans, faced a bleak employment picture on the eve of World War II. World War I had blocked the flow of immigrant labor to American industry and at the same time had stimulated greater production. Employers had met the new manpower needs by recruiting Negroes from the agricultural South. Industrial prosperity and exclusionary immigration laws sustained the demand for black workers through the twenties. But the labor surplus that accompanied the great depression allowed employers to become more selective, and as a result they frequently substituted white workers for Negroes, wiping out earlier gains.[1]

The outbreak of World War II did not appreciably lessen the suffering of Negro workers. Despite the manpower shortage created by the draft and by high levels of wartime production, employers were reluctant to use black labor. Pressure from the black community compelled President Roosevelt to issue Executive Order 8802 on June 25, 1941, which created the nation's first Fair Employment Practice Committee[2] and government pressure through the FEPC combined with the tightening labor market to force more employment of Negro labor. But, while industry employed more Negroes, black occupational distribution did not significantly improve. Most of the movement, for both male and female black workers between 1940 and 1944, was from the farm to the factory, not upward within the factory.[3]

Negroes found jobs primarily in the war-related basic manufacturing industries which held government contracts and were therefore subject to FEPC supervision.[4] Widespread growth of black employment in basic industries improved the economic position of Negroes, but the low quality of the jobs indicated employer reluctance to break traditional segregated patterns. Although there were large percentage increases of blacks in skilled and white collar jobs during the war, the actual numbers were so small as to be meaningless.[5] At the beginning of the war employers limited newly hired Negroes to unpleasant tasks with low status, such as janitorial and service work, or work with noxious and unpleasant material, such as that in foundries and paint rooms.[6] As the manpower shortage increased, however, Negroes began to find jobs as semiskilled operatives in manfacturing plants. The wartime economic expansion opened up large numbers of more desirable (higher paying) jobs to white workers. The upward mobility of the white work force opened semiskilled, skilled, and even some white-collar positions that could be filled by blacks without seriously altering the basically discriminatory makeup of the occupational distribution.[7]

Nothing more clearly illustrated the inherent racism in the economic system than the extravagant praise lavished on firms which made even minimal attempts to upgrade black workers. The Governor's Interracial Commission of Minnesota noted that only a lack of resources prevented it from compiling an "honor roll of every war industry in Minnesota that has upgraded any Negro worker," but it did feel compelled to "record the names of some of the larger corporations . . . that are now not only employing ten or more Negroes but offering positions above that of janitorial work and unskilled labor to the properly qualified."[8] Even though companies were required by government contracts to practice fair employment, and even though only one firm in Minnesota had a single Negro in a position higher than semiskilled production work, the commission praised the advances in Negro employment being made by Minnesota employers.

Most of the first breakthroughs for blacks occurred in plants specifically created to meet military needs. Once the war-production industries set the pattern of employing blacks, other firms followed when they could no longer find white workers.[9] War industries may have hired Negroes first because they suffered the severest manpower shortages, but war industries were also the only businesses covered by Executive Order 8802.

While actual impact of FEPC is impossible to measure, we do know that the thirty-one companies involved in FEPC hearings during the war sharply increased their rate of hiring Negroes. In 1942 almost all of those companies had a smaller percentage of Negro employees than the average for all firms reporting to the War Manpower Commission, but by the beginning of 1944 all of them employed a greater than average percentage of black workers. Most of the increases were in semiskilled production work. The number of skilled workers remained almost unchanged, and the reports did not even bother to mention the number of Negro white-collar and professional employees.[10]

The shortage of labor and the fair employment practice requirements established the broad trend of increased black employment. Utilization of Negro workers in any given industry, however, depended on the policy of the individual employer. A few companies, like Ford at its River Rouge works, had a history of hiring black production workers and even some black skilled workers,[11] but most employers hired Negroes for production work for the first time during World War II. Firms which did not have a tradition of employing any Negroes at all hired them in larger numbers and promoted them more quickly than companies with some history of hiring blacks. Apparently employers found it more difficult to break the habit of only hiring Negroes for menial occupations than to start off the employment of Negroes on an equal basis.[12]

The industries which most readily assimilated new black workers were those that produced products unique to the war economy, such as tanks, warships, and guns, and those which could expand the use of Negroes in such traditional black areas as the foundry. For example, in rubber production, the percentage of Negro employees rose from 3.3 in 1942 to 9.5 in January, 1945,[13] but there was virtually no improvement in the kinds of jobs available. An industrial relations director recalled that when his firm attempted to install black workers in an all-white department of an Akron tire plant, "within minutes every machine in the department was silent. The personnel man led the Negroes out, the machines were turned on, and that department remained lily-white."[14]

There were many war industries which neither set up new plants nor hired large numbers of new employees in the hot, dirty jobs traditionally reserved for black workers. Despite FEPC, opposition from white workers was frequently strong enough in these plants to prevent or severely limit the number of black employees. Opposition to hiring Negroes was sometimes so intense that companies went to the expense of recruiting and transporting unskilled, untrained whites from distant parts of the nation rather than hire the trained Negroes in their own communities.[15] On a number of occasions when employers contemplated hiring Negro women, their white women employees exerted considerable pressure to prevent such a move. The white women feared that industrial employment of Negro women would dry up the supply of domestic labor, or at least drive up the wages for household service. In some communities middle-class housewives believed there were secret "Eleanor Clubs," named after President Roosevelt's wife, subversively undermining the American way by persuading Negro women to leave their service jobs and seek work in industry.[16]

Usually, however, employees opposed black workers because they were black, not because of the impact their employment would have on the labor market. During the war black workers did not economically threaten white workers, but white workers protested the employment of Negroes nevertheless. When the pressures of technological change, labor shortage, and government supervision forced the automobile industry to upgrade its Negro employees, the companies experienced a series of strikes. Unlike the rubber tire plant mentioned above, however, the automobile companies stood firm, and Negroes moved into production jobs.[17]

The aircraft industry was an important exception to the generalization that new rapidly expanding war production industries led in the hiring of Negroes, but it was the exception that proved an important aspect of the rule—Negroes only got low status jobs. Not only did the aircraft industry employ an unusually large number of skilled workers, but it was also a glamor industry which used the appeal of its product to attract the highest quality workers. The aircraft manufacturers considered Negroes inferior workers and feared the blacks would prevent the companies from securing the highly skilled whites they needed.[18] In 1941 North American Aviation officials said Negroes "will be considered only as janitors." Vultee was scarcely more progressive. Its management told investigators, "We may at a later date be in a position to add some colored people in minor capacities such as porters and cleaners."[19] However, many northern aircraft plants abandoned some aspects of their discriminatory employment practices as the war progressed, the manpower pool grew smaller, and federal pressure increased.[20]

FEPC played at least an indirect role in practically all breakthroughs in Negro employment. The wartime FEPC required government contractors to recruit, hire, train, and upgrade workers "without regard to their race, creed, color or national origin." Moreover, circumstantial evidence that indicated an employer sought data that could be used to discriminate counted against the company in a hearing. Thus, while it was not technically improper for a company to ask the racial, religious, or national background of a job applicant, such questions were thought to "create favorable conditions" for discrimination, and to "lend support to the conviction that discrimination exists."[21] The same held true for the absence or near-absence of minority workers in any given plant.

FEPC operated under the assumption that personnel techniques that singled out Negroes, such as requesting racial identity on application forms, would be used against the black applicant. But under its "color-blind" interpretation of equal employment, FEPC was unwilling to support any personnel policy which distinguished between blacks and whites, even if it benefited blacks. The commission unquestioningly accepted the philosophy of the American Creed. The ideal of FEPC, which would remain the ideal of fair employment forces until 1963, held that all workers, white or black, were to be judged purely on their objective merits. Executive Order 8802 declared it the "duty of employers and of labor organizations . . . to provide for the full and equitable participation of all workers in defense industries, without discrimination because of race, creed, color, or national origin."[22] FEPC interpreted this provision quite literally. Some employers attempted to hire Negro workers at a rate that reflected the percentage of Negroes in the labor pool area, but FEPC forbade such activity because the quota system worked "to the disadvantage of individuals in both minority and majority groups by permitting considerations of race rather than those of qualifications and availability to operate."[23] The commission admitted that such quotas did occasionally benefit Negroes, but in its zeal to be democratically color-blind FEPC ruled that the executive order prohibited "discrimination against white as well as against colored employees."[24] During the 1960's a more sophisticated understanding of black employment problems led the government to alter its disapproval of gathering racial background data and of the use of benign quotas. However, most other guidelines developed by FEPC stood the test of time.[25]

The war markedly improved the Negro employment picture, but as the manager of a North Carolina cigarette plant said, "During the war we did things we wouldn't do normally."[26] Wartime events did not necessarily have a lasting impact on the attitudes and activities of the business community. Americans accepted emergency measures, from rationing and bond purchases to fair employment practice, because they were temporary. The end of the war would mean no more brown-outs in the home and no more "brown-ins" on the job.

The end of the war presented no problem to those employers who had hired blacks on strictly pragmatic grounds. They needed workers in order to produce. Blacks were the only workers available, so they hired blacks. Once the war was over and they could once again indulge their preference for white employees, they quickly slipped back into traditional employment patterns. Southerners in particular had never considered the American Creed applicable to blacks and eagerly welcomed the return to normal.

Northern employers, however, had frequently based their prewar rejection of black workers on assumptions that blacks would do poor work and prompt employee unrest. In other words, the northern businessman discriminated against blacks on economic grounds. As with their southern colleagues, northern employers hired blacks because of pressures generated by the wartime emergency. However, the end of the emergency did not restore the *status quo ante bellum* in the North because black workers had proven their ability not only to master the technicalities of factory work, but had also proven their ability to operate in the industrial social environment. Thus, it was more difficult for the northern employer to continue to justify discrimination under the aegis of the Capitalist Ethic. By proving that blacks could be successfully employed, the war had opened the way for equal employment forces to exploit the idea of fair play contained in the American Creed. Julius Thomas, director of the industrial relations department of the National Urban League observed, "It will not be easy to tell the average Negro youngster that he will not find employment in this or that vocation after the war. He will promptly reply that his father or mother held that job in a local war plant in 1944."[27]

The status of the postwar economy was the dominant factor in determining the direction of Negro employment. Immediately after 1945 blacks were more afraid of losing jobs because of the economic slowdown involved in the transition from a wartime to a peacetime economy than because of a reversion to prewar hiring patterns. To counter the expected layoffs of blacks, some manpower experts suggested that employers grant

Negroes adjusted seniority, or that they racially balance any layoffs they were forced to make.[28] But a system of proportional layoffs would not only have protected black workers in newly acquired jobs, it would have also threatened union seniority rights and the accumulated seniority of returning veterans. The business community would not consider an attack on anything so fundamental as seniority rights.

The Negro workers' position looked particularly perilous because they had made their greatest gains in those industries that would suffer the most during reconversion. "Nothing but another war would revive production in ammunitions, explosives and firearms, aircraft, and shipbuilding to their wartime levels," noted two students of the labor market. "Consequently, the Negro worker will be subjected to the hazards of finding employment in new industry and will have the additional difficulties of transferring his war-learned skills or of obtaining retraining."[29] Under the best circumstances economists expected severe layoffs of blacks in almost all industries, if not as the result of reconversion or of a general recession, then as the result of displacement by returning veterans.[30] Fearing that extensive Negro unemployment would contribute to a recession, create a dangerously dependent group of people, and possibly lead to race riots, such as those that followed the end of World War I, concerned economists called for extensive federal control of the labor market through full employment legislation, a peacetime FEPC, federal control of industry location, and a fully coordinated United States Employment Service to encourage labor mobility.[31]

Reconversion had the expected detrimental effect on black employees in war industries. In several Connecticut war plants, for example, black workers had constituted between 8 and 25 percent of the work force during the war. By 1948 the number of Negro employees had fallen to less than 10 percent in the plant with the most black workers and to less than 3 percent in the plant with the fewest.[32] However, the negative impact of reconversion on black employment was mitigated by the continued expansion of the economy. Domestic consumption maintained production at a level high enough to allow consumer-oriented industries to absorb the black workers who had lost their jobs in war production plants. In the spring of 1947 the occupational distribution of employed Negroes was unchanged from the war period, indicating that black workers had not lost their wartime advances.[33]

The continuing manpower demand meant that economic conditions were conducive to a movement for a permanent peacetime FEPC, but there was strong political opposition. Congress killed President Truman's attempts to extend Executive Order 8802 into the postwar era and continued to oppose the idea of a federal FEPC during the late 1940's.[34] However, several states and cities passed fair employment legislation prior to 1950.[35]

In 1945 New York consolidated and extended several previously existing antidiscrimination statutes in the Ives-Quinn Act, which was the nation's first FEPC law. Connecticut, Massachusetts, New Jersey, New Mexico, Oregon, Rhode Island, and Washington followed New York's lead and passed antidiscrimination laws during the late 1940's.

Businessmen who supported FEPC legislation in the late 1940's were, for the most part, strong believers in the American Creed who were nevertheless cautious about hiring blacks because they feared such a policy would put them at a competitive disadvantage. Despite arguments that hiring blacks would be good for the economy,[36] FEPC supporters had no illusions about their fellow employers and believed that only legal coercion could convince their competitors to engage in fair employment practices.[37] The American Friends Service Committee clearly recognized the inability of businessmen to live up to the American Creed and at the same time remain true to the Capitalist Ethic. AFSC consistently argued that legislation would strengthen the hand of those employers who wanted to act "democratically" but were afraid to do so.[38]

Many businessmen wanted an FEPC law because it would relieve them of having to weigh the relative merits of the American Creed and the Capitalist Ethic. Without a law, no matter what the democratically disposed employer did, he lived in a state of cognitive disequilibrium. Either he sacrificed profits for equal opportunity or vice versa. The owner of a national chain of women's specialty shops who had been forced by community pressure to stop hiring blacks in a southern location said that more than half of the employers he knew wanted to desegregate but were afraid to. He felt that the lack of fair employment legislation gave "undue advantage to the relatively few hate mongers," who could cause enough trouble "to discourage even the most stouthearted believer in democratic employment practices."[39]

By the same logic the New York City West Side Association of Commerce opposed state FEPC legislation. The New Yorkers did not oppose fair employment. Quite the contrary, they believed that racial and religious discrimination should be declared unconstitutional. However, unless an equal obligation were placed on all employers in the nation, the west side businessmen warned that the state would lose business to areas unencumbered by compulsory adherence to the American Creed.[40]

Despite the increase in business support for FEPC in the postwar years, the majority of businessmen opposed such legislation. However, northern businessmen could not oppose FEPC on the grounds that equal opportunity did not apply to blacks, and so they opposed FEPC legislation because it would constitute an infringement on their managerial freedom.[41] The right of the employer to choose his workers was fundamental. Thus, northern businessmen opposed a requirement to do what they all said they were already doing (or at least in favor of doing) because it was a dangerous encroachment on their liberty. The various drives for state and federal fair employment permitted discriminatory businessmen to unite in opposition to Negro employment while maintaining a facade of propriety. Instead of confronting the fundamental issue of employing Negroes, the business community attacked the less embarrassing problem of government interference with their personnel policies.

Obviously those hiring policies which business was so staunchly defending were less than perfect examples of the American Creed in action. William R. Thomas, a member of Ford's industrial relations planning department, was unique only because he articulated the racist assumptions which stood just behind the shining shield of managerial prerogatives which so many discriminatory businessmen carried. Thomas voiced concern that FEPC legislation would disrupt informal work groups. He believed efficient work groups depended on good informal social relationships, which in turn depended upon ethnic compatibility. Thomas claimed that disruption of ethnic homogeneity among work groups would lead to unnecessary disruption of production. He was not, however, so callous as to deny blacks any role in his operation. Thomas pointed out that "Negroes associate themselves with porter jobs; Irish with police positions; Poles with heavy construction work; and Greeks with food services."[42]

Small businessmen, ever sensitive to their precarious position in the economy, and highly protective of what they considered their essential rights, objected strongly to the idea that they might have to hire those whom they did not like. F. A. Virkus, a spokesman for the Conference of American Small Business Organizations, complained, "Already it is difficult enough for small business to succeed financially, in the face of taxation, shortage of venture capital, government regulation, unionization with its accompanying rigidity of wage scales, material shortage, and a host of other plagues," and he was not sure small business could bear the additional burden of nondiscriminatory hiring. Virkus claimed that the right to hire and fire was the cornerstone of small business management and that any regulation of that right by the state was a blow to "the economic foundations of our country."[43]

Virkus' comments were typical of the antigovernment position taken by many conservative opponents of FEPC. Conservative businessmen clearly saw equal employment legislation in the broader context of the battle between free enterprise (the very soul of the Capitalist Ethic) and collectivist totalitarianism.[44] Donald R. Richberg, who had promoted business interests during the NRA days of the New Deal, was the most widely quoted anti-FEPC theoretician. According to Richberg, "discrimination in the choice of companions is the very essence of social liberty [and] discrimination in the choice of business associates is the very essence of economic liberty." Thus a fair employment practice law deprived the employer of his economic liberty and deprived his employees of their social liberty, thereby destroying freedom of association and liberty of contract.[45]

The belief that FEPC threatened basic American freedoms fitted well into the mood of the business community during the Truman administration. That was the period of the "sell America" campaign which emphasized the automatic, self-correcting virtues of the free enterprise system. Profits depended on efficiency. Efficiency assumed a rational utilization of manpower, and the rational utilization of manpower precluded racial discrimination. According to the true believer of the Capitalist Ethic the system structurally prevented unfair employment policies. Said one spokesman for the business community, "American businessmen are, for the most part, honest and fair in their dealings with others. They are universally free from prejudice and they do not practice oppression upon their employees. *They would not be successful if they did those things.*"[46] The very idea that there might be a flaw in the perfect jewel of capitalism aroused the ire of conservative employers like the speaker at a national small businessmen's meeting. "The battle line is drawn," he warned, "statism against freedom, dictatorship against democracy, communism against Americanism, paganism against Christianity."[47]

The superpatriotic, "sell America" type of rhetoric which marked many of the attacks on FEPC legislation was derived in part from the intense anticommunism which accompanied the beginnings of the Cold War. It followed logically that if antidiscrimination legislation were an infringement of economic freedom, and if infringements of economic freedom were a dangerous blow at the free enterprise system, then FEPC must be a communist plot since communists were the people most anxious to destroy the American economy. Referring to the FEPC referendum which California voters defeated in 1947, one FEPC opponent told a Senate committee, "Communists, fellow travelers, parlor pinks, left wingers and radicals of all hues were its protagonists and FEPC propaganda emanated from those sources."[48] But even hard-line anticommunist conservatives were unwilling to simply discard the idea of racial accord. Using a time-honored southern rationale, they stood the American Creed on its head by arguing that Negro workers were not unhappy with their situation and that FEPC legislation was "part of the Communist strategy to disrupt and disorganize the United States by causing friction between the colored and white races while pretending to be devoted to equalizing them."[49]

Discriminatory businessmen preferred to attack FEPC legislation rather than to attack the idea of employment integration. Few of them would publicly admit that they did not want to employ Negroes, so they had to reconcile their supposed opposition to discrimination with their opposition to legislation which would outlaw discrimination. As businessmen steeped in the conventional wisdom of the free enterprise system, employers right-eously attacked encroachments of the state, but as moral men and as be-lievers in the American Creed they had to demonstrate that FEPC would cause more harm than good, that it was the wrong way to achieve the right end. By predicting that an antidiscrimination law would increase race hatred, antiintegrationists could excuse their unwillingness to live up to the letter of the American Creed in order to conform to its broader spirit. The representative of several large southern industries made this point by quoting *Plessy* v. *Ferguson,* the 1896 Supreme Court decision which had upheld segregation: "Legislation is powerless to eradicate racial instincts, or to abolish distinctions based upon physical differences and the attempt to do so can only result in accentuating the difficulties. . . ."[50] In New York, the state Chamber of Commerce feared an antidiscrimination law would "attract an undesirable element from outside the State and it might give rise to burning resentment leading to possible race riots, pogroms and other evils."[51]

Racist businessmen predicted an anti-Negro backlash because they shared the widely held belief that discrimination was an instinctive re-sponse to racial differences which could not be eliminated by law. In a folksy "common sense" discussion of FEPC, George H. Fisher, the chairman of the labor committee of the American Society of Industrial Engineers, explained that "unlike some of our modern well-educated theorists," practi-cal old-time personnel men were "scientists enough not to try to force elements together which were naturally antagonistic . . . just as a farmer separates a horse and a mule when they refuse to pull together."[52] Fisher's view of race relations left room for cooperation only when it occurred "naturally." He made his peace with the American Creed by endorsing equal employment when it sprang spontaneously from the heart of the white worker.

Most businessmen, however, did not see pseudoscientific barriers to racial cooperation. They believed that a slow, patient evolutionary process of education and moral persuasion could eliminate discrimination but that legislation could not. Proper moral behavior, said the businessmen, was a matter between a man and his God, and it was up to the churches to instruct and enforce ethical activity. One business spokesman charged that church support for fair employment practice legislation was "nothing less than a confession of the bankruptcy of their own spiritual and moral leadership."[53]

By emphasizing that economic integration would come only when education and persuasion had changed the hearts of the people, "moderate" businessmen were placing their confidence in the basically democratic instincts of the American people. Thus, they believed the ideal of the American Creed would triumph where force would fail. Pointing to a few isolated breakthroughs in Negro hiring as proof that progress was being made, Ralph Van Nostrand of the Merchants and Manufacturers Association of California contended that "good community public relations, education and understanding are doing in a voluntary way, what the policeman's club cannot accomplish."[54]

FEPC supporters relied heavily on the fundamental argument that the legislation was merely a legal implementation of a widely accepted ideal—it was part of the American Creed. But because most business opposition focused on the law's presumed violations of managerial prerogatives, much of the FEPC propaganda was defensive. The most effective argument pointed to the success of the New York State law, which was not only the first but also the strongest state antidiscrimination statute.[55] The New York experience confirmed predictions that neither FEPC nor Negro job seekers would harass the business community.

Proponents of FEPC laws implicitly conceded the argument that an FEPC limited the employer's freedom to run his business the way he saw fit. They countered along three lines. First, FEPC was only one of many laws which society needed to insure proper behavior, and it was the nature of laws to restrict the freedom of some to insure the freedom of others. Second, supporters of the legislation carefully explained that the employer could still apply all his traditional standards in all areas except race and religion.[56] Finally, pro-FEPC forces contended that the laws were not designed to alter basic attitudes, but rather to proscribe specific kinds of activity. They were aimed not at prejudice but at discrimination.[57] On the other hand the supporters pointed out that "forced" integration could change people's attitudes by demonstrating the inaccuracy of the presumptions which underlay their discriminatory behavior.[58] But when pressed to the wall FEPC proponents had to concede, as did one businessman, "in the final analysis, perhaps the strongest arguments in favor of FEPC are neither economic nor political, but moral."[59] In an age when religious values were generally banished from the business world, this was a weak reed upon which to rest an entire movement.

3

Business Counterattacks:
Voluntarism and Breakthroughs

During the early 1950's, growing public acceptance of black employees combined with the business opposition to FEPC legislation to produce some token steps toward equal employment opportunity. The breakthroughs of the Eisenhower era indicate an increasing compatibility between the demands of the American Creed and the Capitalist Ethic. The chance of a successful local FEPC law was directly proportional to public acceptance of Negro employees. Thus, as the businessman's social environment demanded a more rigorous application of the American Creed to black workers, it also reduced the potential cost of hiring Negroes. At the same time the businessman might be able to reap public acclaim by giving a few symbolic jobs to blacks and forestall government intervention in his personnel policies.

Businessmen who had fundamental ideological objections to FEPC legislation, and who were not merely erecting respectable facades over their own racism, sought to demonstrate their genuine commitment to equal employment opportunity in the immediate postwar years by forming voluntary organizations to further the principles of fair employment.

The idea of community voluntary race-relations committees had first become widespread during the war. After the Detroit race riot of 1943 more than two hundred and sixty cities set up race relations committees. While most of the committees supported FEPC legislation, at the same time they urged businessmen to adopt voluntary fair employment codes. Critics claimed there was a contradiction in the committees' position, and feared that the voluntary codes would serve no function except to take "government off the spot, inhibit pressure for adequate legislation and replace an enforceable legislative device by a pious hope."[1]

The wartime voluntary action groups were not notably successful in bringing about any degree of fair employment beyond that required by Executive Order 8802, which had established the wartime FEPC. Because the voluntary committees were created as emergency war measures, their members frequently lacked a long-range commitment to the problems of the black American. A particularly nasty example was the Fair Employment Practice Forum in an Ohio city which was headed by the president of the city's industrial association, a man who blamed most of the city's race troubles on the municipal administration during the depression which "treated the niggers so well that they came here in droves."[2] This ill-starred experiment in voluntary fair employment activity collapsed when the group's black representative from the state employment service married his white secretary. The director felt that such an act was more than he or any other member of the group could swallow and accounted for the city's continuing reluctance to do anything about employment discrimination.

The movement to establish voluntary fair employment practice committees reemerged after the war. Frightened by the growing trend toward municipal and state FEPC laws and confident that the public mood had softened sufficiently to minimize negative economic effects, a number of state and local chambers of commerce began to discuss elaborate voluntary equal employment plans. The first, and most widely publicized, voluntary fair employment plan emerged in Cleveland, Ohio in 1949. Municipal FEPC legislation was pending before the city council. Although the city council had defeated an FEPC ordinance in 1947, the legislation seemed sure of passage in 1948 until the chamber of commerce suggested a voluntary plan in place of the legal requirements.[3] Clifford F. Hood, president of American Steel and Wire Co., and Elmer L. Lindseth, president of the Cleveland Electric Illuminating Co., led Cleveland business opposition to FEPC. Lindseth, who was also president of the chamber of commerce, admitted that Cleveland employers discriminated against Negroes, but argued that a voluntary plan would reduce discrimination more than legislation.[4]

The city council agreed to suspend action for ninety days while the newly formed Cleveland Committee on Employment Practices attempted to tackle the problem of discrimination. The chamber of commerce financed the committee, which consisted of sixteen members. The chamber appointed eight business members, and Cleveland's mayor, Thomas Burke, named eight others to represent unions and minority groups.[5] Under chairman William L. Ong, assistant to the president of American Steel and Wire, the committee launched an intensive advertising (or, as they called it, "public education") campaign to persuade employers to voluntarily hire Negroes. The committee mailed information pamphlets and requests for cooperation to 8,200 businessmen. One hundred and fifty, or fewer than 2 percent, responded favorably.

In addition to contacting employers the committee attempted to convince the public that voluntary fair employment was a viable alternative to FEPC. The advertising agency of Fuller & Smith & Ross, which itself had voluntarily begun to employ blacks, donated its services to prepare car cards, posters, spot announcements, and speeches to carry the message to the people of Cleveland. The committee spent more than thirty thousand dollars in its fifteen-month public education campaign.[6]

The voluntary plan failed to break down the barriers to black employment. Favorable coverage of committee efforts in the business press consisted almost exclusively of case studies and examples, a sure sign that the program was failing to place large numbers of Negroes in new jobs.[7] As a result of the campaign some individual firms did begin to hire Negroes in white-collar and professional jobs, but high visibility jobs in high visibility firms (especially in banks and department stores) remained closed to blacks. Supporters of the voluntary plan claimed that the educational campaign had broken down racial barriers and that a significant number of Cleveland businesses had revised recruiting, placement, and promotion procedures to eliminate racial bias. Critics welcomed any change in attitudes that may have occurred as a result of the advertising but pointed to the lack of actual job progress as proof of failure.[8]

Originally intended as a way to stop FEPC, the voluntary plan actually prepared the Cleveland business community to accept FEPC legislation. In January 1950, when the city council again considered an FEPC ordinance, the chamber of commerce reluctantly supported the move. Support was not unconditional, however. Despite a year and a half of "plenty of good will but practically no jobs,"[9] the chamber of commerce initially opposed the legislation, but when it became clear that the ordinance would pass in any event, the chamber had second thoughts. Since it was no longer in a position to block FEPC through suggestions of voluntary action, the chamber sought to soften the objectionable sections of the proposed ordinance. Businessmen feared the punitive aspects of the ordinance. They believed the commission might be antibusiness and that unscrupulous lawyers would use the ordinance to get new cases. To meet these objections the council gave businessmen one-third of the seats on the fifteen-man commission which would administer the ordinance. They declared that only principals, not lawyers, could file complaints and required two sets of conciliation hearings before any punitive legal action could be taken against an employer.[10] One newspaper accurately assessed the situation when it commented, "This ordinance is not just government regulating business, but it's business helping to regulate itself."[11]

The Cleveland voluntary equal employment plan demonstrated business reluctance to accept the idea of equal employment except under pressure, and its ability to mold to its own ends those pressures it could not avoid. The voluntary nature of the Cleveland program, legitimized by the formal support of the chamber of commerce and some key business leaders, allowed businessmen to meet new community standards for fair employment with a minimum of action. By expressing support for the voluntary program businessmen demonstrated their allegiance to the values of the American Creed. By taking small symbolic steps such as removing racial designations from job application forms and help-wanted newspaper advertisements they could demonstrate their social responsibility without significantly altering their traditional employment patterns and risking possible white disapproval.

The failure of the voluntary plan to place significant numbers of Negroes in nontraditional jobs made it difficult for the business community to oppose the FEPC ordinance. Having tried and failed to solve the discrimination problem themselves, the logic of their position compelled businessmen to accept legislation. Moreover, the successful voluntary integration that took place in a few firms reduced the fears other businessmen had about hiring blacks. The successfully integrated firms served as models for those companies forced to integrate by the ordinance.[12] But the business community accepted the ordinance itself only reluctantly and then only after a successful attempt to modify the legislation to make it more acceptable to the business community and to give businessmen a dominant voice in the administration of the code.

Despite its failure to prevent a municipal FEPC, the Cleveland plan prompted the Illinois State Chamber of Commerce to launch the biggest and most successful anti-FEPC voluntary fair employment plan. There was some precedent for business-government cooperation for equal employment in Illinois. During World War II the Chicago Mayor's Committee on Race Relations appointed a subcommittee composed of the presidents of sixteen of the city's most important businesses. These chief executives conducted a survey of ninety-four Chicago companies which employed a total of 50,000 Negroes to determine company experience with black workers. The subcommittee concluded that integration could take place successfully in Chicago plants and that Negro workers could perform as competently as white workers.[13]

The mayor's committee gave blacks new job opportunities, but it certainly did not give them equal job opportunities. While virtually all Chicago businesses employed black workers in some capacity by the end of the war, significant gains were limited to semiskilled production positions and to some unskilled office jobs.[14]

Postwar equal employment activity by the Chicago business community appears to have been minimal. A staff member of the Chicago Association of Commerce and Industry claimed that the association regularly held conferences on fair employment practice, but if this was true, the meetings do not seem to have made much of an impact on the business community, or on the association itself.[15] The president of the association expressed a biased attitude toward Jews, and the organization did not have any black workers on its staff.[16]

Concern with the fair employment problem surfaced again in late 1949, when, for the second time, the lower house of the Illinois state legislature passed an antidiscrimination bill. The Association of Commerce and Industry set up an informal committee on fair employment practice. The committee tried to persuade employers who were sympathetic to the idea of increased Negro employment to act on their principles. The casual nature of this effort cannot be overemphasized, and it appears to have had little impact. Chicago businessmen who were widely known as leaders in the field of Negro employment refused to become deeply involved in the association's activities, and even their superficial participation aroused the suspicion of more conservative employers.[17]

The Illinois State Chamber of Commerce took the threat of FEPC much more seriously than the Chicago Association of Commerce and Industry. Unlike the desultory city group, the state chamber of commerce launched a major voluntary equal employment campaign to head off an FEPC bill that was given a good chance of passage in 1951. The state chamber of commerce knew of the Cleveland experience, but felt it could succeed where the Ohio city had failed. The Illinois chamber believed that the Cleveland plan had placed too much emphasis on educating the public on the problems of Negro employment (thus contributing to the passage of the FEPC ordinance) and not enough on convincing the business community to hire more blacks.[18]

A special seventy-five man committee of the Illinois chamber of commerce conducted a state-wide survey of business integration practices and attitudes. Questioning three hundred top executives, the committee discovered that strong opposition to Negro employment was limited in the state, and that objections were strongest in the south. Of the firms contacted, 57 percent employed no Negroes at all, and of the 43 percent which did hire black workers more than 80 percent barred them from all but unskilled jobs. Despite this overwhelming record of discrimination, 70 percent of the employers indicated support for the chamber's voluntary equal employment opportunity program.[19] The businessmen probably recognized that a voluntary gesture of acceptance of the ideal of equal employment might forestall legislation which would require them actually to hire blacks.

The chamber of commerce voluntary program called for a series of regional conferences for top executives and personnel men. Training schools to instruct lower-level personnel men in the attitudes and techniques of employment integration were to follow. The chamber planned to set up a counseling service to assist companies experiencing difficulties in the integration process and, with the help of outside groups, hoped to locate and place black workers. In conjunction with the counseling program the chamber planned to set up a clearinghouse to circulate experiences with employment integration.[20]

The *pièce de résistance* of the program was to be a movie demonstrating the value of integrated employment and countering all the common objections to hiring Negroes. The original script for this film called for the chief executive of the fictional company to admit that he had not been forceful enough in expressing his support of equal employment opportunity when he discovered that his personnel department had regularly been turning away Negroes and Jews. In the final version the company president merely corrected his staff without admitting any responsibility. This cut was made because one of the employers financing the venture objected to the implication that the company president might have been in some way responsible for discrimination. The man in question was the chairman of the board of one of Chicago's most important firms, and an immovable hard-liner in his own refusal to give customer-contact jobs to Negroes in his company. [21] The executive's position was not hypocritical because the chamber of commerce was not actually trying to implement an equal opportunity program. The chamber wanted to get more but not necessarily better jobs for Negroes. The film-makers deliberately shied away from any discussion of the existing lack of opportunity for blacks and refused to deal with the implications of the American Creed for employment practices. Instead the film took a very narrow Capitalist Ethic focus, emphasizing the economic benefits of using the entire pool of available labor.[22]

The Illinois State Chamber of Commerce achieved its primary goal. In 1951 the state senate again refused to pass the FEPC bill. But because the threat continued (the state lower house passed an FEPC bill every other year until 1961 when the law was finally enacted) the chamber of commerce continued its program in at least a moderately active form until 1954.

Although the Illinois State Chamber of Commerce chose to ignore the implications of its integration activity for overall values, other business supporters of voluntary fair employment practices faced the demands of the American Creed more squarely. Throughout the early 1950's businessmen argued that voluntarism and education would end discrimination while preserving the individual flexibility necessary for maximum profitability.[23] In 1954, the governing board of the National Association of Manufacturers adopted the following official policy: "Freedom of opportunity for every individual to work at an available job for which he is qualified is an objective of the American way of life. Employment of individuals and their assignments to jobs should be determined by matching the individual's skills and qualifications with the requirements of available positions. These objectives can best be achieved through voluntary methods."[24] States such as Wisconsin that passed FEPC laws without enforcement provisions seemingly bowed to the irresistible logic of the voluntary compliance argument. In 1952 an Indianapolis businessman told a television audience that compulsory legislation was "the easy way out. If we can just get someone else to take over our responsibilities. That does not build strong people, neither does it build a strong nation."[25] Even in states which had an enforceable FEPC, the tide of business cooperation and voluntary action flowed strongly. In the mid-fifties, New York businessmen, who had lived with an antidiscrimination law for more than a decade, banded together to encourage each other to live up to the spirit of the law.[26]

The voluntary integration programs of the early 1950's were a clear expression of business ambiguity toward equal employment opportunity. They were an attempt to comply with the spirit of the American Creed without living up to the practical requirements embodied in an equal employment policy. Most businessmen did not want to hire Negroes, or were afraid to do so. Yet pressure from fair employment legislation, or the threat of such legislation, and the growing number of successful pioneer employers meant that businessmen who had previously ignored the question of employing Negroes had to come to some conscious decision about what they would do.

The voluntary plans were designed to relieve pressure on the business community, not to solve the problem of employment discrimination. Thus the business response to FEPC reflected the anti-Negro feelings that still permeated the business community in the 1950's. In the more liberal areas of the Northeast and the Midwest employers frequently accepted the abstract ideal of fair employment, but even in states with FEPC laws, employment of Negroes in nontraditional jobs was token at best. For example, immediately after the war, the liberal New York papers, the *Herald-Tribune,* the *Times,* the *Post,* the *Eagle,* and *PM,* each had one token black reporter. The conservative papers had none, and only the communist *Daily Worker* had a significant number of black staff members.[27] In 1948, when 125 white editors were asked if they would hire Negroes for their professional staffs, only 20 bothered to answer and 14 said they would not.[28] The six who said they would hire Negroes may very well have been like the New York *Post* city editor who told a job-seeking Negro, "Oh yes, we expect to employ a Negro any day now, but it will be either Walter White or W. E. B. DuBois."[29]

A 1951 survey of Negro employment practices in Connecticut, which like New York had an FEPC, disclosed a systematic pattern of discrimination. Employers hired a few nonwhites in professional and white-collar jobs, but on the whole they relegated Negroes to semiskilled and unskilled positions. Most employers merely ignored FEPC, although businessmen in one Connecticut city actively opposed it with an educational campaign that taught managers how to legally circumvent the equal employment law. Businessmen there also circulated a letter which warned employers against cooperating with investigators who were trying to discover the effect of the law on black employment.[30]

Reluctance to hire blacks was also reflected in a survey of minority employment practices in the San Francisco Bay Area in 1949. More than 40 percent of the employers who mentioned Negroes as a minority group said they would not hire them, or would prefer not to hire them for any job, and fewer than 20 percent said they would use Negroes in white-collar positions.[31] Another survey of San Francisco in 1955 indicated that business attitudes toward employing blacks had not changed much in six years. More than a quarter of one hundred employers questioned did not even claim to have a fair employment policy. Of the remaining 75 percent only 12 percent actually had some sort of formal nondiscrimination policy. The others had merely responded affirmatively when asked if they favored an integrated work force. Needless to say, actual employment of Negroes was considerably below even these rather unimpressive expressions of good will.[32]

Even at the end of the 1950's many employers remained reluctant to extend themselves on behalf of black employment. A questionnaire survey by the Minnesota Advisory Commission to the U.S. Commission on Civil Rights in 1960 disclosed not only severe underutilization of the black labor force, but a strong disinclination on the part of employers to take even pro forma steps to express their support of fair employment. Of 922 firms that responded, only 582 answered the question that asked what they had done to assure fair employment. Of these, almost half admitted they had done nothing.[33]

The growing willingness of firms to extend equal opportunity to blacks was clearly a function of the changing social and political environment. Business sensitivity to the American Creed was dependent upon continuing external pressure. For the business community as a whole demands for employment integration increased steadily after World War II. Employer response in the isolated cases where pressure slackened demonstrated the superficiality of business commitment to the American Creed.

Illinois Bell Telephone practiced just such equal employment opportunism in its treatment of black clerical workers in Chicago. In the late forties and early fifties, during the peak of the Illinois FEPC drives, Illinois Bell began hiring black clerical workers in its Loop accounting department, and by 1951 Bell employed Negroes in most of its downtown Chicago offices.[34] However, in 1952 Illinois Bell began transferring its downtown operations to suburban locations. Over a period of seven years outlying offices took over almost all the work done downtown. Each time an office closed the company transferred its Negro workers to one of the remaining downtown offices (which were closer to their homes) while the whites moved to the new location. At the same time, Illinois Bell almost stopped hiring any new Negro employees. Even after the independent union which represented the clerical workers complained, the company did no more than install a token number of black workers in its suburban branches.[35] Unlike retail outlets which were dependent on walk-in customers and had to hire blacks to attract a growing black population, the telephone company was able to follow the white population to the suburbs and leave its black employees behind in the central city.

In 1952, a National Urban League survey of thirty industrial cities disclosed widespread discrimination against Negroes in skilled and white-collar occupations. Discrimination occurred despite the manpower demands of the Korean War, and despite the antidiscrimination clause in the government contracts which many of the offending companies held. The report noted that southern employers were particularly blatant in their discriminatory practices.[36] Whereas many northern employers appeared willing to employ a minimum number of Negroes in professional, managerial, and skilled occupations, southern managers maintained a much more rigid stance. In the Upper South Negroes managed to keep the better positions they had gained during the war, but in areas of the Deep South postwar formalization of employment policy and job standards actually led to a decrease in the number of black workers.[37] Southern businesses continued widespread discrimination against blacks well into the 1960's, although instances of token Negro employment did begin to appear in individual firms in some areas.[38]

Despite general business reluctance to remove the ceiling on Negro jobs during the 1950's, there were some employers who pioneered in placing blacks in nontraditional positions. The changing employment policies of retail store owners are particularly interesting because retail merchants were extremely sensitive to alterations in the public mood. They were highly vulnerable to protests from both the black and white communities and had to be sure the balance had tipped in favor of equal employment before they began hiring blacks. Moreover, the reaction of stores' low-paid, status-conscious, white-collar sales people was an excellent barometer of how sincerely the white public had accepted the American Creed.

Some isolated Negroes held retail sales positions before the war, but, with rare exceptions, only in stores with predominantly black clientele. G. Fox of Hartford, Connecticut, was apparently the first major department store to employ Negroes in white-collar and professional positions. G. Fox started to treat black and white employees equally in 1942, and promoted black workers to sales, clerical, and other nontraditional jobs. In 1945, Fox placed a Negro in a management position on its personnel staff.[39]

The G. Fox policy, although a major breakthrough in both the nature and number of jobs given to blacks, was not immediately followed by other northeastern department stores. Even after the passage of the New York State Fair Employment Practice Act in 1945 department store owners in New York City refused to hire blacks in other than stock and service jobs. In early 1946 there were few if any blacks in store jobs which required them to meet the public. However, by the spring of 1947, nine of the fifteen largest New York stores had at least one black sales person, and one had fifteen.[40] A study done that year indicated that the public completely accepted the black sales help.[41]

Breakthroughs in Negro retail employment were made in a number of northern cities in the years 1947-48. Besides New York, stores in Boston[42] and Minneapolis[43] began to hire blacks in response to FEPC laws, pressure from civil rights groups, or a combination of both. Philadelphia stores also hired their first black sales help in the late 1940's. Immediately after the war Philadelphia store owners had rebuffed attempts by the American Friends Service Committee to persuade them to hire black sales personnel. The manager of one of the largest Market Street department stores told an AFSC interviewer in January, 1946, that he would not employ a Negro unless all stores moved together. He feared a single pioneer would lose business to nonintegrating stores.[44] His position was fairly typical. He accepted the ideal of the American Creed, but the practical constraints of the Capitalist Ethic prevented Negro employment. One personnel director explained that progress would come slowly, and although she did not expect to see such a revolution in her lifetime, eventually Negroes would hold every kind of job. Fearful gradualism marked most Philadelphia merchants but perhaps none more so than the president of a large department store. After demurring for the usual reasons of customer and employee reaction, the store executive explained that the problem would be solved only through "amalgamation," which he felt would take centuries.[45]

Employer fears of customer and employee reaction to black workers were reenforced when one of the largest of the Philadelphia stores unexpectedly found itself pioneering in Negro employment. In an advertisement for sales help the store had neglected to include the usual "whites only" designation. One thousand two hundred people applied for the advertised positions. One-third of the applicants were black, and the store personnel department rejected them out of hand. The rejected applicants made their feelings known in the black community, and the store suddenly found itself under extreme pressure to hire Negroes in nontraditional jobs. To placate the black community the store agreed to employ Negro sales people, only to discover that its white workers began to object. The store backed down in the face of employee opposition, and the black workers were not hired.[46]

Throughout 1946 and 1947 a coalition of Philadelphia civil rights groups made a concerted effort to persuade store officials to open up their hiring practices. Although the employers expressed sympathy for the movement, particularly when the efforts were of the gentle Quaker variety, they adamantly refused to move until the city passed an FEPC ordinance in March, 1948. Subsequently the stores, whose managers had predicted no substantial progress for generations, peacefully and successfully integrated their white-collar positions.[47]

Despite the successful integration of the department stores in New York, Boston, and Philadelphia, store managers elsewhere were sure their cities, their customers, or their employees could not be counted upon to agree to the hiring of blacks. Although Philadelphia stores hired Negro sales people in 1948, as late as 1954 only one store in Chester, Pennsylvania, a small city with a large black population less than ten miles from Philadelphia, had a black sales person. Moreover, although she was a college graduate with professional social work experience, she worked in a second-rate store.[48] The same kind of discrimination existed in Wilmington, Delaware, barely twenty-five miles from Philadelphia. In 1949, a store owner who had a strong personal commitment to the American Creed promoted a stockgirl to a sales position, but opposition from white employees forced her to request a transfer back to stock work. When she subsequently attempted to help on the sales floor during peak periods, customers complained and the employer stopped even that token gesture toward employment integration. It was not until 1953 that Wilmington public opinion had mellowed enough to permit a store to use a black stock girl in sales during peak periods without incident.[49]

In the South blacks held nontraditional retail positions in a number of isolated instances. Southern employers most likely to hire black sales people operated their own small stores which did not cater to an exclusive class of customers. These employers broke with the traditional southern pattern of employment discrimination because they worked closely with their employees and came to regard them as individuals. Once the formal employer-employee barriers were down it was easy for the southern shopkeepers to fall into the paternalistic acceptance of blacks which remained as a legacy of the antebellum period. Ironically, this attitudinal anachronism provided, in isolated cases, an alternative route to equal opportunity outside of the American Creed. During World War II, for example, the owner of a Greensboro, North Carolina clothing store had hired a Negro janitor. By 1955, the black man had become a salesman on a par with the store's white personnel. Despite the fact he had not finished grammar school, and reportedly spoke English very poorly, he got along with his co-workers and was popular with customers. When asked if he employed Negroes at any of his other stores, the owner replied, "It has never occurred to me. This boy came to me twelve years ago and showed so much ambition and aptitude that I let him grow as fast as I could."[50]

Any guilt feelings businessmen may have harbored as a result of their unwillingness to live up to the American Creed usually surfaced only after their consciences had been pricked in the pocketbook. Businessmen integrated their work forces most easily when there was minimum conflict between the American Creed and the Capitalist Ethic. When the public expected (or at least accepted) equal employment, *and* either blacks or the government demanded it, *and* there was sound economic reason for hiring blacks, then firms would fall into line quickly. Just such a situation emerged among downtown Chicago stores between 1950 and 1953.

During World War II some Chicago stores employed Negroes in nontraditional jobs, but still in a service rather than in a white-collar capacity. A department store manager found that wartime wage controls prevented him from getting eighteen-year-old, size-sixteen blondes for his store restaurant. Only older white women or Negroes would work for the government-controlled low wages he was forced to pay, and the owner found younger blacks superior to older whites. The store manager did not extend his favorable experience with Negro waitresses to other areas of his firm, however.[51] With the exception of one high-quality women's store which hired "medium brown" women for service positions, no other major downtown store in Chicago employed any black workers in a nonmenial capacity prior to 1950.[52]

The drive for an Illinois FEPC and the shift of whites to the suburbs prompted Chicago retail employers to reassess their discriminatory policies in the immediate postwar years. Retail merchants in Chicago played a major role in the fight against an Illinois FEPC. Both the city and the state merchants' associations lobbied effectively against equal employment opportunity legislation. At the same time they faced increased demands to hire Negroes from black and white civil rights groups, and from their own lobbyists. In 1950, one of the retailers' legislative representatives compensated for his opposition to FEPC by pressuring the store owners to proceed with employment integration voluntarily. The lobbyist had agreed to work against FEPC legislation because he earnestly believed that voluntary action could bring about implementation of the American Creed while preserving maximum business freedom. But the failure of firms to begin hiring blacks placed him in a state of value-action incongruence which he resolved by threatening not to lobby when the legislature next considered FEPC.[53]

While the store managers' own lobbyist pushed for voluntary action, downtown retailers discovered that their customers were also demanding black sales people. Although there had been no systematic exclusion of Negro shoppers from Loop stores during the war, relatively few Negroes had patronized the larger department stores.[54] During the late forties and early fifties, however, larger numbers of black Chicagoans began to shop in the Loop as whites began moving to the suburbs. Black shoppers expected black sales people, and despite the fear that Negro clerks would offend their white customers, many employers were not willing to sacrifice the additional patronage by discriminating against blacks.[55] The manager of a chain of women's shops who was among the first to employ blacks boasted that his success led other specialty shop owners on State Street to come to him for advice. He told an interviewer, "These shops realize that the upper middle class is moving to the suburbs and large department stores are going after them with branch operations. They realize that to survive they have to cater to the people remaining in the city."[56]

In 1949 the first major downtown department store decided to begin hiring Negroes in white-collar positions. Store management apparently believed the propaganda of the retail merchants' anti-FEPC campaign and felt obligated to prove that voluntary integration could work. Moreover, the store's personnel director had a social service background and was instrumental in convincing management that black workers could work successfully in a major Loop department store. This moral commitment to hire blacks was undoubtedly strengthened by the steady pressure from black action groups, especially the Congress of Racial Equality, which had picketed the store in protest of its hiring policy.[57] In July, 1950, the store hired a college-trained black man to work as an administrative assistant. When he became familiar with company procedure, the store moved him to the personnel department to help coordinate the integration of the rest of the firm. But management trusted him with the delicate task of hiring other Negroes only after he cleared himself of suspicion on several counts. First he assured his employers that he was unsympathetic to communism even though he had worked on a black newspaper which was widely accused of being "communistic." He also demonstrated his conservatism on personnel matters by telling management that he "did not believe that a firm should go out and hire Negroes without considering problems generic to the hiring of Negroes and further should not push the matter if all factors were not propitious to the situation."[58]

Although cautious before it began to integrate, the store moved fairly rapidly once the policy change was made. Within three months there were more than eighty blacks on its staff. A subsequent personnel director said overqualified applicants swamped the store. People with master's degrees were asking for stock jobs. But however qualified they were, the store found that their black workers suffered from the disabilities of ghetto culture. Management discovered a number of the new black employees selling marijuana, and subsequent investigation disclosed that others, including a store guard, had lied about police records. Despite these minor drawbacks, the bulk of black workers performed admirably and gained high acceptance from their supervisors.[59]

Rank and file employees reacted more negatively than supervisors to integration. Although there was little overt opposition, the Negroes felt, or were made to feel, unwelcome at employee social affairs, and on a number of occasions were told not to use certain lockers or rest rooms. Part of the problem may have derived from the failure of management to inform their employees of the new hiring policy. Older workers in particular felt threatened when they found management "sneaking" Negroes into the store.[60]

Whether or not it was true, store personnel believed that much of the initial difficulty was due to the activity of the pioneer employee. Other black employees believed he had hired too many blacks too quickly and without sufficient quality control. Many employees believed the pioneering black manager was "an entirely too bright young man." According to one source, the pioneer Negro lost his position after a couple of years when he became "too friendly" with white women and took one to lunch in the executive men's dining room.[61]

Despite some initial difficulties, the store maintained its new employment policy and willingly became a symbol of racial progress on State Street. It accepted the annual human relations award of the mayor's commission and freely shared its experience with others who sought guidance. It is indicative of the quick change of mood that once a major store had broken the ice, a smaller, less important firm complained that it had been hiring Negroes long before the big store and resented the larger firm getting all tne *good* publicity.[62] All the important State Street stores but one and many outlying stores followed the leader. They followed so quickly that the American Friends Services Committee, which had been instrumental in assisting the first store, found itself swamped by requests for qualified black employees.[63] Once they accepted the idea of hiring blacks, several shops discovered that they didn't have to do anything to implement their new policy because Negro workers who had been "passing" admitted their ethnicity.[64]

Although most stores seemed eager to jump on the integration bandwagon, some nonretail firms took a dimmer view of the break in the color line. The head of a Loop business organization expressed strong criticism of the department stores which had integrated (he admitted some of his objection was based on his southern background and personal aversion to Negroes) and contended that the stores had hired blacks only because there was a labor shortage and that integration would not last.[65] His cynicism was not entirely unfounded since one of the State Street stores admitted that it indeed was employing Negroes because the labor market was tight. In fact, the market was so tight that the store wanted to wait until it loosened up a bit lest the personnel department be tempted to fill all open positions with available black applicants.[66]

The one major holdout among Chicago department stores demonstrated how a limited amount of personal bigotry and a great deal of institutional racism could combine to prevent action even in the face of overwhelming pressure to integrate. The most prestigious of the major downtown stores adamantly refused to follow the trend because management believed that the store had a "distinct personality" which made it more susceptible to customer retaliation. While stores which catered to the general public might not suffer as a result of Negro sales people, a store which served an "exclusive" clientele operated in a more rarefied socioeconomic environment, farther removed from the American Creed—but no less responsive to the Capitalist Ethic.

Part of the store's reluctance to hire blacks arose from conflicting beliefs among the firm's administrators. Some executives, including several at the highest level, felt sympathetic to the equal employment drive, but they were stopped by a single highly placed individual whose racial attitudes had caused him to withdraw his daughter from college because the school had a Negro guest speaker.[67]

In mid-1950, the executives of the holdout store informed AFSC that they would hire blacks only when to do so was no longer a controversial issue. They explained that they could not even hire blacks in traditional jobs because the store had a policy of promoting from within, and since Negroes could not be promoted to customer contact jobs, it would not be right to hire them for any jobs. The personnel director also claimed that he had received hundreds of letters from customers who had threatened to take their business elsewhere if the store were integrated.[68] Furthermore the store management objected to the pressure to hire blacks as an infringement of their freedom to employ whomever they wanted.[69]

By the end of 1952 other firms in the Chicago area began to apply strong pressure on the holdout. Its irreconcilable position had become an embarrassment to anti-FEPC forces and had caused a split in the previously unanimous opposition to FEPC. Several of the first firms to employ Negroes, including some which had actively lobbied against FEPC, came to the conclusion that voluntary integration activity had reached a dead end and that only legislation could bring about complete fair employment. Those employers who continued to oppose fair employment legislation sent a delegation to visit the holdout and explained that unless the store changed its policy the state legislature might very well pass an FEPC law, in which case the high executive would have cut off his nose to spite his face.[70] The store's managers, however, would not budge. They admitted in early 1953, as they had three years before, that they would integrate someday, but it would be at a time of their own choosing, when they could be absolutely sure they would meet with no unfavorable reaction from either their current employees or from their customers.[71]

In fact, the store did integrate in 1953, but not because it was the date of its choosing. Sight unseen, the store hired an applicant for a management position on his merits. He turned out to be black. The store refused to honor its commitment to employ him, so he turned to the Mayor's Commission on Human Relations. Although the commission had enforcement power only when dealing with public contracts, it was able to hold public hearings on complaints—which it threatened to do. Faced with the adverse publicity of public exposure, and with a supertight labor market, the store hired a black clerk-typist and five other Negro workers.[72]

Lacking any fundamental commitment to the American Creed, this store was able to hold out against a wide variety of forces that normally pushed employers into providing better jobs for black workers. Sure that their establishment was unique and that it had a special image to uphold, the management refused to be persuaded by the examples of others. Fearful and conservative, the employers assumed their customers shared their bigotry. Yet, three years of constant pounding by integrationist forces appeared to have had some effect. The problem of black empoyment had become a constant topic of discussion in management circles, and management had come to accept the inevitability of Negro employment someday. Thus when the city moved to expose, if not punish, their exclusionary policy, the store capitulated. The attitudes of the public and of the business community in Chicago had moderated sufficiently to make public hearings unpalatable enough to cause the store to violate its image and its principles, even in the absence of an FEPC law.

Spurred perhaps by the continuing tight labor market, several major Chicago industrial employers joined the retailers in hiring either their first black workers or blacks for the first time in nontraditional jobs.[73] Nevertheless, Negro employment in nontraditional jobs was spotty at best. Despite six years of organized support for voluntary equal employment, in 1956, a group of Chicago businessmen, the Mayor's Committee on Community Welfare, could not find a single firm in the city that did all its hiring entirely on the basis of qualification. Many firms expressed support for the idea of equal employment, but the committee concluded that substantial progress would not be made until an FEPC law was passed.[74]

Voluntary plans, although designed to head off FEPC, convinced some employers that legislation was necessary. Operating under the threat of legislation, under pressure from civil rights groups, and under persuasion from their own voluntary fair employment groups, businessmen in the 1950's placed a small number of black pioneers in nontraditional jobs. Such placements were tokens, and most employers continued to discriminate against most black applicants. Nevertheless, in many industrial states and some municipalities, the early fifties saw a small but growing acceptance of the idea of fair employment and a tolerance of legislation toward that end.

4

Opposition to Employment Integration:
The Plant

The voluntary fair employment activity and token placements of the early 1950's were an attempt by some elements in the business community to live up to the American Creed without sacrificing profitability. These early postwar applications of the American Creed grew out of the developing popular and government demands for equal employment that had arisen during World War II. Where the pressure to integrate had become acute (but not yet law) businessmen who felt uncomfortable discriminating against blacks could satisfy both their consciences and the demands of society through a minimal change in employment procedure.

Although the few breakthroughs of the 1950's were important indicators of the kinds of general changes that would follow in the 1960's they were the exceptions rather than the rule. The business community widely opposed employment integration during the 1950's. For a significant number of businessmen the refusal to hire Negroes did not come from weighing the conflicting demands of the American Creed and the Capitalist Ethic and opting for the latter. These businessmen suffered no cognitive dissonance when they discriminated because they were racists for whom the American Creed was a whites-only ideology.

Racist explanations for excluding blacks from employment decreased during the 1950's and virtually disappeared during the following decade. Employers may not have changed their personal attitudes toward blacks, but they recognized a liberalizing public attitude toward race relations, and they sought to present a position more in line with the American Creed.

Once employers recognized there was a growing public demand for fair employment they found themselves faced with a dilemma. Most whites (including many of the businessmen themselves) still opposed equal employment and presumably any attempt to hire blacks would be costly in terms of employee and customer reaction. On the other hand, articulate segments of the public, the government, and sometimes the employers themselves accepted the ideal of employment integration, and any refusal to follow that ideal required some rationalization. The most obvious, the most rational, and the most frequently used explanation was that, whatever its abstract merits, fair employment would create unnecessary expenses and was therefore a violation of the Capitalist Ethic.

Even though fears of high cost kept most businessmen from integrating their firms during the 1950's the period was marked by increasing demands for black employment and therefore an increasing amount of business rationalization as to why no blacks were hired. Although constant discrimination in the job market and inferior educational facilities had combined to severely limit the number of Negroes trained for skilled and white-collar jobs, there were almost always more qualified black workers than there were businessmen willing to employ them. The availability of qualified blacks and the pressure to hire them made it difficult for employers to ignore the problem and depend on established institutional procedures to deal with Negro job seekers. If blacks were denied jobs, managers had to have a policy to explain why. When the president of a large Chicago store, who later became a national leader in the fight to solve minority problems, was asked in 1955 why he did not employ any Negro clerical help, he explained that his staff had a predilection for beautiful red-headed Irish girls. In other words, it was the fault of the system, not his personal bias that had led to the racial imbalance. Additional discussion forced him to admit that having been confronted with the situation, he had to make a personal decision, and he promised to do what he could to promote integration in the future.[1]

The reasons businessmen refused to hire Negroes between the end of World War II and the beginning of the civil rights revolution in 1960 fell into three major categories:

Personal racism—Some employers objected on inherently racial grounds to employing Negroes. These businessmen either simply did not like Negroes, or they objected to on-the-job social contact between whites and blacks, or they believed that Negroes had racial traits that made them inferior workers.

External racism—Many employers, who usually claimed they had no personal objections to hiring blacks, assumed that their employees, their customers, or the community was biased. These businessmen feared that others would react adversely to black employees and that their business would suffer.

Inertia—A third group of businessmen were afraid of being pioneers. They had no specific objections to employing Negroes, but they wanted to wait until someone else hired blacks first. Large numbers of businessmen who would otherwise have been willing to integrate, refused to do so because others in their geographical region or in their industry had not.

The statement of Paulsen Spence at the 1947 Senate hearings on an FEPC bill reflected the full spectrum of racist thought as it applied to the employment of Negroes. Spence based his assessment of blacks on the belief that they were behind whites on the evolutionary ladder and had less experience with civilization. Specifically, Spence made the following generalizations about the habits and abilities of Negroes: 1) "The average Negro is dirty," 2) "A substantial portion of the Negroes are affected with venereal diseases . . . no self-respecting white woman would use a toilet that had been used by a Negro," 3) "The Negro is completely unreliable," 4) "No matter how hard they try, there are few Negroes who can resist the temptation to steal," 5) "The Negro is further handicapped by the fact that he will not work for another Negro," 6) "Likewise, I doubt if there is a white man in the whole South who would work under a Negro," 7) "The Negro . . . has practically no mechanical aptitude, and figures such as are used by a bookkeeper are a complete mystery to him," 8) "The Negro is not an immoral person, but rather an unmoral person. I doubt if the average Negro of either sex has morals much different from Falla."[2] Spence was unusual in his forthrightness and willingness to sum up the racist's view, but many of the sentiments he expressed were shared by respectable businessmen both in the South and in the North.

Investigating business race relations in 1946, Everett C. Hughes found that despite their experience with Negro employees during the war, businessmen continued to think of the Negro as "a creature unfit for any but the marginal positions in industry because of his laziness, primitiveness, and childishness, yet full of an unjustified desire to have what he does not have and should not want to have, up to and including marriage with the manager's secretary."[3] Southern employers were particularly apt to hold racist stereotypes, but during the 1950's many northern businessmen also regarded blacks as racially inferior. As late as 1966, 21 percent of northern business managers and 68 percent of southern managers in one sample asserted that they did not think Negroes were as intelligent as whites.[4]

Businessmen who believed that Negroes were biologically inferior found it not only easy, but natural, to support segregation, and they viewed integration as a violation of eternal truths. The spokesman for an ad hoc, small-business, anti-FEPC group explained that segregation was "natural law" because "even the birds of the air, the beasts of the field, the bugs and the worms in the ground choose to associate and work with their own kind."[5] Belief in the inherent inferiority of Negroes or in the natural law of segregation were general values that manifested themselves in the specific fear of social integration. Exactly what constituted social integration was, of course, a matter of individual interpretation. In the early 1950's social integration frequently meant any contact as equals between blacks and whites, but in later years the line was sometimes more finely drawn. In 1962, an important Georgia manufacturer of office supplies who had integrated blacks into most areas of his company below the white-collar level explained that he was willing to extend economic opportunity on a nondiscriminatory basis, but he would not be "a party to any deviations which might savor of social integration." Apparently he believed that promoting Negro women to clerical positions was tantamount to social integration.[6] If an employer believed, as did one Indiana businessman, that the framers of the "Constitution" [sic] were referring only to white Protestants when they said "all men are created equal," and that God did not intend intermingling, then the closer the contact between black and white, the more un-American and blasphemous such activity would be.[7] And in fact, the closer the form of contact between the races, the more employers (and whites in general) objected. Thus individuals who expressed no opposition to employing Negroes, nevertheless, refused to do so for fear that equality in employment would lead to more intimate personal contact, which the employers considered improper.[8]

Since the closest socially recognized form of intimacy was marriage, businessmen frequently pointed to interracial marriage as the reason they would not hire Negroes. A New York employer who affirmed his strong support of equal opportunity indicated he would not hire a Negro secretary because he did not want his daughter marrying a colored boy. When asked what the connection between these two situations was, he replied, "Well, the line has to be drawn somewhere, and I draw it at personal intimate relationships."[9] Managers frequently objected to intermarriage in terms of their expectations for their own children, and then they transferred this concern from the family to the firm. Businessmen who viewed their employees in a strong paternalistic light acted in what they considered their employees' best interests when they refused to bring blacks into their corporate families. Both the chairman of the board and the president of a large Chicago financial institution liked to view their company as a cross between a social club and a family. They provided employees with all kinds of fringe benefits, including free meals in the corporation's own restaurant. Because many of the young employees married each other (the president had met his wife there), the management carefully screened all applicants as to "character and social acceptability." Whatever their character, Negroes were considered socially unacceptable as marriage partners.[10]

In the South fear of intermarriage continued to be a deterrent to fair employment well into the 1960's. During the early years of the civil rights movement the executive vice president of the Retail Merchants Association of a progressive southern city rejected the idea of employment integration on the grounds that "Martin Luther King and the NAACP has as its ultimate objective, intermarriage, and all other activities are directed toward this end."[11]

The businessman who rejected blacks as potential employees because he did not want his daughter, or for that matter anyone else's daughter, to marry one, rested his argument on the cornerstone of American racism. Although some employers rejected blacks as suitable mates because they attached specific unacceptable qualities to them, most employers who refused to hire Negroes out of fear of intermarriage did not feel compelled to give reasons why they wanted their employees to avoid social contact with blacks. The fact that Negroes were Negroes was sufficient in itself. The discriminatory businessman had four hundred years of racial exclusiveness to support his position, and even the most persuasive proponents of integration seemed to be at a loss for an appropriate response.

The employer who would not hire blacks because he wanted to protect the racial purity of whites was expressing his racism in a purely social manner. Businessmen seeking to prevent social relations between blacks and whites could not defend their positions from a strictly economic point of view. Whatever his employees did with each other after work was (barring negative community reaction) literally none of his business. However, when the employer's racism manifested itself by finding fault with specifically work-related traits, the racism cloaked itself in the Capitalist Ethic. If, due to biological shortcomings, Negroes were inferior workers, then opposition to integration made good business as well as good social sense. By and large, businessmen assumed Negroes were unreliable, unambitious, unintelligent, and unacceptable to white customers, and thus were incapable of filling responsible positions.[12] The imaginative employer could find proof of these childlike characteristics in every aspect of black behavior. A Baton Rouge employer complained on the one hand that Negroes were lazy because they would not work longer hours when he offered them higher wages, and on the other hand that they were unreliable and undependable because they quit his employment to take higher-paying jobs.[13]

While some employers attributed highly specific physical traits to blacks, such as the ability to withstand heat or an insensitivity to toxic chemicals,[14] the most consistent physical stereotype was the classic concept of "strong back, weak mind." Thus blacks were frequently considered only for jobs which required a maximum of stamina and a minimum of intelligence. So ingrained was this stereotype that firms which had successfully used Negroes for years, such as an Atlanta steel company, simply phased them out with the coming of mechanization on the assumption that blacks could not do any work of higher levels.[15]

To a limited extent businessmen's negative attitudes toward blacks during the 1950's stemmed from their experiences with Negro workers during World War II. But, while some employers generalized the poor performance of a few blacks to the entire race, many more employers unrealistically generalized their exceptionally good experience with pioneer black workers during the 1950's. Throughout the war, due to the severe manpower shortage, many employers hired poorly qualified blacks because they were the only workers available. Not surprisingly, these businessmen were dissatisfied with their Negro employees and used their unhappy wartime experiences to justify discriminatory postwar employment policies.[16] In the decade after the war, however, business experience with blacks was, for the most part, favorable. Many pioneer black employees were overqualified, and their outstanding performance on the job gave rise to high expectations for black workers in general. Businessmen who employed blacks during the fifties rejected the racist stereotype because experience taught them it was not true. They could conform to the American Creed by offering employment opportunity to blacks while getting more than their money's worth in talent.

Beginning sometime in the 1960's, however, as the pool of overqualified black workers dried up, there appears to have been a resurgence of negative business expectations toward black capabilities. Unlike earlier racist stereotyping that grew out of ignorance, this later downgrading of black ability appears to have been based on experience. A study by Dwight Vines in 1967 found that both in the North and in the South managers who had *no* experience with Negro employees tended to expect *higher* quality work from blacks than managers who had experience with them. Vines found increasingly favorable managerial attitudes toward Negroes, but he also found increasing dissatisfaction with the performance of Negro workers.[17] It would seem that despite some poor on-the-job performance by blacks, businessmen during the late 1960's were placing greater importance on equal employment than on equal performance. Some businessmen may have claimed they were getting inferior work from black employees, but the expectation of poor quality work from Negroes ceased to be a generalized stereotype.

Whether or not they were personally biased against blacks, employers were often reluctant to admit that they had violated the American Creed by finding blacks unacceptable for employment. Businessmen preferred to see themselves as helplessly caught in the trap of other people's racism. Aversion to Negroes on the part of others was the single most important reason cited by businessmen for their failure to employ black workers between the end of World War II and the beginning of the civil rights movement.[18] In 1953, the executive director of Minnesota's Fair Employment Practice Commission observed that "while we have encountered some evidence of prejudice, we do not find strong expressions of it on the part of those who make employment policy." He found that the problem was "a very general feeling of fear that prejudices on the part of fellow workers, union members or customers will cause friction in the company or the union or will cause a loss of trade."[19]

Unlike the fear of blacks, which was racist and was condemned by the American Creed, the fear of losing trade was good business and was approved by the Capitalist Ethic. By transferring the source of discrimination from himself to others, the businessman not only absolved himself of guilt for acting unfairly, but also rationalized his unfair employment policy. The entire burden of responsibility fell from the employer's shoulders when he attributed racial bias to others. He could adopt a position of moral purity while perpetuating an admittedly immoral policy. The fault lay in the system. Capitalism was responsive to the demands of the people and the capitalist could change only after the people had changed.

Businessmen often ascribed the severest racism to their female employees. There was a persistent belief among employers that women were particularly prone to Negrophobia and the more women a businessman employed the more likely he was to reject the idea of Negro employment.

The employers' expectations of female opposition to blacks was not necessarily based on an accurate assessment of the white women's actual feelings. Blood's study of the integration of Minneapolis-St. Paul retail sales personnel provides a good example of such unwarranted fear. A third of the managers Blood questioned predicted difficulties when they introduced blacks into their white-collar, predominantly female labor force. In fact, when integration occurred, there was practically no opposition at all.[20] A 1955 incident in a North Carolina furniture company illustrates how far out of touch employers could become. The personnel manager of the company called one of his top secretaries into a conference in order to demonstrate to a visitor the extent of white aversion to working with blacks. Much to his chagrin he discovered that the secretary, although a local girl without a college education, had no objections whatsoever to working alongside Negroes. She explained to the incredulous personnel man that she entrusted the care of her children to a Negro maid—with whom she ate lunch—and therefore could not see why she should object to a similar pattern at work.[21]

Because most women were white-collar workers who depended to some extent upon job status to compensate for the typical low pay of clerical help, employers faced the double problem of status threat and female reaction when they employed Negro office help. The office manager in a Chicago garment factory said he had no objections to hiring black clerical help but doubted if he could "attract high class white personnel for employment after employing Negroes." It took a visit to a successfully integrated department store to convince him that job status was not inversely proportional to the number of Negroes on the staff.[22]

Even businessmen who had successfully integrated their firms continued to believe that whites resented interracial employment. As late as 1962, several Atlanta employers refused to allow their firms to be used as examples of employment integration because they said their white employees did not want it known they were working with blacks.[23] There is some evidence to indicate that the introduction of blacks into an all-white work force did have a detrimental impact on employee morale,[24] and antiunion employers feared that white employee backlash might take the form of unionization.[25]

Quite clearly some managers were placing their own prejudiced thoughts in the minds of their employees. Nevertheless, the pattern of employers assuming worker opposition was too consistent to imagine that it was based solely on the racism of businessmen. Employers who had been "burned" during the war, like the North Carolina mill owner whose workers had not only walked off the job when blacks appeared but who had also refused to touch any of the "contaminated" thread which the blacks had spun, continued to shy away from blacks in the postwar years.[26] Throughout the 1950's many employers who attempted to employ blacks found themselves facing vociferous employee opposition, and fainthearted employers who took their workers at their word remained opposed to integration.

When employers did move to hire blacks and refused to be intimidated by white resistance, they seldom suffered any prolonged trouble.[27] This was true partly because employers did not attempt to hire Negroes in regions where the white population was vehemently antiblack. Nevertheless, the extent of employee Negrophobia is certainly open to question. Even in a hard-line southern city like Dallas, at least one clothing store successfully integrated its work force as early as 1952.[28] In most cases employers were not ready to test the depth of employee prejudice, but the case of a medium-size machine shop in Dallas demonstrated that even a timorous move to employ Negroes could meet with unexpected acceptance from white workers. The president of the firm, which made gears, had suffered from high turnover among his white employees. In 1953, at the risk of being branded a "nigger lover," he decided to train blacks. He believed that Negroes would provide him with a more stable work force because they would not be lured away by the aircraft plants which were pirating his other workers—aircraft companies did not employ blacks at skilled jobs. After secretly training the Negroes at night, the president broke the news to his day workers, apologized, explained his economic predicament, and assured them that the blacks would not get their jobs. He even admitted to the men that he was prepared to back down if there were widespread opposition. There was none.[29]

Worker opposition to blacks did not necessarily die after the employer placed Negroes on the job. While most early fair employment policies were implemented smoothly, there were numerous instances of continued employee resentment even after blacks had begun to work. Particularly during the early fifties when virtually no blacks held nontraditional jobs, whites were extremely concerned about the structure of white-black relations on the job. Established job patterns relegated Negroes to inferior positions. Therefore any job at which a Negro worked was *ipso facto* a low status job and a threat to the white workers who shared it. When a Dallas retail store promoted a Negro employee to a cashier's position in 1954, white girls complained and demanded that she wear a uniform. The store complied and satisfied the white objections by forcing the black girl to wear a badge of service.[30] This case was not unique. White employees frequently insisted on some kind of distinction between black and white workers, usually demanding segregation of work places, lunch rooms, toilets, and company recreation facilities.

During World War II, Executive Order 8802 had prohibited discrimination in hiring in industries holding government contracts. The executive order, however, did not deal with on-the-job segregation of working quarters and plant facilities and the wartime Fair Employment Practice Commission did not attempt to do what committee member Mark Ethridge said "no power in the world—not even in all the mechanized armies of the earth, Allied and Axis," could do, that is "force Southern white people to the abandonment of the principle of social segregation."[31] Wartime acceptance of on-the-job segregation was not limited to the South. When RCA brought the first Negroes into its Indianapolis plant in 1942, the company agreed to provide segregated facilities "as a concession to the expressed will of the white workers for the purpose of achieving the introduction of Negroes.[32] When integrated facilities had the support of management the War Labor Board supported such a move against the objections of the workers, but when management was willing to accede to their white employees' demands for segregation the government agencies went along.[33]

The physical demands of production militated against continued extensive segregation on the work floor after World War II. In the traditionally unpleasant or menial jobs assigned to Negroes, segregation existed by department, but once blacks began to move into production-line work such segregation became difficult to maintain. It was awkward to try to turn white jobs into black ones and uneconomical to separate blacks and whites working at the same job. Some plants did try to keep their workers separated, however. In 1954 the personnel director of the Chicago branch of a major insurance company hired eleven Negro clerks and placed them in a separate office in the cellar. The manager supplied the segregated unit with its own air-conditioner and Coke machine and, in the absence of complaints, was convinced that the segregated Negro women were happy. He was so sure that the black clerks were content that he invited a visiting antidiscrimination field worker to interview them. The personnel man seemed genuinely shocked and confused when the questions of the visitor brought the black workers' resentment to the surface.[34]

Managers explained the maintenance of on-the-job segregation by claiming that Negroes had certain characteristics that made them unacceptable to white workers. During World War II, workers in a Connecticut factory complained that Negroes were dirty, louse-infested, and diseased. "Diseased" in these cases was usually a euphemism for venereal disease, a belief which manifested itself in "elaborate efforts to avoid using the toilets Negroes used."[35] Venereal disease particularly frightened whites and was a major theme in plant desegregation battles. A midwestern employer explained that he found that Negroes had a higher incidence of venereal disease than whites, but that during World War II he had hired them anyway as long as they agreed to get the disease treated. Since the company hired its first black workers only at the lowest level, and gave them no opportunity to advance, it is hardly surprising that white workers concurred with the management's decision to segregate sanitary and eating facilities.[36]

When first employing Negro workers a number of employers instituted physical examinations, including blood tests, to forestall possible employee objections to dirty and diseased coworkers.[37] Although a "hypothetical program" for the integration of Negro employees, drawn up by the American Friends Service Committee in 1950, did not "recommend additional Wassermans unless all employees got Wassermans," it then cited the cost of these blood tests for venereal disease as the only additional expense a company might undergo as a result of employing Negroes.[38] As late as 1966 a southern firm required its black employees, but not its white workers, to obtain a report on their health from the public health office on communicable diseases.[39]

White fears of Negro-borne diseases commonly led employers to separate "social" facilities for black and white workers. During the 1950's throughout the South and in many areas of the North dining rooms and bathrooms were strictly segregated. Frequently the segregated facilities paralleled departmental segregation. The separate and usually inferior toilets and lunchrooms assigned to blacks matched their separate and usually inferior jobs.

In several instances when employers attempted to integrate facilities during the 1950's opposition came from black as well as white employees. Some older black workers, fully aware of the social implications of integrated bathrooms and cafeterias, feared the conflict they believed would ensue. When, in 1955, the vice president of a major Dallas department store suggested to an older black employee (the head of the maintenance department) that the cafeteria be integrated, the employee, who had been with the firm for 25 years, demurred. He explained that as long as the black workers ate in the kitchen no white woman employee who might have a grudge against one of the Negro workers could use his proximity in the waiting line as an excuse for claiming he had gotten fresh with her. The vice president admitted he had not considered the problem in that light, and he called off the move.[40] There were additional instances in Raleigh, North Carolina, and in Indianapolis where Negro maintenance workers refused to use company dining facilities which were open to all employees. In the Indianapolis case the black workers refused to attend a newly integrated company picnic in 1953 and asked that they be given their traditional separate outing.[41]

Objections to integrated facilities on the part of black workers were relatively rare and limited to situations in which the Negroes were otherwise relegated to an inferior status. By far the largest number of objections to integration came from white workers, and most of their objections centered on integrated toilets. In the South, part of the problem arose from southern laws, ordinances, and commission rulings that required plants to have separate bathrooms for black and white men and women.[42] Such laws could be a real deterrent to smaller companies' considering the integration of their staffs. When a small firm employed Negro janitors a small third toilet met the legal requirements, but bringing black women into the labor force presented a more difficult problem. Employers thought they would have to construct another complete bathroom to meet the needs of the new black employees, and the expense was often inhibiting, especially when coupled with strong opposition from white women.[43] A major national food chain fired the black women in several of its North Carolina branches in 1957 when the state inspector demanded that the firm add a fourth rest room. All the company's stores in the state had been built on the assumption that Negro women would never be employed, and for reasons of room or expense, local managers were unwilling to expand their facilities to meet the demands of the law.[44]

Until the late 1950's employers in the North as well as in the South had to face the problem of integrating the washroom. Indeed, the problem may have been somewhat more acute in the North because, unlike southerners, northerners had no generally accepted method of dealing with white objections to sharing facilities. Southerners, whether or not under the aegis of the law, differentiated between economic and "social" integration by maintaining segregated facilities even for an integrated work force. Northern employers, on the other hand, faced either the ire of their white employees if they integrated social facilities, or the awkward alternative of establishing segregated facilities in a society that did not condone this kind of blatant racial discrimination. Well into the 1950's many northern employers continued to react with ambivalence and confusion when employment integration forced them to face the great water closet crisis. One Chicago insurance company tied itself in knots over the problem of social integration. The firm, which had traditionally hired Negroes only as messengers, agreed to open all positions to black applicants. But the messengers had their own lounges and rest rooms, and the management was not sure what to do with the new black employees. On the one hand management did not want to extend to black women the segregated pattern they had established for the black men, but on the other hand if the company did not provide the newly hired black women with separate toilets then the managers worried that they would have to integrate the men's rooms.[45]

Toilet trauma did not strike southern employers widely until after the Kennedy administration. Most southern employers considered the employment of Negro workers sufficiently daring in itself without attempting to compound their troubles by integrating their nonwork facilities. In some cases southern management went to astounding lengths to assure their black workers of separate but equal toilets. In 1952, a Dallas food company was able to solve a minor personnel emergency by installing a sanitary napkin dispenser in the Negro women's rest room after difficulty had developed over the black workers using the machine in the white rest room.[46] Frequently separate but equal toilets were more separate than equal. A small Dallas garment manufacturer hired his first black power machine operators in 1953. He set up a partition to divide them from his white workers on the work floor, and made the black workers use a small, inadequate toilet while his white girls used a much larger wash room.[47] Perhaps the most extreme example of the two-toilet syndrome occurred in 1958 in an Atlanta company where the owner bowed to employee demands and made his Negro porter use the segregated toilet of a company in the next building.[48]

Under considerable pressure from the government, from elements within the business community, from some unions, from civil rights organizations, and frequently from parent companies headquartered in the

North, southern firms began to desegregate toilet facilities during the 1960's. By that time public opinion in the South had evolved to the point where many white workers could accept shared facilities, but employers did not always recognize that their employees' attitudes had changed. In 1963, the Retail, Wholesale and Department Store Union forced the Suffolk, Virginia, plant of the Planters Peanut Company to integrate blue-collar jobs, plant entrances, water fountains, and the cafeteria, but the company balked when it came to desegregating the blue-collar rest rooms.[49] The firm claimed it would lose two hundred of its two hundred and fifty white employees (it had 1,250 black workers) if it eliminated the separate toilet facilities. The union complained to the federal government's Committee on Equal Job Opportunity, which threatened to cancel the firm's government contract unless the company integrated its washrooms. Faced with the possible loss of business, the company complied with the union demands and did not lose any of its white workers.[50]

In the North, the attitudes of both employers and employees toward integration changed at approximately the same rate. However, in the vast majority of the cases reported from the South in the period after 1960, southern management appeared considerably ahead of the southern work force in accepting racial integration. This is not to say that southern businessmen were in the vanguard of social and economic progress in their part of the country, but rather that employers were vulnerable to external pressure and therefore made changes in personnel policy before their white work force was willing to go along. Employers faced with loss of contracts or legal action could and did enforce nondiscrimination and integration on the line, but social pressure was frequently sufficient to maintain segregation in work-related facilities even after racial designation signs came down.[51] By and large southern management believed that southern white workers looked upon desegregation as inevitable. Employers thought white workers would try to delay integration by every means at their disposal but in the end would live with it.[52] And indeed there were examples of successful integration of facilities in southern companies. Workers in a southern industrial plant decided they would rather be clean than continue to boycott an integrated shower,[53] and textile plants in Alabama reported that within a few weeks of integration in 1967 workers had ceased to use the paper cups at drinking fountains and the disposable toilet covers in the rest rooms.[54]

The demands by employees for duplicate toilet facilities suggest the fear of sexual contact between races that frequently complicated attempts to integrate employment. While the taboos against mixing the races were stronger in social than in economic activities, many white workers and employers considered the mere presence of a member of the opposite sex and race a potential social hazard. In 1952 a small Charlotte, North Carolina, manufacturer commented that he believed that Negro and white men could work together and that Negro and white women could work together, but that a white woman working with a black man would have "lost something," would have "been degraded."[55] Even when employers allowed blacks and whites to mix on the job they could demand that male Negroes adopt a socially subordinate role in their contact with white women. For example, a long-time black employee of an Atlanta insurance firm was reprimanded for complimenting a white female employee on her hairdo and for addressing her by her first name—as she had always addressed him.[56]

Since whites were most willing to accept integration in employment and least willing to accept it in purely social activities,[57] employers frequently feared that they would face their most difficult integration challenge in those areas where the company sponsored social activities.[58] By and large, however, these fears seem to have been ungrounded. Company-sponsored athletic teams usually had no problem absorbing blacks. The white bowlers of one midwestern firm even offered to dissolve their team when they could not find a bowling alley that would allow blacks to play.[59]

Sexually mixed social activities were somewhat more of a problem, but even at dances and dinners whites accepted the presence of blacks. A survey of forty-four firms in the upper Midwest in 1949 indicated that Negroes successfully participated in the social activities of 71 percent of the companies.[60] However, the definition of "successful integration" has to be understood in context. In the mid-fifties an executive of a New York firm which "successfully" included Negroes in its social programs said, "I don't think they mix socially. You have to draw the line. They brought their own friends to the Christmas parties. They know their place."[61]

Perhaps because of the tradition of paternalism toward the Negro, some southern firms allowed blacks to attend company social programs during the 1950's before they would give them full job equality.[62] But after 1960 the solutions to the problem of social integration appear to have polarized among southern firms. Firms which had traditionally sponsored extravocational social programs either continued them with full black participation or they were disbanded. One very thorough survey of management practices after the passage of the Civil Rights Act of 1964 indicated that many southern companies folded their social programs in the face of employee resistance to black participation.[63] But at the same time in the same states there were companies that successfully integrated parties, picnics, luncheons, and dinner-dances with no employee opposition.[64]

During the late 1940's and the 1950's the personal racism of many employers prevented them from instituting fair employment policies. Although such men sometimes used economic excuses to explain their discriminatory practices they were not in fact choosing the Capitalist Ethic over the American Creed but were merely catering to their own personal prejudices. Some of those employers who rejected blacks for reasons of external racism were in fact projecting their own personal hates onto their employees. Other employers, however, who might have personally accepted blacks, truly feared the costs of a negative reaction from their employees if they integrated. For these businessmen external racism was a genuine economic threat which forced them to choose between their individual acceptance of the American Creed and the Capitalist Ethic which prohibited unnecessary business disruption. This fear of friction between blacks and whites was so strong that many employers attempted to maintain separation on the job and in plant facilities even after they had begun to extend some measure of equal opportunity to Negroes.

5

Opposition to Employment Integration:
The Community

Even those businessmen who honestly believed that white workers would seriously object to integration, and therefore claimed economic considerations prevented them from hiring blacks, were dissembling to some extent. External racism on the part of employees was rarely strong enough to significantly endanger company operations. After all, employers held the ultimate economic whiphand over their employees, and businessmen were not inclined to cater unduly to workers' whims except when they coincided with the employers' own interests. Thus, with only an occasional exception, when a strongly motivated employer put integration on a "take it or leave it" basis, white workers were not willing to sacrifice their livelihoods on the altars of bigotry.

While employers feared the reactions of those over whom they held economic sway, they were even more afraid of the external racism of those upon whom they were economically dependent—their customers and the community at large. If a businessman were willing to fire a white employee who openly opposed integration, the worker had to have a profound commitment to his racist values to undertake the personal disruption of leaving one job and hoping to find another. However, the customer who objected to blacks in a business had merely to walk into another firm and transact his business there. While there was usually a high correlation between the attitudes of the community and those of a company's employees, if there were differences, the community attitudes had a much stronger impact on business thought. From the perspective of the Capitalist Ethic the reaction of customers was much more important than that of employees. While the "customer is king" concept may have been overemphasized in the perpetuation of the myth of free market capitalism, it was nevertheless an important consideration in the minds of many businessmen, particularly in the retail and service industries.[1] Employers, always sensitive to their customers' feelings, assumed that their patrons would object to Negroes dealing with them as equals and catering to their intimate personal needs.[2] The vice president of an Atlanta credit company explained that his firm would not hire black investigators because it would be extremely embarrassing "for a white person to be asked personal questions about his friends and their habits by a Negro."[3]

Prior to 1960, many employers were so convinced that their customers would reject Negro sales and service personnel that even firms with a black clientele excluded blacks from their staffs. Despite the fact that Negro organizations had been agitating for equal employment opportunity at least since the 1930's,[4] many employers continued to insist that Negroes objected to being served by members of their own race. In fact, there are a few substantiated cases of black customers objecting to Negro sales or service personnel. In 1953 a Greensboro, North Carolina, furniture dealer claimed that his uncle attempted to allow Negroes to run an outlet in a black neighborhood, but that "not one of them called him to express appreciation for having given this sales position to a Negro but many of them complained to him for having sent a Negro to transact business with them."[5] For the most part, however, managers merely assumed that their black customers shared the values of the white society and would feel demeaned if served by a Negro. In 1955 a Chicago insurance executive predicted that if he "opened a Southside office in the Negro section and hired Ralph Metcalf, Jackie Robinson or other famous Negro athletes to work there, the Negroes wouldn't go there."[6] And as late as 1962 an Atlanta furniture store owner explained that in order to "satisfy customers of both races white salespeople only are employed."[7]

As was so frequently the case in the history of American race relations, the black worker was discriminated against both coming and going. If some employers who had black customers refused to hire black salespeople because both their white and their black customers might object, many more refused to hire black sales or service personnel because they had few black customers and did not want to attract any. The general opinion in the business community until well into the 1960's was that Negroes could only be used to cater to Negro clientele.[8] If there were few or no potential black customers, then many businessmen shared the attitude of a Chicago broker who could not understand "why we should have to go way down and look for employees from the Negroes when we are able to reach out and hire the best in the community."[9]

A 1953 article in the trade magazine *Sales Management* aptly illustrated the assumptions which limited business use of Negro sales and service personnel. David J. Sullivan, a black marketing and management consultant, discussed in some detail the hiring and use of black salesmen. The entire article was predicated on the assumption that Negroes would only be used to sell to members of their own group: "To sell effectively to retailers in Negro areas is it necessary to employ Negro salesmen? . . . Do retailers in Negro neighborhoods prefer a Negro or a white salesman to call on them? . . . The answer in both cases is 'yes' [sic]." Sullivan went on to discuss the cultural uniqueness of the black community, and concluded that only black salesmen could overcome the obstacles to profitable sales in Negro neighborhoods. Nowhere in the article did Sullivan even hint that blacks might be able to sell to whites.[10] The idea that Negro sales and service personnel should be used primarily with Negro customers continued to exert great influence on employers into the mid-sixties, especially in the South. As late as 1963, Negro baseball star and businessman Jackie Robinson encouraged businessmen to hire more blacks sales people by emphasizing, "you will demonstrate to the Negro consumer that you want his business . . . [and] you will find you have won the consumer loyalty of the Negro."[11]

Employers based their fears of customers' objections to black sales people on the same stereotypes which made employers fear their employees' opposition to blacks. Employers widely held, for example, that Negro men could not serve in any position which brought them into contact with white women, especially in the woman's home. In Columbus, Ohio, the manager of an office of a large life insurance company agreed in 1952 that Negro policyholders and employees should not be forced to do business in a special segregated office. Despite his inclination toward equal treatment, however, the manager resisted the suggestion that black men be used as premium collectors. He said that collectors called at the homes of policyholders and that they dealt mostly with white married women whose husbands would object and whose neighbors would talk if a Negro man visited them during the day.[12]

Employers' fears, of course, were not entirely unfounded. The Columbia, South Carolina, branch of a national retail firm, somewhat atypically, used a black appliance repairman as early as 1952. During one of his house calls a white woman accused him of "frightening her." The man was brought to trial (the specific charges are unclear) and was found innocent only after his supervisor interceded on his behalf. The store itself assuaged the woman's fright with two hundred dollars and started keeping a file of complimentary letters on all its Negro employees to use in such cases in the future.[13] A similar incident occurred in 1954 in Chicago, when an investigating company which had been using Negroes in Negro neighborhoods decided to use them in white areas as well. Not only did the clientele object, but one of their men was picked up by the police on a loitering charge after a woman complained about him being in a white section of town.[14]

Throughout the 1950's, in both the North and South businessmen believed the public still would not accept the implementation of the American Creed and they invariably sought justification in the Capitalist Ethic. In every kind of retail and service industry and in many manufacturing firms, the response to the question of integration was the same—"our customers would object and we would lose business." The comments in 1952 of a man who was later to become one of the South's leading spokesmen for moderation and integration are indicative of the depth of potential opposition to black sales people. Not only did this Atlanta businessman personally reject the idea of hiring Negro stenographers, but he said that if Rich's (the leading Atlanta department store) "put on a Negro sales girl I would never let my wife shop in that store again. . . ." He went on to bolster his self-proclaimed position as "a long way ahead of the others . . . and a southern liberal" by praising Booker T. Washington's accommodationist Cotton States Exposition speech.[15]

It need hardly be said here that, for the most part, the fears of massive customer resistance in the North were unfounded. Stores which placed blacks in sales positions rarely experienced sufficient public disapproval to even warrant mentioning. A few dissatisfied customers occasionally cancelled charge accounts and there were isolated incidents of unpleasantness, but by far the vast majority of employers discovered that the public was much more willing to accept Negro sales people than they were.[16]

It appears that both southern employers and southern consumers were slower to accept black sales personnel than northerners. Large numbers of southern employers continued to use customer nonacceptance as an excuse for not hiring blacks, at least until the passage of the Civil Rights Act of 1964. Interviews with numerous businessmen in Atlanta, Georgia, during the early 1960's disclosed widespread agreement that firms would lose white business if they employed blacks in customer contact positions.[17] Atlanta firms that had begun to integrate in 1962 were reluctant to advertise their activity for fear of alienating, or further alienating, their customers.[18] They need not have been. Under pressure from boycotts and sit-ins a group of almost a dozen stores in the city hired their first Negro sales help during the Christmas rush of 1962 and received no adverse public reactions.[19] The following year the manager of a home-delivery bakery not only agreed to hire his first black routemen, but also agreed to assign them without regard to the racial makeup of the neighborhoods, thus breaking the taboo against black men calling on white housewives.[20]

By the mid-sixties many national firms had begun to use Negro outside salesmen without regard to the race of their potential customers. Public attitudes had changed to the point where Negro salesmen in the North and Midwest were in a position to tap the guilt feelings which a

hundred years of agitation against the evils of discrimination had culti-
vated. White customers were frequently eager to give orders to black men
as a way of demonstrating their freedom from prejudice.[21] Nevertheless,
even among the supposedly sophisticated and progressive giants of American industry old stereotypes continued to play a role in determining
personnel policies. At the end of the 1960's, steel executives still felt that
Negroes were generally so socially unacceptable that they could not be
hired as salesmen because "certain social contacts away from a business
place are important. For example, a salesman may be expected to take his
client to dinner or discuss a contract over cocktails at a private club."[22]

Internal racism, that is, personal employer bigotry, was the first possible barrier to black employment. But even when they accepted the
American Creed many businessmen rejected employment integration because of external racism from the white employees and customers. Public
opposition to integration was the final category of external racism which
stood in the way of black employment. The public can be defined as those
people who, though not necessarily the firm's customers, influenced the
social, political, and economic climate in which the company operated.
Although businessmen frequently equated specific powerful local figures
with the public, they could also mean the more amorphous collection of
customs, social patterns, mores, and habits which established the intangible
real boundaries of corporate action.

The businessman who molded his actions to fit public opinion could
not cite the immediate costs or profits of integrating. Nevertheless, the
Capitalist Ethic underlay business decisions based on conformity to local
values. The atmosphere of community respect and goodwill so necessary
to smooth day-to-day operations was a product of good local citizenship,
and that meant adhering to community hiring patterns. Two surveys
taken a decade apart disclosed that when businessmen did integrate they
counted "public image" and "favorable community relations" as the
most important benefits gained from employing Negroes.[23]

The search for public approval was indicative of the secondary role
the American Creed played in the businessman's decision-making process. Even when the employer personally accepted the ideal of equal
opportunity and believed he could surmount the obstacles of employee
and customer opposition, the fear that he might offend some vague community standard was frequently enough to preclude black employment.
In such situations the businessman played a passive role and allowed
social forces to determine the timing and extent of integration. By remaining morally neutral the management of the company followed what it
perceived as the path of least resistance. Such a stand gave maximum
weight to organized power blocs within the community during times of

social flux, and maximum weight to local social patterns during times of stability.

Because of their monopolistic status, public utilities offer a unique illustration of the relationship between public opinion and the Capitalist Ethic. Even though they were frequently among the first companies in a region to hire Negroes in nontraditional jobs, the utilities consistently soft-pedaled their pioneering during the 1950's. In 1950, a midwestern telephone company refused to allow the American Friends Service Committee to use it as an example of successful integration because they feared that other businessmen would accuse them of pioneering only because they were a monopoly that did not have to face competition.[24] On the other hand, those utilities which refused to integrate placed great emphasis on their vulnerability, as controlled monopolies, to public opinion. In 1952, an eastern telephone company fired a newly hired black girl because white employees objected to her. Their personnel man explained that the white objections were indicative of public sentiment and that "a public utility could not crusade, nor could it be far behind nor too far ahead of the general community feeling."[25]

During the 1950's public opinion in the North shifted sufficiently to become a force for, rather than against, integration. In 1955 conservative businessmen in Indianapolis cited the "favorable climate" as the reason for initial black employment.[26] Those employers who continued to resist integration were less able to hide behind the Capitalist Ethic. Racism could no longer be cloaked in acceptable economic terms, and businessmen began to experience the conflict of values that arose when violations of the American Creed went unjustified. A group of Columbus, Ohio, businessmen who had previously been able to hold off the demands of black pressure groups became "scared to death" when white groups began pushing for equal employment opportunity in 1953. They were afraid that there was a major movement behind the fair employment drive which would "some day bring forth a big editorial or publicity about their policy of discrimination."[27] By 1958, the mood of the country outside of the Deep South had moderated enough to allow how-to-do-it books on employment integration to discuss the pros as well as the cons of publicizing steps toward equal employment opportunity.[28]

In the South, where segregation and discrimination had not only been a long sanctioned historical practice, but where formal ideological justification for discrimination also existed, employers were likely to attribute discrimination to "local custom." Local custom reflected not only the desires of the dominant segment of society (not always the majority in the South), but also the quasi-legal mores of race relations to which all citizens were expected to conform.[29] Southern employers were fully aware during the early fifties that change was in the offing, and many of them expressed their willingness to begin hiring blacks when the time came—but not until then.

Even when national companies hired integrated work forces in their plants outside the South, local custom dominated their employment patterns below the Mason-Dixon Line. In 1954 a manufacturer of electrical equipment decided to open a plant in Raleigh, North Carolina. The industrial relations manager reported that the city's responsible citizens, "and I don't mean Rotary and Kiwanis," demanded that the firm agree to abide by the city's segregated employment practices. The company had three options: 1) not to move to the city, 2) move, but refuse to abide by local patterns, and 3) move and knuckle under. It chose the third option and operated under the constant scrutiny of the city's first citizens, who made sure that the firm towed the color line.[30]

When a businessman was confronted by public opinion, either from common citizens or from pillars of the community, he was dealing with a tangible situation. The employer could judge the impact of his integration activity through community feed-back and adjust his policy accordingly. So long as the Capitalist Ethic took precedence over the American Creed, public opinion was the final arbiter of whether or not to integrate. However, public opinion could change without the employer realizing it, and, as long as there was no pressure for integration, many businessmen clung to policies which were no longer demanded by community mores. Such employers were tradition-bound. A survey of more than one thousand discriminatory firms by a special Pennsylvania commission in 1953 revealed that well over a third of them listed "tradition" as the cause of their discriminatory policies.[31] The report did not disclose what the firms meant by "tradition," but it is possible that in the early fifties some of them may have been entirely innocent of any conscious effort to exclude blacks from their firms. An Indianapolis insurance executive expressed surprise in 1952 when an equal employment opportunity worker asked why he had no black clerical workers. The manager said it had simply never occurred to him to ask that question. He had no answer, and he promised to begin actively looking for Negro clerical employees.[32]

For firms like these, discrimination did not exist because of a conscious decision on the part of management not to hire blacks but rather was the result of a failure of management to make a firm policy in favor of fair employment. As soon as such firms realized that no cost was involved in living up to the American Creed, the low-key, low-pressure tactics of pro-fair employment groups, including the usually circumspect activity of state FEPC's during the 1950's, were frequently strong enough to prompt them to adopt a formal fair employment policy. Tradition-bound companies usually existed in northern industrial states where public opinion had come to oppose discrimination. In many cases it took only a minor incident to bring the shift in public opinion to the company's attention.[33]

A closely related, but somewhat different set of rationalizations and justifications came into play when the businessman perceived his role not as one of passive response to public opinion or community standards, but as a creative force within the community. Ideally, employers liked to limit their community leadership to broadly acceptable activities, such as support for charities, education, and noncontroversial civic improvement. Thus, there would be no conflict between a businessman's role as a power in the community and his need for good public relations. The equal employment issue placed the employer on the horns of a dilemma. While Negro employment was clearly a problem that called for decisive business leadership, it also threatened to expose the employer to adverse publicity no matter what he did, either from the opponents or proponets of employment integration. Joseph Ross, a Detroit department store executive, explained that the businessman had "been trained all of his life in the tradition of his craft to be a useful citizen in his community, but never to get involved in controversial issues."[34] Faced with the unavoidably controversial issue of fair employment, during the 1950's businessmen usually decided that they owed greater allegiance to the patterns of the local community than to the ideal of the American Creed—at least when it came to hiring blacks.

Even when equal employment was required by law, the extent to which employers hired blacks was almost invariably determined by the prevailing racial attitudes of the local community. Very rare were men like the manager of an Indianapolis variety store who said that he was a citizen of the company, not a citizen of the community, and would abide by community patterns only to the extent necessary to maximize profits.[35] Much more common were remarks like, "our recruitment has been limited to white workers because of the responsibility we owe this community."[36] In 1953, when one of the nation's largest steel corporations was challenged by black leaders to do something about discrimination in the Philadelphia area the company assured them that it wanted to be a good neighbor and work along with residents and other businesses in the area. But the company made quite clear that because of its size and the potential impact of any of its decisions on the community, it would not take the lead in pushing to end discrimination.[37]

Except for instances in which the business community feared economic disruption, employers usually opposed attempts to alter community race relations patterns. The urge to conform to community patterns of employment was so strong that even firms which pioneered in placing

Negroes, thus deviating from the accepted norm, expressed their policy in conservative rather than liberal terms. International Harvester, which in fact did break community patterns, albeit cautiously, privately admitted that "when they went into a community they studied very carefully what other business practices were, then I. H. went just as far in its integration as the most progressive company in that vicinity and then just a little farther."[38] In public statements, however, this policy was interpreted as meaning that "when International Harvester enters a new community its plant adopts policies generally in consonance with community patterns."[39]

A series of events at the end of 1963 served to focus public attention on the problem of the corporate role in the community. In September, the Student Nonviolent Coordinating Committee (SNCC) accused the United States Steel Corporation, along with a number of other Birmingham, Alabama, employers, of encouraging by silence the racial violence that had recently led to the bombing of a church and to the death of four black children there.[40] SNCC's charges were followed four days later by a similar accusation from Charles Morgan, Jr., a Birmingham lawyer. Morgan told a Yale University audience that Roger M. Blough, chairman of the board of U.S. Steel (and a graduate of Yale Law School), could telephone Alabama's governor, George C. Wallace, and tell him, "frankly, a) the Birmingham schools aren't good enough and b) the Negro children should be admitted by nightfall. . . ."[41] Within a week groups were picketing U.S. Steel's office in New York City.[42]

Under the threat of contract cancellation from the federal government, Tennessee Coal & Iron, the U.S. Steel division in Birmingham, had begun to eliminate some of the more blatant forms of anti-Negro discrimination practiced in its plant, such as its dual seniority system. However, Arthur V. Wiebel, president of Tennessee Coal & Iron, rejected suggestions that he exert pressure within the business community and the city to ease racial tension. Wiebel and other businessmen did talk with government conciliators and sign a newspaper advertisement calling for the employment of black policemen.[43] But on the one hand Wiebel claimed that U.S. Steel did not have much economic power in the community, and on the other he insisted that the firm would not do anything "because the minute that would happen, people would say: 'There's U.S. Steel trying to run Birmingham.'"[44] Roger Blough backed up Wiebel at a news conference when he stated, "for a corporation to attempt to exert any kind of economic compulsion to achieve a particular end in the social area seems to be quite beyond what a corporation can do."[45] Despite encouragement from newspapers and the President of the United States, the company stuck to its position that "any attempt by a private organization like U.S. Steel to impose its views, its beliefs and its will upon the community by resorting to economic compulsion or coercion would be repugnant to our American constitutional concept. . . ."[46]

While it may be questionable whether Roger Blough actually refused to exert his influence in Birmingham because of constitutional scruples, at least he cannot be accused of hypocrisy. Neither U.S. Steel nor its representatives were in the forefront of the drive for economic civil rights or in the movement to promote social consciousness among businessmen. The same, however, cannot be said of the Crown-Zellerbach Corporation. For a number of years in the mid-sixties this San Francisco-based paper company was one of the important big business advocates of increased black employment. James P. Mitchell, Secretary of Labor in the Eisenhower administration, an important, socially concerned businessman and a senior vice president of Crown-Zellerbach, became a leading spokesman not only for extending equality to Negroes but for actively going out to recruit and train qualifiable Negroes. Mitchell based his advocacy on a number of the standard arguments: it was morally and socially right, it would undercut radical demonstrators, and it was cheaper than other methods of solving the problem.[47] As the head of a special committee appointed by the mayor to study the problem of Negro employment in San Francisco, Mitchell had recommended that the mayor establish another commission to set up a privately financed training program.[48]

Mitchell's stand brought him and his company widespread recognition in the firm's home city. By 1964 northern white attitudes had changed to the point where people not only accepted equal employment opportunity but could applaud Crown-Zellerbach's call for extra assistance to help blacks achieve economic equality. However, when faced with a much cruder form of discrimination, in a much less enlightened environment, Crown-Zellerbach's vaunted liberalism failed to materialize. At precisely the same time that Mitchell was exhorting his colleagues in the Bay Area to go the second mile, Crown-Zellerbach was trying to turn its back on the racial problems of Bogalusa, Louisiana. Crown-Zellerbach had acquired its Bogalusa plant in 1955. For almost ten years it maintained segregated facilities and separate lines of promotion for blacks and whites. Not until the federal government began to put pressure on the company did it slowly and reluctantly begin to alter its discriminatory practices.[49]

Crown-Zellerbach's reluctant acquiescence to the fair employment demands of the federal government may have been less impressive than the company's West Coast rhetoric, but it was positively radical compared to the firm's response to racial upheaval in the city of Bogalusa. Bogalusa had chosen to ignore the Civil Rights Act of 1964, and Crown-Zellerbach, which provided 70 percent of the town's income, chose to stand back while the Ku Klux Klan intimidated the few whites who supported the law.

Not until word of Crown-Zellerbach's callousness got back to San Francisco, where public pressure was exerted against the company, did the firm express its support for equal rights for all citizens in Bogalusa. Violence continued in Bogalusa, and the company continued to hide within its shell, insisting that civil rights were a community not a company responsibility.[50]

The Congress of Racial Equality, which had come to Bogalusa to help the black community gain its rights under the Civil Rights Act, instilled a new militancy in the people. In early 1965, the company which had only recently desegregated its water fountains, suddenly found itself confronted with a black work force that challenged the firm, not in the community, but within its own walls. The company may have been reluctant to act outside of its immediate jurisdiction, although it apparently would when sufficient pressure was brought to bear, but when blacks started protesting Crown-Zellerbach's employment patterns the firm could no longer hide behind claims of corporate noninvolvement in civic affairs. Demands by the black community for improved job conditions overflowed into general civic disorder which ended only after the home office sent one of its vice presidents to Bogalusa to oversee negotiations with the protesters. Robert F. Collins, a lawyer for the black protest group, announced "the real issue is what, if anything, the company is willing to do to compensate for the past discrimination. To merely say that at this point you are going to be fair is not enough."[51] The company, whose northern spokesman had been nationally honored for his calls for hiring qualifiable blacks, was reportedly "appalled" at this suggestion. The company, whose northern spokesman had urged his fellow businessmen to act in order to forestall government action, responded to southern demands for better economic treatment with the comment, "This company cannot be expected to solve these problems by itself. The government will have to lay down industry guidelines."[52]

The U.S. Steel and Crown-Zellerbach incidents illustrate the difficulties faced by firms when they attempted to reconcile their internal employment policies, the demands and expectations of their immediate community, changing national standards, and the requirements of governmental bodies. Executives of both companies had refused voluntarily to intervene on behalf of blacks in the community. When circumstances forced them to contend with the de facto power they wielded, they both chose to deny the obvious and retreat behind ideological arguments for noninvolvement. Writing in *Harper's,* David G. Wood, himself a steel executive, called U.S. Steel to task for failing to act. Using the same argument Crown-Zellerbach used in San Francisco, but not in Bogalusa, Wood called on industry to move ahead, both inside and outside the plant. If they did not, Wood warned, businessmen were inviting government interference into the conduct of business "in a situation where it is right and we are wrong."[53]

Wood was only one of a number of voices that began to call for increased corporate participation in the social affairs of the community in the mid-sixties. Some of the calls for business involvement were extensions of business' safe and long-accepted role as a mainstay of the Community Chest and a governmental ally in making noncontroversial civic improvements.[54] More socially concerned employers, however, denounced individual action and called for corporate commitment to solving the community's social problems. In 1967, Elisha Gray, chairman of the board of the Whirlpool Corporation, said,

We businessmen can put together more sheer power for good or for evil than all the rest of the elements of the community combined. Our, call it influence, call it clout, by any name it is the ability to get things done. Most of us, however, and you can include me until recently, have not wanted to throw our weight around. We have not felt it the province of business to get into social problems. Whatever personal comfort you may get from the individual approach it won't do a thing toward curing problems of such great dimensions. I believe the job can only be done by organized, unanimous, mass assault by businessmen.[55]

As government and public pressure grew during the 1960's firms increasingly began to ignore local custom and started to emphasize their responsibilities to a constituency beyond their immediate community. This new found sense of national social responsibility reflected the changed relationship of the Capitalist Ethic and the American Creed. The black revolution of the early 1960's and the Civil Rights Act of 1964 made it economically wise to adhere to the American Creed. Leadership suddenly became a practical policy. Companies began to take positions like that of the Caterpillar Tractor Company, which told its management, "we should be prepared to contribute strong leadership to community endeavors to alleviate the long years of injustices which exist for so many minority group people."[56] Thus businessmen brought pressure on their own to extend open housing to blacks in Chicago,[57] lobbied for open housing legislation in Delaware,[58] put pressure on the directors of local recreation facilities to extend equal treatment to blacks,[59] and generally began making themselves visible in areas traditionally considered outside the proper sphere of business. Things had gone so far by 1967 that Edward C. Logelin, Chicago regional vice president of U.S. Steel, told a college business symposium, "more and more business is finding it must be concerned with other than its commercial aspects. . . . The problems [of society] cannot be solved by government alone, but rather the private sector will have to supply many of the answers and all of the wealth that will be required."[60] U.S. Steel had at least learned the rhetoric of the new era.

After 1960, leadership, that is, a willingness to be first, became a popular virtue in the eyes of businessmen. But prior to the Kennedy administration even businessmen who fully accepted the importance of the American Creed (with some important exceptions which will be discussed in later chapters) were afraid to be the first to employ blacks. In a confidential interview in 1955, one of the nation's most important management consultants observed that "most businessmen are not bigots, but they are cowards."[61]

A detailed consideration of the variables responsible for a firm assuming the leadership role in equal employment are beyond the scope of this study. However, as far as businessmen themselves were concerned, company size, length of time in the community, and sometimes the nature of its ownership seem to have been the most important factors in determining an employer's willingness to pioneer.[62]

While large corporations were not necessarily in the forefront of social innovation, throughout the 1950's small businesses often waited for larger companies to take the lead in nondiscriminatory employment, and the limited available data indicate that larger companies were more likely to begin hiring Negroes than smaller firms.[63] The personnel director of a small Chicago packing house indicated in 1951 that he would like to promote blacks to supervisory positions but did not dare proceed until the large meat packing companies began doing so.[64] Similar views were held by many managers of smaller businesses, including the president of a Columbus, Ohio, bank who refused to employ blacks because it would be "highly contrary to established Columbus tradition . . . until some of the larger banks had made a move first."[65] On the other hand, there were firms, like U.S. Steel in Birmingham, which claimed they would not act precisely because they were dominant and did not want to be accused of trying to control the town.

The herd instinct is strong in the business community. No employer likes to break a new trail into controversial areas, but once a pioneer indicates a new direction many other employers are eager to follow his lead. Virtually all organized efforts to crack the employment barrier attempted to exploit the businessman's propensity to follow by holding up to reluctant firms examples of successful employment integration.[66] Where leaders existed who were willing to be used as examples, this technique could be very successful since many employers quite consciously modeled themselves after the most progressive firm in town.[67]

In his study of department store integration in Minneapolis-St. Paul during the late forties, Robert O. Blood, Jr., found that when one company advanced a Negro to a job above the generally accepted level for blacks other firms usually followed suit. Blood referred to this process as the "domino theory of employment breakthrough."[68] For the theory to work, not only did the dominoes have to be lined up, but the first one had to fall, or be pushed over. The first domino frequently had a very broad base and was not easily tipped. Indianapolis department stores were under pressure to upgrade Negro employees after 1951, when they began losing black workers to Indiana Bell Telephone and to the Finance Department of the Army which maintained a large office in that city.[69] In May of 1952, the personnel manager of one of the city's major department stores determined that the time had come to hire blacks as sales clerks. He had the reputation of being an "excellent combination of idealist and realist," and other managers had said that when he began hiring Negroes they would know that the time had come for action. The personnel manager took his leadership role in the business community quite seriously but preferred to give another store the opportunity to be the first in the city to move on this particular issue. He devised a plan whereby the other store would place a black worker on the selling floor on Monday morning and he would follow on Tuesday. He believed that a third store would then be willing to employ black sales people on Wednesday.[70]

The other stores were not willing to conspire to integrate. They played Alphonse to the first store's Gaston, and nothing happened during the first part of the summer. Because the first store had always dominated patterns of retail conduct in Indianapolis, other employers refused to budge until it acted.[71] An American Friends Service Committee field worker in Indianapolis then accused the personnel man of the key firm of being "the greatest single obstacle to integration in the city." This charge apparently stung, and the personnel man showed the accusatory letter to the store's president. The president manfully suggested that the integration take place while he was on vacation. That way there would be no way of appealing the decision up the line.[72]

On September 16, 1952, the personnel manager announced at a meeting of the merchants association that two Negro sales clerks were starting work that morning. He explained that he had held off, hoping that someone else would move first so that his store would not always get the credit for being the most progressive firm in town, but since none of them would, he felt compelled to take the step.

Other companies in Indianapolis were favorably impressed by the experience of the pioneer, and within three months the Indianapolis outlet of a major national chain had promoted two blacks, one to head its service station, and one to a sales position in the store. The other two of the three big department stores in Indianapolis were a bit slow to come around, and the personnel manager of the pioneering store jocularly, but significantly, teased their management as "being slow in recognizing that a new community pattern had taken place," to which one of them responded that he himself would begin employing blacks within a month.[73]

The pattern of integration in the department stores of Minneapolis-St. Paul, Indianapolis, and Chicago demonstrated the importance of leadership, albeit reluctantly assumed leadership, in breaking with tradition. The inaction of the banks of Chicago is a good example of how the failure on the part of any businessman to take the lead could greatly impair progress. As early as 1950, one Chicago bank which did a large amount of business in the black community began hiring Negroes, but the president of the institution did no proselytizing himself and would not let his bank be used as an example by groups who were attempting to get other banks to adopt fair employment practice.[74] In 1952, a second Chicago bank hired its first Negro white-collar worker. It had been the subject of extensive pressure from the black community which had exploited the bank's close ties to the labor movement to embarass it into employing blacks.[75] Since the situations of both banks were atypical, neither constituted a precedent for the rest of the financial community.

At a meeting of Chicago bank personnel directors in 1952, those present agreed that when the time came they would all hire blacks simultaneously, but they could not agree on when the time would come. The vice president of the most important bank in Chicago, the institution which could set the pattern for the industry, refused to employ Negroes because he believed if he changed his policy the other banks would feel morally committed to follow him, and he certainly did not want to run the risk of being labeled a moral leader.[76] Two years later, despite constant requests from the black community and fair employment groups, Chicago area banks had still refused to hire blacks. Banks in outlying areas said that they were waiting for downtown banks. Middle-sized Loop banks said they were waiting for the industry leaders, and the industry leaders dragged out all the excuses in the book to explain why they were not ready to integrate. They feared their employees would object. They feared their customers would object. Negroes had too high a crime rate, and too many of them were on relief, and if the banks gave them jobs they would just attract more undesirable black immigrants from the South. Management said that such a controversial step had to be initiated by the banks' boards of directors, and the members of the boards said that it was an operational matter which should be decided by management.[77]

Finally in the spring of 1955, the bank which had previously refused to integrate because it did not want to exert undue moral pressure on its fellows began hiring blacks in nontraditional jobs. The bank had been under fire from various Chicago organizations since 1950. The Urban League, the American Friends Service Committee, and the Chicago Commission on Human Relations had all approached, cajoled, and threatened the institution, but to no avail. The deciding factors apparently were "a gentle prod by government people" and a meeting with executives from similar institutions throughout the nation, many of whom had successfully employed Negroes for some years and wondered why their Chicago counterpart had not acted.[78] Like the management of the first two pioneers, the leaders of the third bank to integrate refused to urge similar action on their colleagues. Each bank had started an equal employment policy for internal reasons, and while they might have been able to bring pressure on other banks, their managers apparently valued their friendships with other bankers too highly to endanger these relationships with social pressure.[79]

The blame for the resistance of the Chicago financial community to integration cannot be laid entirely at the feet of the three pioneering institutions. One of the most influential of the Loop banks was controlled by an ardent racist,[80] and other internal factors undoubtedly played a part in preventing the dominoes from falling. The failure of the pioneers to be leaders also was extremely important. The pioneers were so circumspect about their employment policies that the neighbor bank of one of them could explain his lack of black workers by pointing out that because the bank's owners were Jewish they had to be extremely conservative and "conform to the standards set by other large banks in the community," even though an integrated bank was located next door.[81] It was not until 1957 that some of the more important downtown banks began to hire Negroes. This was more than seven years after the first breakthrough, and almost three years after the second.[82]

The emergence of plans for cooperative action to achieve integration simultaneously among businesses reflected the businessman's fear of moving ahead of his colleagues in the controversial area of equal employment. Both the Indianapolis retail stores and the Chicago banks made abortive attempts to coordinate the introduction of black workers. This hide-in-the-crowd approach had wide business support and was recommended by some integrationist advocates.[83] In the 1950's employers as divergent as a Philadelphia banker and a North Carolina shoe manufacturer called for coordinated action in order to protect individual employers from customer retaliation and from the charge of breaking local custom.[84] Even in the mid-sixties the President's Committee on Equal Employment Opportunity proposed this technique of unified action to persuade reluctant southern employers to comply with the law.[85] It was not, for the most part, until after the passage of the Civil Rights Act of 1964, that company executives occasionally felt brave enough to take the position of the corporate personnel manager of Owens-Illinois who said, "We hope to chart an independent course of our own so that we will be ahead—a little bit ahead—of the law and the average company. We would like to be two or three years ahead of the times but not twenty."[86]

Even when businessmen personally accepted the idea of fair employment and believed they could overcome objections that might arise within the plant, they frequently still refused to employ blacks out of fear of community opposition. Basically businessmen viewed themselves as chips floating on the stream of society. They sought to follow the strongest currents of customer response, public opinion, community mores, and colleague reaction, rather than attempt to risk the danger of being swamped by moving against the tide.

6

The Rationale of Integration

Between the end of World War II and the beginning of the Kennedy administration, increasing numbers of firms reluctantly and slowly began to employ Negroes and advance black workers to positions previously barred to them. While personal and external racism were sufficiently strong to prevent the majority of employers from hiring blacks, nevertheless the trend during the late 1940's and 1950's was toward larger numbers of blacks in better jobs. The improving Negro employment situation was based, to a large extent, on factors beyond the control of the business community. State FEPC laws, increasing federal pressure for equal employment, the manpower shortage of the Korean War, and a growing public demand for fair treatment of blacks all forced businessmen to reconsider their stands on black employment.

Whether or not there were compelling practical or economic reasons to integrate, an important segment of the business community sought to develop a rationale for integration which would explain the changing pattern of Negro employment in terms of morality, ethics, and the American Creed of fair treatment and equal opportunity for all citizens. Pioneering employers of the 1950's, more than any other group of businessmen, had to come to grips with the full implications of the American Creed. Even when the motivation for black employment was more practical than ideological, large numbers of pioneers seized the American Creed as the most satisfying justification for their change in policy. For the businessman with a strong personal commitment to human equality, the American Creed stood as legitimate in its own right. But for the employer who was under pressure from forces besides his conscience, the American Creed provided that wonderful little extra which transformed a mere business decision into an act of Christian virtue and an affirmation of the American dream.

The single most important factor in the liberalization of hiring policies after World War II was the adoption of state fair employment practice laws. By and large, businessmen opposed the passage of these laws[1] and were less than enthusiastic in complying with them once they were passed. Yet, in those states that had strong enforcement procedures (usually also an indication of strong popular support for the FEPC laws) businesses did begin to grant equal employment to job applicants. In 1948 the American Friends Service Committee (AFSC) drew up a list of corporations which had good reputations for fair employment. Of the sixteen firms on the list, fourteen were located in New York State (nine of those in New York City), one was in New Jersey, and one was in Chicago. New York and New Jersey both had very strong antidiscrimination laws, and the Chicago firm, International Harvester, was a national leader in the movement for integrated employment.[2]

New York led the way both legislatively and in terms of public attitudes which made it comparatively easy for New York businessmen to employ blacks. In other states, without strong FEPC laws and with more public antipathy toward integration, employers who allowed Negroes to pierce the job ceiling could not protect themselves from criticism under the aegis of legislation. In the period before the legal and popular pressure of the civil rights revolution, many pioneering businessmen justified their unorthodox employment practices on ideological grounds.

The American Creed was the most important ideological argument businessmen used to defend their employment of Negroes. The discrepancy between the American Creed[3] and the actual treatment of Negroes became particularly evident during World War II. When the wartime FEPC forced a New Haven firm to hire Negroes, management told the white workers, "millions of American boys of all races, colors and creeds are now fighting shoulder to shoulder to rid the world of a system which is based on racial intolerance and the crushing of personal liberty." The company explained that many of the same undemocratic tendencies existed in the United States, even in New Haven, but that industry could "do more than any other single agency to contribute to a solution by showing its willingness to employ those who are best qualified for employment opportunities."[4] Black men are dying in a war against racist totalitarianism; how can we then deny them equal job opportunity in the war effort at home?—this was a standard, and frequently telling, argument which employers used to convince their employees to accept black coworkers.[5]

While many businessmen used justifications based on democratic philosophy when explaining why they employed Negroes during World War II, references to the American Creed were usually window dressing for the more cogent pressures of the wartime FEPC and the manpower shortage.[6] The three-step procedure developed by a West Coast aircraft company to try to calm white workers when they objected to new black employees demonstrated the reality of legal compulsion which lay beneath the ideological facade of the American Creed. First, the company used the stock "black soldiers are dying" argument, to which it added that the company needed black manpower to help the home-front war effort. Second, the firm made a humanitarian appeal to the whites, explaining that "they have to have money to buy food and clothing just as we do." If these two somewhat abstract appeals were not sufficient grounds to accept the new black workers, the management pointed out that Executive Order 8802 forced the company to stop discriminating and declared that any employee who objected would be fired.[7]

The wartime rhetoric of patriotism and democracy may have been a convenient facade to cover up the actual compulsory sources of integration, but there was too much truth in the moral arguments for them to lapse along with Executive Order 8802 at the end of the war. William F. Rasche warned the Milwaukee Employers Association in 1946 not to slip back into prewar discriminatory employment habits. Among other reasons, Rasche explained "that in a world in which the combined populations of all the countries on the globe consist of colored and white people in the ratio of two to one, we will sacrifice our position of world leadership if we fail to practice our principles of American freedom and justice at home."[8]

The antifascist patriotism of the war quickly became anticommunist patriotism in the postwar years. Those who opposed equal employment legislation sometimes branded its proponents communist.[9] Occasionally those who advocated voluntary fair employment were also viewed as dangerously left. The president of an insurance company told an AFSC field worker in 1952 that talk "about helping businessmen find pioneer placements . . . was a fine way to introduce subversive people into a business" and that for all he knew the field worker might even be a communist.[10] However, it was also common to find businessmen espousing integration as a method of fighting communism. The American Creed of equal opportunity was in theory, if not in fact, the human corollary of the free market and was therefore theoretically anticommunist. However, like the arguments which stressed patriotism during World War II, arguments emphasizing anticommunism during the Cold War appear to have been mostly the payment of lip service to the prevailing mood. It is unusual to find records of businessmen who advocated the anticommunist approach in private. When the national personnel director of a large mail order house did mention anticommunism in a private discussion in 1950, he did so not in terms of his own personal convictions but rather as a suggested method of most efficiently reaching other businessmen.[11]

If there was a dearth of private comment favoring integration as a way to stem the red tide, there was a surfeit of it in published sources.

Supporters of FEPC in the state of Washington in 1949 tried to convince the legislature that communists wanted the bill defeated because it would deprive them of a valuable source of propaganda.[12] Throughout the Truman and Eisenhower administrations supporters of economic equality for blacks, whether through legislation or through voluntary action, commonly exploited the fear of communism in advocating their cause.[13] As late as 1960, Frank M. Folsom, president of RCA, said that "job discrimination against any of our people on the basis of race or creed weakens us in the face of adversaries who would destroy our democratic system."[14]

Anticommunist arguments for fair employment picked up logically where antifascist arguments had left off. During both World War II and the Cold War patriotic arguments directed against the nation's enemies served to link the essentially conservative ideals of nationalism with the progressive values of employment integration. Moreover, by taking the offensive, fair employment proponents tried to stop short those who attacked their cause as disruptive and communistic. However, the concern with tying fair employment to the antired bandwagon was as much a public relations maneuver as an expression of business ideology.

By the standards of the 1970's the actions of pioneering fair employers personally committed to the American Creed appear to have been half-hearted tokenism. Their policy of hiring an extremely limited number of blacks, frequently overqualified, did not even attempt to meet the fundamental problem of mass unemployment and underemployment in the black community. But those business pioneers in the forties and fifties were far ahead of most of their colleagues, and their successful experiments with integration eliminated many of the racist arguments on which discrimination had rested for years. The favorable experience of businessmen with pioneer placements in the 1950's effectively cleared the ground for the civil rights onslaught of the 1960's, which was able to build on the pioneer experience by demanding more extensive integration than would have otherwise been possible.

In the vast majority of cases in which a company voluntarily played a pioneering role in integrating its work force, a single "great man" who believed the American Creed was more important than the Capitalist Ethic was responsible for the policy.[15] In the absence of obvious external pressures the pioneering businessman frequently ascribed his decision to employ blacks to ideological motivations. Such an employer did not act on the basis of the Capitalist Ethic rationale traditionally accepted in the business community; instead he frequently claimed he was answering an inner call, variously referred to as ethics, morals, principle, conviction, or liberalism. These terms were the employer's name for the reason he chose to follow the American Creed even when it appeared to be in conflict with the

Capitalist Ethic.[16] Exercising personal conviction through equal employment was usually the prerogative of the firm's owner or chief executive although there were numerous cases in which a highly motivated personnel manager was able to institute integration because his superiors were passively sympathetic.[17]

In rare instances a businessman was able to combine his commitment to fair employment so closely with his business philosophy that he simply refused to admit any possible contradiction between the demands of running a firm and the problems of employing Negroes. To such men the American Creed was part and parcel of the Capitalist Ethic. For example, a small Columbus, Ohio, appliance dealer began hiring Negro salesmen in the early fifties. He was a man totally devoid of racial prejudice who could not understand what was so unusual about his personal philosophy or his personnel policy. He was unconcerned with the fact that he was one of the most important pioneers in Negro employment in Columbus. He said he did what he thought was right, did not care how other businessmen acted, and refused to have anything to do with the campaign to change discriminatory employment practices in the rest of the city.[18]

The attitude and employment practices of the Columbus appliance store owner represented the unusual case of a petty capitalist actually living up to the logical requirements of his code of values. At the other end of the scale were paternalistic businessmen who employed Negroes because doing so fulfilled some personal whim. Paternalistic employers virtually divorced their black employment policies from their general philosophies. To them, hiring Negroes was a kind of charity that could be indulged in with little or no regard to the overall impact of such activity on the business.

The owner of an important national producer of dairy products in Greensboro, North Carolina, exemplified the attitudes of employers who bestowed equal employment as a favor. This rather eccentric individual believed that workers could not be productive unless they lived in good neighborhoods so he personally inspected his workers' living quarters, and if he found them unacceptable the employee was required to move. The general manager of his plant and the Negro woman who was his public relations director both reported that the employees formed a union in the early fifties only after the owner had spent three years persuading them to organize. Once the union was formed, the owner began promoting Negroes into all of his production jobs and even into some white-collar positions.[19] The owner had agreed to begin integration of the secretarial help in all his offices but stopped hiring blacks when the union he had urged the workers to join turned out to be a Frankenstein's monster. Rather than remain an independent union it affiliated with the Teamsters and began to make demands. This so upset the owner that he completely reversed field, abolished all his "humanitarian" programs, including integration, and began to spend all of his time trying to get rid of as many workers as possible through automation.[20]

While a certain amount of paternalism probably played a part in many decisions to integrate, in most it was not a clearly dominant factor. Since in the second half of the twentieth century paternalism is not a highly regarded trait, businessmen who sought to explain their inner drives to employ Negroes had to find a more acceptable reason than paternalistic pity. Yet the large numbers of businessmen who claimed they integrated because of personal values were surprisingly inarticulate about the exact nature of their convictions. There were employers, of course, who explicitly cited the American Creed as the source of their integrationist beliefs. The president of the New York Life Insurance Company explained he had worked his way up from clerk to president and felt every other person should have the same opportunity. His own southern upbringing had made him acutely aware that the dream was being denied to Negroes, a situation he felt was both logically and religiously wrong.[21]

More commonly, integrationist businessmen did not articulate the specific philosophical origins of their commitment to fair employment. Instead they explained their actions by using vague terms which indicated a personal sympathy for the concept of the equality of man. When store managers in Minneapolis hired their first Negro sales women in the late 1940's they frequently referred to their own "liberalism."[22] The owner of a chain of Washington, D.C., drug stores was equally imprecise as to his motivation when he told a congressional committee why he placed his first Negro pharmacist in a store in an upper-income white neighborhood in 1951. He explained his move by saying simply, "our company felt an obligation toward these people. . . ."[23] Similarly, when a progressive young businessman took over the presidency of a Chicago photographic equipment company he informed management that lack of any black employees in the company was an indication that the firm "was not fulfilling its obligation to society."[24]

The imprecise references to "liberalism" and "obligations to society" with which so many businessmen explained their decisions to hire blacks reflected both the business community's grasp of the essential demands of the American Creed and business reluctance to forsake the practical concerns of commerce for the abstract problems of moral philosophy. Although they seldom explored its philosophical subtleties, a minority of businessmen clearly accepted the American Creed as the major reason for hiring blacks during the first decade after World War II.

Because there were significant numbers of businessmen who accepted the fundamental principles of the American Creed, appeals to that philosophy could be used successfully as a catalyst for those employers who had guilt feelings about their failures to live up to their values. The American Friends Service Committee established its Employment on Merit (EOM) program to take advantage of the personal values which predisposed some employers toward fair employment. AFSC used businessmen who were willing to give up several years of their careers to go out into the business community to talk to employers on a one-to-one basis. The field workers attempted to crystallize the nebulous feelings of support for equal opportunity into direct action in hiring and promoting blacks. The one-to-one conferences were patterned after the moral suasion techniques of the Colonial Quaker, John Woolman. The EOM program was predicated on the assumption that businessmen could be convinced to put their beliefs about equal opportunity into action. Although AFSC field workers often used practical arguments, they did so only so far as such arguments were compatible with their ethical values.[25] The AFSC-EOM programs frequently faced charges of duplicity for advocating moral suasion on the one hand while on the other it supported drives for fair employment practice legislation. AFSC took this apparently contradictory position because it recognized, without explicitly admitting so, that there was an element of truth in the anti-FEPC charge that morality could not be legislated. Thus AFSC hoped to improve opportunities for blacks by encouraging employers to see the inner light. But AFSC also believed that its technique of individual conversion helped the FEPC cause because of "its ability to win over employers ideologically, because it softens up the business community for FEPC and . . . it will produce some actual living and breathing white and Gentile employers favorable to FEPC. . . ."[26]

The AFSC approach struck a responsive chord in many employers. The chairman of the board of a Chicago steel products company approvingly noted that "businessmen do have a conscience and can be reached, and AFSC gives them a way of acting on it." He followed this comment with the observation that many employers did not like any suggestion that they integrate, but that the voluntary moral suasion approach of AFSC was better than a law.[27] Impending FEPC legislation had an uncanny ability to stimulate moral commitment.[28] One of the leaders of the Ohio State Chamber of Commerce admitted that as long as the chamber was opposed to FEPC legislation it had some "moral responsibility to do something on a voluntary effort."[29]

Large numbers of businessmen felt ambivalent about their discriminatory practices. Although they could defend their antiblack policies on Capitalist Ethic grounds, religious values provided a chink in their armor of selfishness which was exploited by integrationist forces. In 1954, one highly motivated manager of an Indiana agricultural cooperative tried to use economic arguments to convince his superiors of the validity of integration but failed. He discovered, however, that some of his bosses were quite religious (even numbering some Quakers among them) and that their religious beliefs combined with the democratic elements of their cooperative ideology made them much more receptive to moral arguments.[30] The existence of untapped religious commitment in the business community led one AFSC field worker to report that she had told the sympathetic but inflexible president of an Ohio manufacturing firm that she hoped "God will work on his conscience and keep him awake nights."[31] Calling upon God to disturb the sinner's slumber apparently had some efficacy because there is at least one report of the president of an Ohio bank "lying awake nights trying to figure out where he could place a Negro in his organization." An emotional turmoil that was undoubtedly aggravated by his position as secretary to the local Urban League![32]

Specifically, religious feelings appear to have been motivating forces for a number of pioneer employers. For these men, the American Creed was part of the Judeo-Christian ethic which, in an almost pre-industrial fashion, took precedence over the Capitalist Ethic. For example, Joseph J. Morrow, director of personnel relations at Pitney-Bowes, cited religious teachings as a rationale for integration when he told a group of Indianapolis businessmen in 1957, that

regardless of the material or social gains to be realized from providing equal economic opportunity for Negroes, there is really only one impelling and unanswerable argument in its behalf for any human—any businessman—who honestly believes in the teachings of the Christian or Jewish religions. These religions are the strongholds of the philosophical idea of brotherhood among men. . . .[33]

Some businessmen, when convinced to integrate by religious conviction, could become positively enthusiastic. The head of one of the sections in an Indianapolis department store was so moved by his desire to demonstrate that "all men are of one blood before God," and by the opportunity to "give leadership toward correcting a moral wrong," that he said he would demand equal employment in his section. If his superior objected because of possible reactions from customers, he said "that he would take the position that since his motivation was that of a Christian he had enough confidence in divine power to know that the Lord would take care of any difficulties."[34]

Expressions of religious concern for the just treatment of black workers were sometimes sparked by more mundane reasons. So long as some businessmen were being forced to render integration unto Caesar, it did not cost them anything to give a little credit to God. In 1955 the superintendent of a national soap company factory in Dallas proudly announced the firm's new policy of hiring on merit throughout the plant. He said the company was acting on this matter because it was "right, democratic and basic to their Christian beliefs." But he also admitted the company had signed a federal contract with a nondiscrimination clause, and if the firm wanted to keep the contract, it had to change its hiring policy.[35]

The evidence seems to indicate that Jewish and Catholic businessmen with liberal inclinations were particularly open to moral suasion. In response to AFSC urgings, the president of a Dallas metal products company gave consideration to a Negro applicant in 1954 (even though, he noted, he once had a black employee whom he let go because he came to work drunk). The employer explained that as a Catholic who sat next to Negroes and Latin Americans in church, he would "like to have the personal satisfaction of knowing that I was doing my little bit in promoting better community relations."[36]

The church also had a liberalizing influence on an Indianapolis bank manager who agreed to open up his employment policy in 1952 after he discovered that his personnel manager had been running advertisements which called for whites only. He commented that unlike some other parents he had not removed his daughters from their private Catholic school when the bishop had ordered desegregation and that he had no objections to his children becoming good friends with Negroes. It was not uncommon to find businessmen who had either been persuaded to moderate their racial animosity because of the experiences of their children or who pointed to their children's attitudes as hope for the future. At the same time they frequently said they themselves were too old to change.[37]

The moral influence of the Catholic Church could hardly have been stronger than in the case of a small Greensboro machine shop. After suffering a ten-year shortage of machinists, the owner recognized in 1955 that Greensboro A&T College was training a large number of black machinists who could not get jobs. He told his four employees of his plan to hire Negroes, and they informed him that if blacks came they would leave. At that point he went to see his priest. The priest told him to return to the shop and tell the workers that integration was the law of God, the law of the land, and the policy of the company. He did so, and three of the four workers, including his secretary, walked out. Nevertheless, he adhered to his policy, filled their places with new workers, and carried on his business in an integrated fashion.[38]

In general, Jews were more willing than Gentiles to pioneer in hiring Negroes. Many of the pioneering employers cited in this study, who cannot be named because to do so would reveal confidential material, were Jewish. Although Jews frequently felt that if they integrated their businesses they would be vulnerable to attack because of their own minority status, they nevertheless had a certain sympathy with the plight of other oppressed groups. The normal ambivalence between the demands of business and the obligations of conscience were thus magnified in the case of Jews. A Jewish banker from Chicago explained that he was brought up in a small southern town and knew what it meant to be discriminated against. Nevertheless, when one of his officers suggested that he hire a black secretary the resulting outcry from his employees was sufficient to have him veto the idea.[39] A Jewish Boston banker who had personally underwritten a mortgage for a black physician when the bank's board refused the loan, explained that if he ever hired Negro tellers he would do so for religious reasons since such a move was economically indefensible.[40] Robert O. Blood, Jr., compared the integration activity of Jewish and Gentile Minneapolis store owners in 1948 and concluded that "the managers of Jewish stores are more liberal in employing Negroes, in appraising Negro ability, and in predicting employee reaction."[41]

The American Creed was increasingly linked with the Capitalist Ethic in the widening wave of employment integration that followed the civil rights movement. As the risks of hiring blacks decreased and the dangers of appearing racist increased, the incompatibility of the two value sets evaporated, and businessmen could righteously attribute their actions to the American Creed while noting, albeit parenthetically, that integration was also good business. In 1963, the public relations firm of Ruder and Finn advised its clients to accelerate their hiring of blacks not because it was good public relations (although it probably was), but because "we all sort of came to the conclusion that there are times in a company's life—like an individual's life, or a country's—when it should want to do the right thing."[42] In a private letter asking AFSC not to give up its Atlanta operation, the president of one of the city's banks said that he wanted to do "the thing that is morally right and in the long run economically right . . . to do what our hearts tell us to do."[43]

Because the American Creed was a widely held (if frequently violated) value, companies which used it as a basis for hiring blacks cloaked themselves in respectability. But by the same token many firms felt that a commitment to the American Creed should be made voluntarily and not forced down the employer's throat. Thus in 1953, a Greensboro electrical equipment manufacturer who was undergoing intensive pressure to upgrade blacks from the government, from his union, from the Urban League, and from NAACP, praised AFSC for using moral suasion rather than the high-pressure techniques of other organizations.[44] When, however, integration was forced down the employer's throat, the American Creed was always a handy way to sweeten the bitter medicine of coercion. For example, in

1945 the management of a New Jersey manufacturing firm told its supervisors that they were "bringing in Negro labor, not only to comply with certain regulations and laws, but also because the management felt it had a moral obligation to fulfill."[45] And it is difficult to imagine a more blatant example of situation ethics than the "Equal Opportunity for Minority Groups" policy statement issued by one firm around 1964. The statement explained the fair employment policy as a "matter of our social and moral responsibility. If there was ever a situation which deserved measurement by our time-honored standard of, 'does it square with what is right and just,' it is this one." Well and good, except the company had preceded this pious plea with a preface that noted, "we are businessmen, not crusaders," and proceeded to explain that the firm had not felt compelled to do "what is right and just" until 1964, because not until that year was there "a public awareness of this matter of employment and development opportunities for racial minorities *now*." Thus the company's need to follow the dictates of the American Creed was directly proportional to the public's demand that it do so.[46]

Not every businessman who acknowledged the legitimacy of the American Creed arguments for fair employment acted upon those beliefs. When told about the AFSC program for placing blacks in jobs not traditionally held by them, an account executive at a larger Chicago brokerage firm expressed strong support of the plan and indicated his willingness to speak in favor of it to other brokers and bankers. However, when he was asked if he would accept a black in his own firm as a pioneer, "this seemed to floor him, and he was at a loss as to how to answer." He finally managed to explain that his was the kind of business that required close contact with clients, knowledge of their economic affairs, a great deal of traveling, and a background in stocks and bonds. All of these requirements presumably meant that Negroes could not qualify.[47] One of the foremost supporters of civic good causes in Indianapolis told an interviewer in 1953 that he heartily approved of the program of employing blacks in nontraditional positions and said he would be glad to make a financial contribution to this worthy activity. When the interviewer explained, however, that AFSC would rather have him hire a Negro salesman than give money, he retorted that giving money for integration was one thing and integrating his store was quite another. He claimed that his store sold clothing to a high class clientele and that he would not hire Negroes because he "had no desire to solicit business for popular priced lines."[48]

The ultimate refuge of the businessman who did not want to mix his conscience with his commerce was a return to the values of the Gilded Age moguls who carefully divided their private charity from their business dealings. In 1955 a Chicago banker noted that "however liberal the present official staff may be . . . doing the right thing on the race question is one thing, to operate a business successfully from both a financial and organizational viewpoint is something else entirely different from the first."[49] One of his colleagues in the Chicago financial community also divided his personal ethics from his business activity when he observed, "bankers are very sympathetic, highly moral and concerned about the affairs of the community. As such, on an individual [as opposed to a corporate] basis they are doing whatever they can to carry out their social concerns."[50]

Evangelism is a common corollary to commitment and a number of integrationist employers attempted to convert their colleagues and their employees with race relations education programs. Proponents of equal employment opportunity placed great stress on the efficacy of education as a method of persuading others to accept their ideology. They believed, as did Myrdal, that Americans "are all good people. They want to be rational and just."[51] If one assumes that businessmen, and their employees, wanted to live according to the American Creed, but were not doing so, then one must conclude, as did Myrdal, "that the social engineering required should have its basis in a deliberate and well-planned campaign of popular education."[52] Many of Mydral's ideas were picked up in the postwar period and provided the basis for several educational campaigns designed to encourage voluntary employment integration.

The American Friends Service Committee started one of the first of these educational efforts with its Job Opportunities Program (JOP) in Philadelphia in 1945. JOP and its successor, the Employment on Merit program, eventually spread to a half-dozen cities over the next twenty years. JOP was predicated on the belief that an educational campaign could help businessmen adhere more closely to their expressed values of equality and brotherhood.[53] AFSC used businessmen as field workers, but businessmen who were willing to give up several years of their time to work for the advancement of black employment were rare indeed.[54] More often than not, even pioneering employers were reluctant to proselytize among other businessmen, so aside from AFSC, integrationist educational efforts in the business community were limited to the very practical, nonmoralistic efforts designed to head off compulsory FEPC legislation.

More commonly employers attempted to transmit their values and beliefs to their own employees through some kind of in-plant educational program. Interest in education to further better race relations during the late forties and fifties may have been as indicative of the business community's fear of employee opposition as it was of businessmen's beliefs in the educability and rationality of men. The businessman who had decided to hire Negroes still had to face his employees, and some employers used educational programs as a way to ease acceptance of the new black workers. If first-line management could be persuaded to support integration, employers were usually able to impose the change on the rank and file. Thus foremen were almost always included in the educational programs while the workers on the line were sometimes excluded. For example, the Pollack Manufacturing Company of Arlington, New Jersey, regularly indoctrinated supervisors during the late forties, but "where it appeared that discussion of the Negro subject might invite troublesome free-for-all arguments," newly employed blacks were simply assigned to their departments without anything having been said to their white coworkers.[55]

While there were occasional firms which ran their own elaborate employee race-relations programs, it was not until 1949, when the National Conference of Christians and Jews (NCCJ) organized in-plant race education programs, that the process of employee indoctrination received widespread notice. Dwight R. G. Palmer, president of the General Cable Corporation and an important leader in interreligious and interracial activities, sponsored the first NCCJ seminar in his Perth Amboy, New Jersey, plant.

Palmer's commitment to equal employment went back at least to World War II. At that time the St. Louis plant of General Cable, which made vitally needed field telegraph wire, suffered a wildcat walkout when black women were introduced into sections of the plant where they had not been employed before. Black men had previously been integrated with no difficulty, but the white women reacted violently to having to work beside black women. An army officer attempted to set up a program to educate the women into seeing the error of their ways. The workers were not receptive and the officer quit in frustration. Other military personnel seemed willing to go along with the white workers and bar the blacks from the plant. The military men believed that the production of wire was more important to the war effort than strict adherence to the nondiscrimination clause in the contract.

Initially Palmer went along with the military decision, but the idea of denying blacks equal opportunity did not rest well with his personal philosophy. While sitting in church during an Easter Sunday service Palmer came to the conclusion that only his personal intervention could solve the problem. He walked out of church in the middle of the service and flew to St. Louis where, despite the pleas of military officers on the scene, he confronted the angry women who had just shouted down the plant manager, calling him, among other things, a "bald-headed son-of-a-bitch."

In a speech that rang all the changes in the integrationist repertoire, Palmer persuaded the women to accept black coworkers. He called upon the women to judge others by what they did, not by their color or religion. He explained that black soldiers and nurses were dying to save democracy. He pointed out to the women, many of whom were of Eastern European background, "our ancestors left the countries overseas to come here and practice equality and live on merit, and live in democracy and in freedom and to get away from all of the crochety stuff that they have over there, social classes and everything else." He then asked them in the spirit of Americanism and in the spirit of Easter to accept "these nice colored girls." His plea worked. Black women were successfully placed on the work floor.[56] Moreover, General Cable continued to employ Negroes and actually increased its percentages of black workers after the end of the war.[57]

In the postwar period, Palmer served on the committee which organized the integration of the armed services and later was the chairman of the Government Contract Compliance Committee under President Truman. Despite his various official positions as an enforcer of executive decisions, Palmer maintained that he was effective not because he represented the power of the President but because he stood as an example of what could be done by a businessman willing to back up his convictions with action.[58] Palmer was not oblivious to the fact that his position as head of a committee that could cancel contracts was at least partly responsible for his successes in persuading other large firms to begin hiring and upgrading Negroes, but as far as he was concerned it played a secondary role.

Dwight R. G. Palmer was a man motivated by a strong personal philosophy which linked Christianity, democracy, and capitalism. He believed that "democracy is an extension into the political field of the religious view which regards every person, whatever his ancestry or social station, as the possessor of an immortal soul destined for salvation."[59] Palmer opposed discrimination because, as he said in an address to the Canadian Council of Christians and Jews, it sapped "the economic vitality of both our countries [Canada and the United States]. . . . It is undermining the political health of our democracies. . . . Most important of all, it is weakening the moral fibre of our nations by a kind of spiritual erosion."[60] As a businessman Palmer understood that people expected him to defend his beliefs on the basis of good business, and in fact he did see a link between democracy and capitalism, but he also believed that human equality could stand by itself without economic buttressing. Thus, he expressed annoyance and embarrassment with the idea that "democracy is good for business; that tolerance pays off in high production and profits; that civil rights are a good investment." He contended that those opposed to hatred and intolerance would act in a democratic manner "even if it were bad for business, which it is not." He concluded that "the undue emphasis put on the economic element in moral behavior is really one of the pernicious products of Marxist propaganda in our generation."[61]

Palmer used NCCJ seminars to inculcate his workers with his sense of moral commitment in the same way he used his positions in the government to inculcate his colleagues with his beliefs. In both instances he was in a position of authority over those to be converted. While Palmer's position of dominance might raise questions about the sincerity of the converts, his insistence that people be educated rather than forced to conform to his standards indicated his strong belief in the acceptability of the American Creed.

NCCJ seminars became something of a fad for several years after the first experiment at General Cable in 1949. The program itself consisted of nine weekly two-hour seminars. The meetings were held on company time, which undoubtedly helped contribute to the remarkably good attendance. Each nine-week session was limited to twenty-five employees drawn from all levels of the firm, from blue collar to management. Guest lecturers and leaders at the seminars discussed such topics as the three major Western religions, the anthropology of race, cultural differences, and prejudice, with the emphasis placed on free discussion. As Palmer put it, "within the limits of common decency, no holds were barred in the attempt to isolate and identify the bacteria of mutual prejudice and interracial myths, and then to examine the pesky creatures under the microscope of frank discussion."[62]

When the program was first instituted, Palmer was not willing to measure the success or failure of the seminars in terms of dollars and cents, although he was willing to say that the discussions had reduced tensions and improved citizenship and the spirit of teamwork.[63] However, by 1951 Palmer was more willing to make specific economic claims for his program. He said, "We found among our personnel a new spirit of cooperation with other employees and with the management. Tensions seemed to ease up. Somehow production records took on a new personalized interest, scrap figures improved, grievances did not come up so often.[64]

Perhaps because employers discovered that the integration process was not as fraught with trouble as many had feared, interest in race-relations seminars flagged after the first few years. Once businessmen realized that the presence of blacks in nontraditional jobs would not bring the walls down about their heads, they took a more cynical attitude toward converting their workers, particularly if the businessmen were not of an evangelical bent in the first place. A couple of New York employers belittled the importance of education in the late fifties when they said "education is ineffective. You'll never change my mind by talking to me. It can't be done. The thing to do is just do it. That's the best education," and "It's not so much what employees feel. They can be controlled."[65]

During the forties and fifties the moral and ethical assumptions inherent in the American Creed played an important part in motivating the placement of pioneer Negroes in nontraditional jobs. For some businessmen, their religious and ethical beliefs were enough to prod them into hiring and upgrading Negroes. Such persons frequently assumed that other citizens shared their basic values, and so they placed a high value on education as a way of promoting fair employment practice. For most businessmen, however, it took direct economic or legal pressure to germinate the seeds of guilt sown by their failure to apply the American Creed to their employment practices.

7

Economic Pressure and Attitude Changes in the Eisenhower Era

Due to general economic expansion and the Korean War, the business community experienced a manpower squeeze during the 1950's. Because there were highly qualified yet unemployed blacks available, businessmen could get superior black workers when they could not find any white workers at all. Therefore, employers had a sound economic reason for employing blacks. Moreover, the Eisenhower administration was encouraging businessmen to increase their rate of Negro white-collar employment, so any move for greater black hiring would not only rest on sound Capitalist Ethic grounds but would also have the support of a Republican administration which was trying to prove that equal employment could be achieved without federal legislation.

Forced to choose between the pull of conscience and the iron law of the Capitalist Ethic, most employers were unwilling to scrap their economic faith no matter what the demands of their religious beliefs.[1] However, if the businessman could demonstrate that equal employment opportunity stood the tests of both finance and faith, he could reconcile his religious and his economic convictions. "Most of us have a difficult time from the moral viewpoint accusing ourselves or to a lesser degree our predecessors of aggressive or even passive resistance to the realization of these rights of minorities," said a Rhode Island utility executive in 1965. He continued, "Let that be so. We wouldn't have so difficult a time of it when we perceive the situation from an economic viewpoint. After all, we are all businessmen; we're in business to make a dollar whether for ourselves or our stockholders."[2]

Ideally the businessman wanted the exigencies of the marketplace to compel him to employ Negroes. The Capitalist Ethic required the employer to maximize profits, which, among other things, demanded that he hire the best possible workers at the lowest possible price. By and large, however, the price of Negro labor, no matter what its actual cost in dollars, was too high because of the reactions of a racist society. But if no white labor were available, then the employer would have to hire Negroes if he wanted to stay in business. The Capitalist Ethic would require compliance with the American Creed, at least for those jobs for which no whites could be found. Thus economic arguments provided the businessman with a completely consistent rationalization: a manpower shortage meant the best available workers were blacks, and therefore hiring blacks conformed to the Capitalist Ethic as well as to the American Creed.

The racial employment policy of International Harvester illustrates the interplay between fair employment values and economic pressure in creating better job opportunities for blacks. Both International Harvester's motivation and the justification used by its management combined elements of the American Creed and the Capitalist Ethic. Harvester originally announced a policy of nondiscrimination in 1919. The 1919 disclaimer of prejudice included the usual "race, sex, political or religious affiliation" wording, but these seemingly liberal sentiments were actually a facade for the final phrase, "or membership in any labor or other organization," which was the firm's declaration of an open shop.[3] Although Harvester had good experiences with its black workers, the company did not develop a positive approach toward minority hiring until after the establishment of the wartime FEPC. Fowler McCormick, who became company president in 1941, the same year the FEPC executive order was issued, decided the firm should not be content with minimum compliance with the law but should become a leader in employing blacks. McCormick's new policy was administered by assistant personnel director Sara Southall, who went on to become a member of FEPC under President Roosevelt.[4]

Even though McCormick pursued a policy of equal employment because it fit into his concept of the American Creed, publicly the company sought to play down the role of ideology in determining its employment policy. McCormick, who had a reputation as a liberal in the Chicago business community,[5] personally believed that his company should be "concerned as much in the interest of employees and customers as in the interest of its stockholders" and that the corporation should perform "a useful economic and social service for the community."[6] However, McCormick's expression of social concern appears to have been unique in the public statements of Harvester management until the mid-sixties. Much more common were such comments as, "We do not wish to crusade. We're not undertaking to establish social equality, a matter of community acceptance;"[7] "Harvester is not running a crusade;"[8] and, "No high ethical or moral tone was taken. Nothing was said about 'loving thy neighbor as thyself.' "[9]

During the late forties and fifties, Harvester spokesmen sought to justify their employment of Negroes by using a combination of arguments which linked the equal opportunity aspect of the American Creed with the broader interpretation of economic self-interest. "The basic philosophy behind the policy," according to Southall, was "that a man has a right to earn a living."[10] Ivan Willis, the head of personnel, said the same thing but added, "It is our belief that if this policy is not followed, our company and the nation are the losers."[11] Willis developed the economic implications of his position when he observed in 1951 that blacks "represent a vast consumer market that will add to national prosperity as rapidly as Negroes can improve their purchasing power."[12] And in its own internal training program the company stressed not only the "right of a man to earn a living," but also the "relationship of the nondiscrimination policy to a democratic society."[13]

There was almost a schizophrenic duality to Harvester's position. On the one hand, they did not want to be seen as social crusaders and liked to emphasize the strictly business aspects of their policy. On the other hand, the company wanted to place its policy within a broader ideological framework of social commitment. While company spokesmen denied the firm had any interest in the problems of blacks outside of the factory,[14] company policy claimed, "We believe we have social as well as business obligations."[15] It was not until after the beginning of the civil rights revolution that International Harvester felt free to crusade openly, stressing that equal employment was good for the country and therefore good for the company. "This is a 'self-interest' motive, of course," said the head of Harvester's employee relations department in 1965, "and we are not embarrassed to say so, but it is also a valid and compelling reason, one in harmony with the democratic principles of our country, as well as in the best Judeo-Christian tradition."[16]

Harvester's attempts to couch its policy in mostly self-interest terms until the mid-sixties reflected both the importance of the Capitalist Ethic in business thought and the ambiguity of equal employment opportunity as a source of moral concern.

When a businessman was faced with clear, immediate, and direct economic retribution if he refused to practice fair employment he had little choice but to comply. Unless he had a very strong personal aversion to hiring or upgrading blacks, unless he would really "rather close first," a strongly enforced FEPC or a civil rights boycott provided sufficient economic pressure to persuade most businessmen to employ blacks. Not as dramatic, but equally effective was the pressure of a severe manpower shortage. In either of these situations most employers would probably have agreed with the wife of one of the partners of a major Chicago stock brokerage who claimed that "contrary to beliefs held by many workers among minority group people, businessmen are really not concerned about the race problem as such, they look at it primarily from the business angle."[17]

Prior to 1960, most businessmen believed that hiring blacks was potentially more disruptive than excluding them—except during periods of severe manpower shortage. Labor shortages also meant increased demand for white labor, and, for the most part, blacks were employed to replace whites who had moved up to better jobs.[18] This, of course, meant that while blacks got more and better jobs, they were still apt to get the most undesirable jobs in a given firm, or in the most undesirable firm in a given region. Moreover, when executives began to to hire blacks for a position, the job often lost status and became less desirable to whites. Thus manpower shortages frequently had the effect not of integrating employment but of turning previously white departments into predominantly black departments.[19]

World War II created an extreme manpower shortage that led to widespread employment for Negroes. Although the wartime FEPC unquestionably had a significant impact on business, its greatest importance may have been the excuse it gave businessmen to hire blacks. FEPC provided the rationalizations and created the psychological atmosphere which eased the employment of blacks who were desperately needed and who might well have been hired even without the executive order.[20] In some cases management perceived the employment of blacks during the war as an extraordinary device to meet an unusual situation and had no intention of keeping black employees after the emergency.[21] Returning veterans who had accumulated seniority while in service displaced some Negro workers, and others lost their jobs when employers reverted to traditional employment patterns.[22]

However blacks did not suffer major job losses after World War II. In the absence of a postwar depression and with the growth of "clean" jobs due to increasing mechanization, most blacks were able to maintain their positions in unskilled and semiskilled jobs as whites moved into new, higher status positions. Having discovered that the black population was a source of reliable labor many employers saw no reason to return to prewar patterns of discriminiation.

In the postwar era, only obedience to the law ranked ahead of the labor shortage as a universally accepted excuse for integration of employment. Businessmen who could not understand why anyone should ask them to hire blacks when they could get all the white workers they needed frequently explained that they would employ Negroes, but only when they could no longer find whites. In 1952, an official of a Texas aircraft company explained that only if the international situation worsened and the labor market tightened would they resort to hiring blacks, and even then the Negroes would be employed on a segregated basis.[23] The same attitude was neatly summed up in 1953 by the manager of a notoriously conservative Columbus, Ohio, firm who said he would not hire Negroes in any positions above the production level because he "did not have any difficulty in finding enough white people, so why should he?"[24]

Beginning as early as 1949, in some areas, and continuing through the end of the Korean War employers in many parts of the country experienced labor scarcity. As during the 1940's, they turned to the black community for the necessary manpower. In early 1952, one trade journal warned, "Plants that, for any reason, have not hired members of minority groups in the past are likely to have to change their policy. No great reserve of unemployed is left to draw on, as there was a decade ago. And in the absence of full-scale war, not enough women to meet needs are likely to be drawn back into the plants."[25] A Philadelphia utility confirmed this prediction in 1953 when it broke a long tradition of barring blacks from clerical and meter-reading jobs. The company was particularly concerned about the latter because it required "high moral character, since the meter reader has to go into a person's home," but because the personnel director was having great difficulty finding enough persons to fill the vacancies in this job, he was willing to begin considering Negroes.[26]

The absence of any major recession in the 1960's meant a continued steady demand for labor, and employers continued to cite their manpower needs when discussing Negro employment,[27] although the coming of the civil rights revolution displaced manpower needs as the primary reason for business interest in the black community. The southern textile industry, which had traditionally used only white workers, finally integrated during the 1960's when higher paying industries drained its white labor pool. Southern businessmen, however, preferred to blame the government for their new integration policy rather than their low wages and the resulting loss of white workers. It was only under prodding from the federal government that southern mills began a widespread movement to employ more blacks in skilled, white-collar, and even some managerial positions. But the vice president of a large textile corporation played down the importance of government pressure. "It was a choice of running the plant or not—we would have hired Negroes for these jobs with or without civil rights legislation," he said. A plant superintendent in Alabama explained, "We hired Negroes and trained them for production jobs, but LBJ got the blame."[28]

Throughout the postwar period, businessmen who explained their use of black labor as a rational economic response to manpower needs frequently assumed that a large untapped pool of skilled black labor existed.

The pool does not seem to have been as deep as some businessmen assumed, and as soon as the first wave of pioneering employers had snapped up the graduate engineers who were working as janitors and the skilled typists who were working as maids, this argument ceased to have much validity. But while the surplus of skilled black labor existed the arguments in favor of using Negro workers could get extremely cold-blooded. One observer has reported that in 1951 the Chicago Urban League tried to find jobs for Negroes by urging employers to exploit the competitively weak position of black workers. Using "strictly business terms," the Urban League pointed out that employers who hired blacks not only expanded their labor market but got a better type of worker because "Negro applicants are usually overqualified and also show greater job stability since limited job opportunities make them hesitant to quit." Furthermore, the League is reported to have told employers that by expanding the labor market they would help drive down the price of labor.[29] In 1952 an executive in an important media survey company who believed the company's owner would be impervious to moral arguments said he might be reached "on a cold turkey basis of better employees at the same or lower rates."[30]

However, most individuals who advocated equal employment practices did not urge clear-cut exploitation of the Negro's weak economic position; rather they said they were concerned with the most efficient use of the available supply of labor. The officers of a plant which broke local discriminatory hiring patterns in a border state immediately after the war explained, "We haven't time to do anything else. We are going into a line of business that is highly competitive, and we will have many problems in engineering, manufacturing and sales. We need the best people we can get, and we can't afford to go into the problem all over again every time we hire a Negro in a new department or upgrade one."[31] Businesses that claimed they were employing Negroes because they needed the best available workers were dealing with some combination of a severe manpower shortage, a relaxation of antiblack social pressure, or readily available, highly skilled, low-cost black workers. All of these were factors which made complete sense in terms of the Capitalist Ethic and also conformed to the American Creed because they did not involve explicit exploitation.

Widespread underutilization of trained Negro workers during the late forties and fifties created a situation in which a good economic argument could be made for hiring blacks as the most qualified people for the job, particularly for smaller firms which chronically lost out in the bidding for trained manpower to better paying large companies.[32] Highly trained blacks found no ready market for their skills and frequently took jobs far beneath their capacities. Thus, the firm which decided to begin hiring Negroes, for whatever reason, could justify its actions in Capitalist Ethic terms. The first black employees were almost always extremely competent employees whose productivity was higher than that of the average white worker.

But businessmen continued to allude to the efficient-utilization-of-manpower argument even after the pool of readily available skilled black labor had dried up. At the heart of the efficient-use argument was the belief that the employer should hire the best available man. This belief conformed to both the American Creed and to the Capitalist Ethic and thus continued to have currency well into the 1960's. In 1964, Thomas F. Hilbert, Jr., labor relations counsel for the General Electric Company, said his firm did not hire blacks merely to comply with the law. "We are mainly acting in our own and our shareholders' self-interest," he explained. "We want the *best* employees we can find, and we would only be penalizing ourselves if we excluded from consideration any group of potential applicants from which we can procure good employees."[33] After having used almost these identical words in a speech in 1965, one businessman went on to observe, "I don't want to imply here that there is a superabundance of qualified Negro applicants for all the job vacancies we have in our community. If this were so, then our failure to take advantage of such a condition would be perfectly obvious to us all."[34]

In its narrowest sense, the Capitalist Ethic requires a company to adopt policies which will maximize profit. But inherent in that definition is the modifier "long-run." Even if black applicants were not superior to whites businessmen could still argue that they derived long-run secondary or indirect benefits from employing Negroes because they were helping to alleviate conditions which led to social and economic disintegration. Long before the turmoil of the civil rights revolution, perceptive businessmen understood the necessary relationship between the elimination of racial discrimination and the existence of the kind of pacific domestic climate in which business operated most efficiently. As early as 1941, the borough president of Manhattan was able to persuade the vice president in charge of personnel of a New York City utility to begin hiring Negro women in nontraditional jobs by arguing that employing blacks would help society and the utility would thus benefit indirectly. The businessman explained to his workers that they as individual citizens and the company as a corporate citizen had a responsibility to solve the social problem of discrimination against blacks. As the borough president had explained it, the problem arose because widespread unemployment among Manhattan Negroes led to a high crime rate. "We have a labor shortage," the executive said. "We have an untapped pool of workers. These workers need better jobs. Society will benefit if they get them."[35]

When speaking about the secondary benefits of nondiscrimination, businessmen usually claimed that fair employment would lead to the expansion of the domestic market and would reduce crime and welfare and their related costs. Public opinion analyst Elmo Roper, one of the most prominent early business supporters of fair employment, viewed increased Negro employment and spending not only as a source of new business but also as a cushion against recession.[36] New York businessman Frederick W. Richmond said, "It is very simple. My business won't grow unless America grows. The more Negroes that can buy cars, the more the auto companies have to expand and buy steel. I can sell equipment to the steel mills."[37] Among others, the president of RCA, the president of Textron, and the president of the Aluminum Company of America were all early advocates of employing blacks to benefit society.[38]

Just in case the lure of potential profits from an expanded black purchasing public was not enough to convince businessmen to hire more Negroes, fair employment proponents regularly pointed out to employers that they were already losing money because of their discriminatory employment policies. "It is generally accepted as fact," said Elmo Roper in 1949, "that the segregated sectors of our large urban centers are the most expensive to maintain. The social cost of crime, juvenile delinquency, the rate of sickness and accidents, is higher in our depressed areas than it is in other parts of our cities. This is a waste of tax money."[39] Seventeen years later Baltimore's Voluntary Council on Equal Opportunity painted a similar if somewhat more apocalyptic picture. Commenting on the falling demand for unskilled (mostly black) workers, the council warned, "Failure to prepare for it can mean a city with a large mass of unemployed among all ranks, but particularly Negro, and a consequent burden upon the rest of the community that will prove unattractive to new industry, drive the established industries out, and bring a state of depression and despair from the top of the business leadership right through the ranks."[40]

The major difficulty with the indirect-benefit argument was its inapplicability to any given firm. If the management of a firm took a traditional narrow view of the Capitalist Ethic it could easily dismiss arguments which depended on generalized social benefit. While it might be true that all businesses would gain if Negro unemployment were reduced, each individual firm could never be sure all other companies would act in a socially constructive manner. If they did not, then the firm which did integrate would run the risk of suffering economic retribution for an action whose benefits would be shared equally by those competitors who did not share in its costs. Thus, a conservative Atlanta business executive could admit in 1962, "The economic status of minority people reflects itself in the social health of the community and in the economic stability of the country," while at the same time cautioning against moving too fast.[41] Since the benefits were to be long-run, businessmen also looked for long-run solutions—until the riots of the mid-sixties demonstrated that the end of the long run had finally arrived.

Before these riots of 1965-1967, employers most frequently cited legal compulsion as their reason for employing blacks. Even more than a labor shortage, the law removed the burden of decision from management's shoulders. The law forced many businessmen to adhere to the American Creed, and permitted them to do what was economically sound, that is hire the best man for the job. Furthermore, obeying the law fit the businessman's image of himself. As one executive put it, "American companies are basically law-abiding; they may seek favorable interpretations of the law, but essentially executives want their companies to be good citizens."[42]

In and of itself the existence of a legal requirement to practice equal opportunity employment was frequently enough to spur management to analyze its employment practices. Large, highly visible firms which were likely to become the target of complaints from the black community were particularly quick to comply with the law. Saying he was pleased with the way the Massachusetts FEPC had worked out, the vice president of one of Boston's largest insurance companies observed, "Perhaps you shouldn't need a law but the fact is we didn't do anything until there was one." He implied that the company might not even have acted then were it not for the law's punitive provision.[43] This manager's reaction is fairly typical of the responses of employers in the industrial Northeast. Although the employers did not want fair employment legislation and were less than gracious in their compliance, they nevertheless recognized that the law reflected a change in public expectations and that the time had passed when personal racism or even fears of racism in others would be accepted as a legitimate excuse for discrimination.

It usually did not take much pressure from a government body to persuade a company to begin hiring blacks in nontraditional jobs. For example, in 1953, the manager of a New York restaurant refused to hire Negro waitresses because he had an "exclusive clientele." A visit from the FEPC commissioners persuaded him to change his hiring policy and his customers accepted the change without objection.[44] Even reluctant employers began to practice fairer (if not completely fair) employment after specific complaints lodged against them were found valid. In a follow-up study of 334 proven cases of discrimination, the New York FEPC found that in 85 percent of the cases there was "definite improvement in the employment pattern as compared with the conditions which existed at the time the original complaints were filed against these firms."[45]

Reports vary on the extent of the success of FEPC legislation in actually procuring new positions for black workers. Most studies seem to indicate that the laws did have some effect and, moreover, had a very powerful educational impact on the attitudes of management and the public.[46] If there was a positive correlation between popular opinion and the enactment of controversial legislation such as FEPC, businessmen were hardly in a position to strongly and publicly oppose antidiscrimination legislation once it had been passed. Employers were sensitive to community pressures, and they opposed the legislative expression of the "people's will" only when it presented an obvious threat to their economic position.

At the beginning of the Eisenhower administration only seven states had compulsory FEPC laws. They were New York, New Jersey, Connecticut, Massachusetts, New Mexico, Oregon, Rhode Island, and Washington.[47] Although FEPC legislation had been introduced into the legislatures of virtually every other state outside of the Deep South, there was no legally enforceable bar to racial discrimination in employment in forty-one of the forty-eight states. In those states only firms which held contracts with the federal government had any legal obligation to practice equal employment. Roosevelt's second FEP Committee had folded in June, 1946. The Truman administration expended its efforts to extend employment opportunity on unsuccessful attempts to persuade Congress to pass a permanent federal FEPC. Until the outbreak of the Korean War, except for airport facilities constructed with federal funds, Truman made no attempts to use the power of the executive office to insure integration in other than government jobs. However, on December 3, 1951, Truman issued Executive Order 10308, which established the Committee on Government Contract Compliance to oversee the nondiscrimination clause which continued to be written into all government contracts. The eleven-member committee existed for little more than half a year before it was forced to resign by the change in administrations. In its final report the Truman committee called for a stronger antidiscrimination clause in all government contracts and suggested that the chief executive create a committee with the specific power to cancel the contract of any employer who did not live up to the letter of the fair employment clause.[48]

During the 1952 campaign Dwight D. Eisenhower promised that "without the impossible handicap of federal compulsion, we can and must provide equal job opportunities for our citizens, regardless of their color, creed or national origin."[49] This remarkable task was to be carried out by the President's Committee on Government Contracts which Eisenhower created in August, 1953, by Executive Order 10479. True to his word, the president gave this new committee absolutely no power. Vice President Richard M. Nixon served as chairman (thus, the Nixon Committee) of the thirteen men who hoped to work a major change in national employment policy through the dynamic force of their personalities and positions. In fact, the Nixon Committee was nothing more than a clearinghouse for information on employer experience with integration and a propaganda agency which coordinated antidiscrimination activity among various governmental agencies and sought to encourage nongovernmental educational programs "in order to eliminate or reduce the basic causes and costs of discrimination in employment."[50]

Business Week overgenerously referred to the committee's first two years as a "comparatively low-geared, behind-the-scenes, but increasingly effective campaign. . . ."[51] It certainly was low-gear and behind the scenes. Positive action by the committee consisted of rewriting the nondiscrimination clause to require contractors to treat employees equally in all aspects of employment, not merely in hiring. It also required employers doing business with the government to post in conspicuous places notices attesting to the firm's nondiscriminatory policy.[52] In only two other instances did the committee do anything that could be even remotely considered helpful to the cause of equal employment. It persuaded the District of Columbia's Board of Commissioners to include the standard nondiscrimination clause in all the District's contracts, and it convinced the Chesapeake and Potomac Telephone Company, which served Washington, to end its Jim Crow hiring practices.[53] The rest of the committee's activity was limited to printing pamphlets, establishing liaisons with private agencies in the field of intergroup relations, and generally keeping out of peoples' way.[54]

In October, 1955, the committee exhibited an unprecedented burst of energy and called fifty-five leading business chief executives to a closed-door White House conference. The conference was the first of a series of similar meetings that Presidents Eisenhower, Kennedy, and Johnson would call. All three Presidents tried to get top business leaders to do some leading in the area of fair employment. The Eisenhower administration had held a few meetings with individual contractors and small groups prior to the October conference,[55] but the October meeting was the first attempt to appeal collectively to the top corporate executives of the country's most important federal contractors. Shortly after the meeting ended Secretary of Commerce Sinclair Weeks commented, "It's hard to believe that it has taken nearly a hundred years for national leadership to call together the people who have the major responsibility for solving this problem, to discuss it with them in free 'give and take' and ask their cooperation."[56] No significant action took place as a result of the meeting, which perhaps explains why future Presidents were willing to call such conferences again.

Commentary on the meeting indicated that the business community fully recognized that its traditional discriminatory personnel policies were not seriously threatened by the Nixon Committee. On the one hand in an article titled "How the President is Winning the War on Discrimination," the trade journal *Factory Management and Maintenance* concluded that the President's committee was determined to wipe out discrimination and was succeeding through voluntary means. The magazine attributed this success to the committee's "prestige in the business circles it deals with, and to its recognition of the fact that discrimination is a difficult problem that cannot be solved by edict or penalty."[57] On the other hand, the failure of the business press to cite hard data, or even token examples of integration, clearly implied that the increased visibility of the President's committee was not to be confused with actual demands that firms live up to their contractual obligations. *Business Week* reassured its readers that "the federal team pointedly noted there would be no compulsory actions to force immediate compliance with the nondiscrimination clause in contracts."[58] "No federal agency has ever canceled a contract because discrimination exists," one trade journal observed, "and there's no indication that the present Administration ever will. Instead, the idea is to persuade contractors to do voluntarily what is legally correct, and to show them how this will help company, employees, and community."[59] It is little wonder that businessmen and "moderate" southerners thought highly of the Nixon Committee. David Sarnoff, chairman of RCA, said with unconscious irony, that he was "impressed not only by the Committee's achievements but also by its practical approach," and he quoted Mississippi editor Hodding Carter to the effect that "there has been nothing sensational about the Eisenhower program—except its success."[60]

Only a Mississippian or a conservative businessman could find "success" in the committee's record. All accounts agree that the Nixon Committee did little to resolve complaints. During its seven-year tenure the committee received 1,042 complaints but was able to resolve only 372, or just a bit more than a third. Moreover, there is no way of knowing what sort of action the committee recommended to the agencies in the 372 cases in which some final action was taken.[61] After reviewing a third of all the complaints filed with the Nixon Committee, Paul H. Norgren concluded that not more than twenty people actually got jobs as a result of the committee's action.[62] This unimpressive record is ironically highlighted by an early comment of Vice President Nixon expressing his hope that the 1955 meeting would convince people that the government was willing to take action. He said, "Most people just don't like to make formal complaints . . . and I am afraid even today there are many people who do not file complaints because they do not know whether it will accomplish anything."[63]

While the President's Committee on Government Contracts may have been little more than an empty gesture in terms of enforcing the legal obligations of government contractors, its actual impact on the business community went somewhat beyond its limited effectiveness in resolving complaints of discrimination. A large part of the committee's purpose was educational, and it could more legitimately claim success in that area than in complaint settlement (but perhaps only because it is more difficult to measure success in changing attitudes). In some cases the positive educational impact of the committee could readily be measured by the change in hiring practices of firms which were not actually accused of violating their contracts, but which for one reason or another came under the committee's purview. One of the country's largest soap manufacturers adopted an across-the-board (i.e., in the South as well as in the North) fair employment policy after Fred Lazarus, president of Federated Department Stores and one of the nongovernment members of the Nixon Committee, applied pressure to the firm's chief executive officer.[64] In its fifth and sixth annual reports the committee listed scores of cases in which it claimed to have been instrumental in bringing about better employment opportunities for black workers. Most of these cases, in which companies employed Negroes in white-collar and skilled jobs for the first time, did not arise from complaints but rather were the result of "direct consultation and negotiation with senior management of selected major government contractors." Fourteen operators at the Chesapeake and Potomac Telephone Company, or one professional and one clerical worker at Litton Industries in San Carlos, California, were hardly the stuff of which real progress was made, but for the companies involved, many of which were in the South, even token employment meant that the door had been opened a crack.[65]

The isolated breakthroughs in black placement instigated by the Nixon Committee proved that those who claimed the employment barrier was an unbreachable wall were wrong. After meeting with the Nixon Committee in 1955, government contractors in Dallas were reported to have "expressed great enthusiasm for the work of the committee and have shown the desire to really move toward employment on merit."[66] While such feelings may not have been immediately translated into practice, they undoubtedly paved the way for the big push that came after 1960.

Having briefly emerged into the public limelight with its "summit conference" for business leaders in 1955, the committee dropped back into the shadows for two more years. It again caused a brief stir of interest in 1957, when it announced that government agencies granting contracts would unilaterally begin to survey major defense industries to see if they were complying with the nondiscrimination clauses. There were no specific threats coupled with the new "compliance review program," although the administration did hint that it might be more difficult for companies found wanting to get contracts in the future. The depth of the committee's devotion to enforcing the contract clauses was well reflected in the observation of one committee official that "most companies co-operate easily enough. But occasionally you have to threaten them with loss of business—not so much an actual threat as a certain raising of the eyebrows or a shaking of the head."[67] There must have been a lot of head shaking and eyebrow raising during the next three years because there certainly were not any contract suspensions, nor was a single company's name ever placed on an "ineligible list" for additional contracts.[68]

The 1957 "tough line" quickly followed the 1955 summit conference into oblivion. Even though the committee experienced its only pronounced and concentrated successes in the period between 1955 and 1957, it simply did not have enough impetus to keep the hard line alive. In 1955 NAACP filed a series of suits against southern oil refiners with the Nixon Committee. As a result the committee forced at least nine southern oil refineries to abolish separate seniority lists for blacks, although substi-tution of departmental seniority in cases where Negroes were in segregated departments frequently wiped out much of the effect. The Nixon Com-mittee also made some attempt to see that companies administered fair tests which would permit blacks to move up the job ladder. Actual ad-vancement of Negroes into better oil refinery jobs was minimal at best, but it was done only under strong government pressure and in the face of reluctant management and unions and of intransigent local custom.[69] The committee spent its final year and a half puttering around making movies, translating its publications into Spanish, and holding confer-ences.[70]

Statistically the President's Committee on Government Contracts was a failure. Subsequent studies have shown that there was no appreciable increase in nonwhite employment in contractor firms over the life of the Nixon Committee. Plants continued to follow local employment patterns even when the firm had officially adopted a national fair employment practice policy.[71] Yet, despite the committee's gross shortcomings, it was instrumental in placing pioneer black workers in many new positions and in forcing many other firms at least to pay lip service to the philosophy of equal employment. The committee may not have wielded anything more lethal than a velvet fist in a velvet glove, but it did help prepare employers, especially in the South, for the new era. A 1960 survey of North Carolina firms holding federal contracts did not find a single company which gave the traditional excuses that customers and white employees would object to integration as the reasons for not giving black workers jobs. There were firms, of course, which continued to use those excuses, and em-ployers who still believed them in the 1960's, but at least among government contractors in one southern state the fabric which had held the prodiscrimination arguments together had disintegrated.[72]

The strength of the Nixon Committee lay in its reinforcing, with the prestige of a business-oriented Republican administration, of the fair employment arguments that integrationist forces had been using since World War II. The committee joined other fair employment proponents in reciting the great catechism of equal employment: integration is good business; businessmen should be leaders in their communities; a fair employment policy attracts qualified applicants; black workers are not inferior to white workers; neither employees nor customers will object to black workers.[73]

The committee's weakness lay in its unwillingness to use its potential strength to demand, rather than suggest, that government contractors practice fair employment. Operating during a time when most of the attention in race relations was focused on the school integration crisis, the Nixon Committee recognized that widespread discrimination against blacks existed as much in the economic as in the educational sphere, but the committee was insufficiently motivated to take the action that might have mitigated some of the destructive force of the civil rights revolution that was to follow in the 1960's.

The testimony of a business representative to the U.S. Civil Rights Commission during the first days of the Kennedy administration neatly summed up both the educational successes and the enforcement failures of federal fair employment activity during the Eisenhower years. Adrian J. Falk represented the California State Chamber of Commerce, the San Francisco Chamber of Commerce, the Oakland Chamber of Commerce, the Downtown Association, and the Federated Employers of San Francisco and its sixteen affiliated associations. Mr. Falk was despondent. It seems that the previous year the State of California had passed a fair employment practice law nullifying a San Francisco fair employment ordinance in which he had placed great faith. Falk approved of the San Francisco ordinance, which he termed a "compromise" program, because it "emphasized that the entire community shares responsibility for bringing about improvement in employment opportunities for minority group members and because it recognized that because discrimination is rooted in prejudice, it is eliminated by persuasion and education rather than by punitive measures." The new state law was unacceptable. First, Falk called the state law "the most restrictive and punitive of all state FEPC laws in the Nation today," and second, Falk complained that "nowhere in the act does the word 'education' occur." Based on his study of "other States and cities so far," Falk concluded that "no FEPC law will be successful to any significant degree without years of education to change the prejudices which cause such discrimination."

Summing up his position, Falk found "the word 'education' has a magic meaning to a great many people. A lot of people are a little bit dubious and afraid of something which says 'you must.' They much prefer the idea of the 'you ought to or let's do it together' kind of approach."[74] Not the least of Falk's "many people" were those in the business community.

The entire period between 1945 and 1960 was one of education, or perhaps consolidation is a better word. The state FEPC laws along with the manpower crunch of the Korean War created a situation in which pioneering became increasingly easy. The law provided protection from racist competitors and the war provided economic impetus. Successful integration in one area provided examples for other areas, and the business community as a whole began to recognize that the Capitalist Ethic and the American Creed were indeed compatible. By the end of the period the conflict between the two values had all but disappeared and the ideological system had reached a point of equilibrium. In the industrial North businessmen could employ blacks without fear of massive public opposition. The American Creed could be fulfilled without fear and the Capitalist Ethic could be adhered to by choosing exceptionally qualified blacks and ignoring the needs of the millions who could never be "Jackie Robinson."

The crisis of World War II had been responsible for establishing the trend toward using blacks in nontraditional positions. The wartime FEPC not only set the pattern for subsequent state fair employment legislation, but it also demonstrated that legal requirements could successfully bring about racial integration, at least under extreme circumstances of national emergency and stringent labor shortage. More importantly, wartime integration demonstrated that blacks and whites could work together. Writing immediately after the war, two close observers of the labor relations scene concluded that personnel men had learned that four of the major anti-Negro employment arguments were untrue: 1) "Negroes have no mechanical aptitudes," 2) "Negroes and whites cannot work together, mix together," 3) "the Negro is more susceptible to disease, has more disease," and 4) "management cannot force Negroes on the blue collar ranks."[75]

Southern congressional opposition blocked attempts to extend the federal FEPC into peacetime, but the Truman years were marked by a series of state antidiscrimination laws. While businessmen opposed the state laws, their opposition was seldom racist in tone. Voluntary attempts to promote economic integration did not always head off fair employment legislation, but they did reflect the basically positive attitudes toward hiring blacks which many managers held. At the same time employers opposed FEPC, they actively sought recognition and approval for action they took in hiring and promoting black workers.[76] The personnel manager of a Dallas automobile plant claimed in 1952 that "if the civil rights talk in Washington does not set progress back . . . the problem will be solved in 1960." His company had begun to use blacks as maintenance men, and he believed that given time the Negroes would move up into higher positions.[77] At about the same time, and with equally unfounded optimism, two fair employment field workers said they believed that "race relations in the United States . . . have passed the point of revolution and reached the stage of negotiation." [78]

The idea that somehow good faith, honest pleading, negotiation, and education would wipe out job discrimination dominated much of the thinking of those concerned with the plight of the black worker. For the most part progress toward fair employment during the 1950's was token. The concept of the pioneer prevailed. Firms pioneered by being the first to hire blacks at particular jobs, and the Negro workers themselves pioneered in the positions. Each token advance was taken with elaborate planning and much trepidation. Caution and moderation were the watchwords. Lemuel R. Boulware, General Electric's vice president of personnel relations, and a man with a reputation as a tough and unyielding executive, summed up the attitude of many prominent businessmen of the 1950's when he said, "What we try to do is develop a natural and unselfconscious association that comes along as fast as we can bring it about naturally. We are just going along as temperately and constructively as we know how with merit as our sole standard at every level of employment."[79]

A 1956 *New York Times* observation that "community sentiment is generally much more hospitable to integration on the job than to integration in housing, schools or social activities"[80] seems accurate as long as the word "sentiment" is emphasized. After surveying the racial attitudes of New York businessmen in 1956, Rosenberg and Chapin concluded that "the job situation is ripe for improvement. The psychological predisposition already exists in good measure; it needs to be more fully crystallized and institutionalized."[81] Although businessmen did not necessarily implement the increasingly favorable public attitudes toward job integration, examples of fair employment were becoming less exceptional, and profession of the ideal of equal employment was becoming the rule in the business community. The "crystallization" and "institutionalization" which would finally do away with the most blatant forms of job discrimination came after 1960, in the form of legal and social pressure. Historically, the civil rights revolution, as it applied to business, was not an attempt to "force" morality, but rather a semisuccessful attempt to force , an already "moral" segment of the society to live up to its convictions.

Nothing more clearly illustrates this change in business concern and orientation than "how-to-do-it" articles on fair employment. Before the civil rights revolution, they recommended elaborate, cautious, and hypersensitive techniques for pioneering, with an emphasis on blue-collar jobs. Although many of the arguments and methods remained basically unchanged, after 1960 the articles tended to be crisper and more to the point. The success of the educational emphasis of the 1950's could be seen in what the articles no longer said, but were able to take for granted.

For example, during World War II the National Industrial Conference Board published ten principles which characterized successful industrial integration programs. Like virtually every other list, it started off with the observation that no program would work unless top management was fully committed to the policy. A postwar article elaborated on this point, suggesting that the employer "put himself through something like a course of reading, conference, round-table discussion, and inspection trips" in order to prevent his integration program from being "half-hearted, unsure, stupid, or trouble-instigating." Once he had convinced himself, the employer was urged to convince supervisory personnel, workers, and the union of the possibility of effective fair employment.[82]

Having thus prepared the way, articles appearing prior to 1960 usually proceeded to devote an inordinate amount of attention to the selection of the pioneer black worker. During the war, NICB had suggested that care be taken to pick "the right type of Negro as the first worker of his race in the plant." Experts on integration urged that the first blacks in a new position be highly qualified, and some writers even suggested that pioneers be overqualified, although others cautioned against this "Jackie Robinson syndrome" for fear it would breed resentment among less qualified white workers and might make it even harder for normally qualified black workers to follow. There was, however, little disagreement on the suggestion that the black pioneers "have more than the usual amount of poise" and that "the grooming of this group should be above average."[83] In addition, many of the how-to-do-it plans included rather extensive suggestions for orienting the new workers, both to reassure the black employees of management's support and to caution them against "undue" sensitivity to the discrimination they would probably face for a while on the job.[84]

During the early 1960's how-to-do-it articles assumed less racism and wider acceptance of blacks in blue-collar jobs,[85] but their gentle urgings of management to proceed carefully at the upper levels were reminiscent of the advice for the integration of all positions during the

fifties.[86] After mid-decade, however, the pressure of the civil rights revolution dominated fair employment practice activity. All the standard integration methods, all the caution, the careful selection and introduction
of pioneers, the concern about customers and the community, almost
faded out of the picture under the civil rights onslaught of the mid-sixties.
The how-to-do-it articles suddenly became concerned with how business
should respond to outside pressure, not from the white community protesting integration, but from the black community demanding it.[87]

In 1963 the *Public Relations Journal* published a list of problems
it believed businessmen should be prepared to meet. The tone and content of the list indicate how quickly the business community could change
its attitudes when circumspection ceased to be a virtue. The article warned
that employers should know: 1) how to enforce antidiscrimination hiring
rules, 2) how to handle unqualified applicants so they would not feel
discriminated against and how to build a case should antidiscrimination
agencies come into the picture, 3) how to seek out the qualified black
workers rather than waiting for them to come in, 4) how to improve
promotion and training programs to maximize the opportunities for advancement available to minority workers, 5) "how to expose the sophis-
tries which might be used to cover up unfair practices," and, an old
friend, 6) how to meet and overcome opposition to fair employment from
employees.[88]

Many of the specific recommendations in the new period remained
the same, but they had a notably bolder tone. Articles began to encourage companies to adopt employment policies that went beyond mere
evenhandedness to consider some of the unique problems of the black
job seeker. In addition to traditional suggestions such as the necessity of
a strong commitment from top management and a full explanation of the
policy down the line, the how-to-do-it articles of the later sixties suggested
that companies review their testing procedures, their application blanks,
their job requirements, their help-wanted advertising, and their contact
with black community leaders.[89] Businessmen were becoming more sophisticated about the nature of institutional racism.

8

Sophisticated Jobs and Sophisticated Racism

During the war and the immediate postwar years most interest in employment integration centered on getting black workers into plants from which they had been wholly excluded or on obtaining promotions for those who were confined to unskilled positions. With the passing years attention shifted from production work to the more prestigious white-collar, technical, professional, and managerial positions. By the late 1950's and early 1960's the business community had become largely concerned with promoting and hiring Negroes into what were considered high-status jobs. This, of course, does not mean that blacks had obtained fair treatment at the blue-collar level, but enough firms in various parts of the country had made enough breakthroughs so that the focus of the equal employment movement could be redirected.

As Negroes moved into higher jobs, increasing numbers of whites felt threatened. From what little work has been done in the area of white gains from Negro subordination, it appears that some groups of skilled, managerial, and clerical white workers may have in fact improved their economic condition by antiblack discrimination.[1] Although there is considerable difference of opinion among economists about the legitimacy of these findings, scholars generally agree that Negro employment did not pose a real economic threat to production workers.[2] Thus, if employee objections to equal opportunity for black workers were at all based on an actual economic competition, opposition should have increased as Negro workers began moving up the occupational ladder.

The objections to working with blacks voiced by white employees[3] were widely accepted by employers throughout the country in the late forties and early fifties. In the South the patterns of job discrimination were so strong that one observer elevated them to the status of "laws." With the usual exceptions to which all such laws were subject, sociologist Donald Dewey claimed in 1952 that in the South: "1) Negro workers seldom hold jobs which require them to give orders to white workers,

2) Negro and white workers do not ordinarily work side by side at the same jobs."[4] In 1952 the laws were as applicable in the North as in the South. Although the laws decreased in importance in the North during the 1950's, they still applied in many areas of the South as late as 1962.[5]

As one might logically expect, because there was less status loss in being equal to rather than subservient to a black, the barriers against whites working alongside Negroes came down sooner than those which prohibited blacks from giving orders to whites. Southall noted an early break with the rule against blacks and whites working side by side in a Tennessee firm which employed Negroes to work alongside whites in the late forties. But she observed that "even here where so much progress has been made, the traditional pattern of white superiority triumphed; for whenever any kind of issue arose, the Negroes, afraid of offending their white associates, refused to stand up for their own rights."[6]

In many instances, particularly in the South, promotion of blacks on a par with whites was barred through contractual agreements with white-dominated unions. The Nixon Committee's campaign against separate seniority lists in southern oil refineries was directed at some of the most blatant examples of discriminatory collusion between management and white workers.[7] Even where there was no formal dual seniority system, many southern plants had informal agreements that blacks would not bid up into white jobs. In 1960, when Negroes in a Texas manufacturing firm demanded their rights to promotion under the contract, the management agreed, but retaliated by halting all hiring of new black workers.[8] The dual seniority system remained common until President Kennedy's Committee on Equal Employment Opportunity was able officially to end a large number of such arrangements.[9]

The abolition of contractual bars to promotion, however, did not necessarily mean upgrading for the black worker. Because many firms did not want to promote Negroes, they made it a practice to hire nonpromotable blacks, that is, workers without high school educations or other skills. Although education was frequently not necessary for success on the job (and in fact was not demanded of white workers), the requirement of a high school diploma was a useful method of keeping black workers in menial jobs.[10] Even when firms did not unfairly apply an educational criterion, just the existence of such a requirement discriminated against Negroes. The dual educational system of the South, with inferior schools for Negroes, virtually insured that a black man would be unable to compete with a white even for jobs in which educational criteria were fairly applied.[11]

The end of job segregation sometimes also meant the actual loss of black positions. There was some truth to the observation that "the ruts into which the nonwhites have been pressed are sufficiently deep that the steam roller of white competition . . . passes over them quite harmlessly."[12] The forces that had made black workers members of a depressed and exploited economic colony within many southern firms were also the forces which protected that colony from white competition. While blacks could not move into white jobs, neither would whites be hired for black jobs, and that situation insured a minimum number of black jobs in many plants. The elimination of racially based occupational enclaves meant that whites were in fact hired for jobs which formerly only blacks had held.[13]

The development of a highly formalized segregated employment pattern in the South was an industrial extension of the general southern pattern in which rigid custom, and often law, formalized the inferior status of the black. The northern employer, on the other hand, did not have any such contractual or quasi-contractual means for hiring blacks at a low level and for keeping them there. When promotable Negroes hired by northern firms demanded their rights to apply for higher jobs on an equal basis with whites, their employers faced, frequently for the first time, the necessity of creating a policy to deal with black promotion.[14] Northern companies which had a strong policy of promoting from within were apt to use the policy as an excuse not to hire any blacks at all. If all employees were potential supervisory or even managerial personnel, and if the management believed that blacks would be unacceptable in positions of high status, then of course management would not hire Negroes at any level.[15] A study in the late sixties of employment patterns among unskilled janitors and material handlers in the Chicago area disclosed systematic discrimination against blacks even in such menial occupations as material handling. The author concluded that Negroes received janitorial jobs but not material handling positions because blacks traditionally carried out custodial work, because janitors were usually isolated from the white work force and would be less apt to upset white employees, and because custodial work was seen as a dead-end job while material handlers were in position to advance to higher paying jobs. At least in firms which paid high wages, material handlers were better educated, younger, and more often white than janitors because these were the qualities necessary for promotion.[16]

For the most part, however, after the mid-fifties it became increasingly more difficult for northern employers completely to bar Negroes from employment. Once blacks were in the work force normal promotions began to occur. Northern employers found that their equal employment policies augumented the natural pressure for promotion exerted by seniority and forced them to upgrade minority workers into supervisory, technical, and sometimes even managerial positions.

When employers began promoting blacks to higher-level jobs they faced many problems analogous to those which had occurred when the first Negro blue-collar workers were hired. The most common fear was that white workers would object to black coworkers. Every time a Negro was introduced into a new occupation or into a new work group, the employer had to face the potential problem of his employees' position. White workers based much of their opposition on the historically inferior status of blacks. Since black workers had traditionally been limited to low-status jobs, any job into which a Negro was introduced *ipso facto* became low-status. Businessmen frequently shared their employees' evaluation. A San Francisco employer complained that "Negroes are degrading to the profession of selling,"[17] and another said his employees would object to black coworkers "because our employees have acquired 'social caste.' "[18]

The problem of social caste or status became more acute when a Negro was placed in a position where he had power over whites or contact with noncompany personnel. Thus, a Chicago personnel man said in 1955 that while he would hire any qualified engineer who came along, he would not place a black in any position, notably sales and personnel, where he would come in contact with other people.[19] Although this Chicago personnel manager's reasoning was quite typical, his refusal to place blacks in the personnel department deviated somewhat from the usual pattern. Employers placed most pioneering black technical and professional employees in internal staff rather than in line departments. Businessmen probably found blacks more acceptable in staff positions for two reasons. First, staff departments had no actual control over any aspect of production, and thus no member of such a department was in a position to give orders to anyone outside of his immediate department. Second, by definition, staff employees exist to provide a service to management, and it may be that whites felt better about blacks working in a department which existed to serve, not to create.[20] According to an Urban League official, Cleveland employers liked to use Negroes to head the mail room. In this way the company could have a black supervisor, but in a relatively invisible low-status department which had a purely service function and which was frequently staffed by young workers, blacks, or other marginal employees.[21]

The personnel department was another popular spot for employing the first Negro on the managerial level. To some extent personnel men hired blacks for their own departments because they did not want to be in the position of telling other departments to do something they had not done themselves. In addition, however, personnel was essentially a staff department which had little if any control over actual plant production and thus was a "safe department" for a potentially disruptive pioneer placement.[22]

Well into the sixties many employers believed that while there might be industrial "poor whites" who had to work alongside blacks, no white was so low that he had to take orders from a black. The placement policies of the electronics industry make it particularly evident that position and power are not synonymous, and that blacks were seldom given the latter to wield. Government pressure, particularly after the passage of the Civil Rights Act of 1964, persuaded many electronics firms to begin hiring blacks. Because of the electronics industry's high percentage of professional and skilled jobs many of the placements were necessarily in positions which blacks had not previously filled. A black engineer in Detroit observed in 1964 that "you may find a Negro with a fancy title and a high salary, but these things are usually meaningless because he won't have responsibility over people."[23] When a manufacturer of electronics said, "You can't put a Negro in a position where he will give orders to a white engineer because it will cause too much friction,"[24] he was only parroting one of the standard clichés of industrial race relations. Employers who were willing to break the first "rule" that Negroes and whites could not work together on the same job were still not willing to break the second rule, "Negroes cannot work over whites in the chain of command."[25] While there are indications that even some blacks objected to Negro supervisors, during the forties and fifties businessmen permitted black supervisors only in those positions where they controlled other blacks, or a mixed crew working in a traditionally black area, such as the foundry.[26]

The "law" which forbade blacks from supervising whites applied equally to the North and South through the forties and fifties. By the mid-sixties, however, the rule had lost much of its force in the North, but continued unabated in the South. More than half of the managers questioned in a 1947 survey of two northern cities said they would have objections to placing a Negro supervisor, administrator, or professional over a group including whites.[27] A similar question asked of a sample of northern managers in 1966 indicated a major change of employer attitudes. Eighty-two percent of those questioned agreed with the statement, "A Negro supervisor would be accepted by white subordinates in my company after he had successfully proven himself a good manager." More than half of these managers expressed the view that black workers would be able to rise above the level of foreman. However, only a third of the southern managers questioned believed that whites would ever accept a Negro supervisor, and approximately the same number thought that a black could rise above the level of foreman.[28]

Once large numbers of blacks began to work in white-collar jobs (large numbers being a relative term), the barrier against black supervisors fell quickly. The widespread fear that whites would not obey when blacks gave the orders, and the objections which whites raised to working under blacks, evaporated as society began to accept blacks as legitimate workers in higher status jobs. Once society accepted, and even encouraged, the use of blacks in desirable jobs, whites no longer had to fear the psychological cost of taking orders from blacks. Even token promotions beyond the white-collar level removed the terrible stigma of being dominated by a member of the "mudsill." The status gain for blacks meant less of a status threat for whites. So great was the change that in 1967 sixty white sales people in Miami, Florida, submitted without protest to the complete supervision of a black man.[29] While opposition to black supervisors was still the dominant pattern in the South, the Miami case would not have been possible even as an isolated example a decade earlier.

White acceptance of black supervisors was closely related to the increasing acceptance of blacks in white-collar jobs. While most white-collar workers below the managerial level were not in positions of power over their coworkers, blacks seeking white-collar employment nevertheless found barriers similar to those that existed for supervisory positions. Because the status of nonsupervisory white-collar jobs was almost wholly dependent upon socially accepted symbols of position, rather than on real power, blacks had as difficult a time breaking into sales, clerical, and technical positions as they had moving into supervisory jobs. Whereas whites objected to being supervised by blacks because it lowered their status directly, they resisted the encroachment of the blacks into white-collar positions because the low social standing of blacks demeaned the status of the job—and job status was frequently all poorly paid white-collar workers had.

Until the beginning of the 1960's, employers' fears of worker and customer opposition were usually strong enough to limit Negro white-collar workers to token positions in isolated locations. Breakthroughs in white-collar employment for Negroes were of primarily symbolic importance and were pursued one at a time. Victories were counted in ones and twos. The Urban League placed a few workers here and the American Friends Service Committee placed a few workers there.[30] The 1958 report of Eisenhower's Committee on Government Contracts, optimistically entitled *Five Years of Progress,* clearly illustrated the token nature of black advancement in industry. The report listed more than fifty firms with government contracts which opened up new positions to blacks. Though all of the firms employed more than a thousand people, and many employed more than ten thousand, the companies averaged fewer than fifteen black professional, technical, or clerical workers each. Even this low average is misleadingly high since three firms had disproportionately large numbers of Negro white-collar workers, and the vast majority employed fewer than ten blacks.[31]

The classic arguments against hiring Negro workers in white-collar positions fell into disuse in the North after 1960 as employers began hiring more blacks for such jobs.[32] While the actual number of blacks involved was pitifully small, and Negro white-collar workers remained severely underrepresented by any statistical measurement, nevertheless, at least in large border and northern cities, the hiring of Negro white-collar workers had begun to move beyond the tokenism of *a* company Negro toward a somewhat wider use of Negroes in higher status positions.[33]

The increasing employment of blacks in white-collar jobs, which might be called "stage two" tokenism, even began to appear in some areas of the South among government contractors during the early 1960's and among nongovernment contractors in the border states. The U.S. Commission on Civil Rights found widespread discrimination against blacks in Washington, D.C., in 1962, yet it concluded that "in clerical and sales work, where customer relations are of prime importance there is evidence that Washington's Negro majority is slowly but steadily influencing changes in employment."[34] Similar studies of Houston, Texas, and Dade County (Miami), Florida, in the early 1960's disclosed the same kind of reluctant but discernible change in employment policies. In both cities tokenism continued to be the order of the day, and blacks were still unable to get white-collar jobs for which they were qualified, but there was "occasional acceptance of Negroes in better than traditional jobs, a change slowly impelled by rapidly growing industry and fast increasing population."[35]

By the beginning of the 1970's the process of token integration in the North had finally worked its way up to the level of management. It is almost impossible to ascertain employers' attitudes toward this final step in the process of economic integration. The Civil Rights Act, the urban crisis, the ghetto riots, and the change of mood in the black community from passive resistance to militancy—all contributed to businessmen's acute awareness of the need for equal employment at all levels. By the late sixties few if any employers were willing to engage in the kind of public rationalization and justification for discriminatory hiring that had marked the black man's steps up the previous rungs on the employment ladder. Despite executives' use of liberal rhetoric there is some indication that the questions and doubts which accompanied acceptance of blacks in white-collar and supervisory jobs continued to exist as Negroes moved into managerial positions, which were both white-collar and supervisory—or at least nominally supervisory.

The first blacks hired into managerial positions frequently found that they were not even tokens but mere window dressing. At least the first Negroes employed in blue-collar and lower level white-collar jobs were expected to do the work for which they were hired. But too often black "managers" were not even expected, or allowed, to perform any managerial work. Public opinion had come to demand a "house nigger," and no matter what their actual training and competence, many of the new black executives were just expected to be the company's liaison with those segments of the community that wanted to see Negro employees in executive positions. A black lawyer in an electronics firm was expected to handle but not to process most of his company's legal papers. His job brought him into contact with the firm's top executives so he could serve as a constant reminder of their liberal policies.[36] In a similar vein a young black professional complained, "I don't want to be hired as an engineer and then find myself assigned as the company's representative to Plans for Progress or some other government-sponsored program in the equal opportunity bag. Above all, deliver me from presiding over the company table at the annual Urban League benefit dinner."[37]

Employers sought and frequently found overqualified black applicants for managerial positions. Although this approach was scored by some observers as an attempt to avoid the problem by choosing employees who had learned to be as "unNegro as the recruiters,"[38] reports indicate that despite their superior qualifications the black executives were not promoted.[39] Hired for decorative rather than functional purposes, the token black managers could serve their purposes just as well in powerless junior positions as in senior positions where they might have real control over the company.

Employers' demands for black employees and the increasing willingness of Negroes to apply for nontraditional jobs did not necessarily mean that large numbers of new black workers would begin appearing in the nation's offices. Employers may have accepted the American Creed sufficiently to hire Negro white-collar workers but they still insisted that the new workers be qualified. Until the early 1960's the term "qualified" frequently meant white, and technical ability was simply unimportant. Thus companies which were the first in their areas to hire blacks sought, and could usually obtain, overqualified candidates. When no Negroes could get any job which required training or skill the numbers of qualified blacks from which the first pioneer firms could choose was relatively large. However by the late fifties even though firms were still seeking black workers with qualifications superior to those of white workers, they were beginning to encounter difficulty in finding them. What had appeared to be a large pool of Jackie Robinsons was quickly drained dry by the early comers.[40] Chronically inferior educational opportunities, coupled with the knowledge that they could not expect to get jobs which required education, meant that few blacks were either able or motivated to gain the necessary training for white-collar jobs. Once hired there was no institutionalized means of replenishing those few highly motivated individuals who had prepared themselves for acceptance in the white business world despite the fact that they had no valid reason to expect that their preparation would actually result in a job.

There is little question that beginning in the early 1960's a shortage of qualified Negro employees began to develop. While employers may have wanted blacks at the managerial level more for their publicity value than for their business acumen, they nevertheless desired, but could not find, Negroes with education in technical and managerial skills. The validity of the qualification crisis was reflected in the response of the organizations working for improved Negro employment opportunity. Formed to deal with economically irrelevant forms of discrimination, i.e., those based on racial grounds, the fair employment organizations suddenly found themselves confronted with economically relevant discrimination, i.e., that based on real inability to perform the job.[41]

Until the early sixties, service organizations such as the Urban League and the American Friends Service Committee could usually meet the lack-of-qualified-applicants dodge by offering the reluctant employer a living, breathing, fully qualified black candidate the next morning. But in 1961 the personnel director of Standard Oil of California, Fred Russell, claimed that "the real problem for the Negro in this area is job qualification. In southern California, at least, I think people are ready to employ Negroes." Russell was a member of the Urban League and was presumably aware of whether or not qualified Negroes were available in his locality.[42] American Friends Service Committee field workers in Atlanta found that by 1962 they were having difficulty coming up with fully qualified candidates to meet employers' arguments that no suitable Negroes ever applied. One field worker observed, "I am beginning to think that perhaps the employer has strong ground on which to stand by using this excuse rather than the fear of what may be the reactions of his white employees . . . because while it is true that a proportion of the staff does resent the desegregating process it recognizes that change is taking place."[43]

In early 1964, the AFSC employment program in Atlanta reported that it was "shifting from major emphasis on confrontation to recruitment and encouragement in the Negro community to prepare for job openings as they are occurring in the post-pioneering stage. . . . Unfortunately," the report continued, "when the nontraditional job occurs we are frequently frustrated in our attempts to recruit qualified applicants."[44] In 1962, Guichard Parris, public relations director of the National Urban League, announced that "state and federal laws have reduced the needs and pressures for getting more and better jobs." Parris predicted that within a decade "most of the [discriminatory] laws and other restrictions shall have disappeared and the Negro will be able to compete in the open market place." In order to enable blacks to compete more successfully the League said it would increase its emphasis on motivating youths to seek training for better jobs, rather than serving only as a placement agency.[45]

Two years later, in 1964, the Urban League established its National Skills Bank, a clearing and coordinating center for placement of skilled black workers. After six months of operation the Skills Bank boasted of placing more than a thousand Negroes, and according to Mahlon T. Puryear, director of the program, "In many cases the jobs were obtained by a major breakthrough in the 'whites only' barrier in the upper echelons of business and industry."[46] But the record of success was somewhat less dramatic than Puryear made it seem. Although the Skills Bank screened more than two hundred thousand individuals during its first year it was able to place only five thousand. The problem did not lie with reluctant employers. Puryear reported that "60 to 70 percent of the largest corporations have placed job orders with the skills bank for talented Negroes. Some of them have open orders with us, more jobs than we can fill some places." Rather, the difficulty lay with the reluctance of many black workers to move to areas where jobs were available and with the lack of professional, executive, and clerical skills among Negro job seekers.[47] The problem of finding qualified workers had become so prevalent by 1967 that 64 percent of more than four hundred employers questioned agreed with the statement "Negroes are apt to be less well trained than whites, so hiring many Negroes will either decrease production or increase training costs."[48]

Despite a great tradition of paternalistic white capitalists urging and assisting education for Negroes, the American business community as a whole did not seem particularly concerned with the lack of trained workers until the advent of the civil rights revolution. The absence of an overwhelming manpower shortage meant that business used blacks in menial capacities, and the rudimentary education which the public schools provided blacks was sufficient to fill the limited intellectual demands of unskilled work. There were some complaints from employers in the immediate postwar years, as there would be again in the sixties, that Negroes needed to be instructed in the responsibility of employment, but the demand for this kind of education was quite different from the demand that blacks receive instruction in a salable skill. Many of the white demands for Negro education in the early period after the war were not for education at all but rather for indoctrination in the attitudes which made successful employees—from the employer's point of view. The business community wanted black workers who were honest and who had a desire to please the boss.[49] On the whole, however, businessmen merely ignored the question of Negro education. Blacks were well enough trained for the jobs available to them and an occasional corporate gift to the United Negro College Fund appeased the spirits of General O. O. Howard and Booker T. Washington.[50]

As legal and social pressure forced employers to increase their hiring of Negro workers for upper level positions, businessmen began to pay more attention to the state of Negro education. The renewed interest in education allowed the business community to let itself off the hook by attributing the scarcity of black employees to the failure of Negroes to "educate them-selves" (as the businessmen frequently put it). By blaming either individual Negroes or the educational system for the economic problems of black men, businessmen shifted the burden of responsibility for Negro under-employment to institutions beyond their immediate control. Implicit in their faulting of education was a generalized acceptance of the complementary values of the American Creed and the Capitalist Ethic. Employers were willing to hire blacks equally with whites (or so they stated) if the blacks were equally prepared. At the same time since most blacks were not equally prepared, the businessman could maintain his all-white professional, techni-cal, and managerial staff.

To some extent businessmen recognized that problems inherent in the country's dual educational system caused Negroes' educational shortcom-ings. Commenting on the failure of blacks to enter management positions in the textile industry, the associate editor of a textile trade journal noted that no Negroes were enrolled in any programs which southern universities offered in the field of textiles. While all the colleges were legally integrated, the magazine observed "that Negro high school students graduating from an educational system that is substandard are going to have an exceedingly difficult time in completing today's university textile curriculum."[51] Yet even when businessmen recognized the source of the lack of training, some drew curious conclusions. The manager of an employment agency in San Francisco observed in 1963, "We have found that the majority of Negro applicants—even those with high school diplomas—coudn't pass the sim-plest clerical tests," from which he concluded not that the schools were wanting but rather that Negroes "are not equipping themselves."[52]

As increasing numbers of blacks moved into upper level jobs, business-men who continued to employ few Negroes needed a new and more sophis-ticated set of rationalizations to explain their failure to hire blacks. The arguments that employees and customers would object, although sanctified by tradition, were becoming embarrassingly transparent. Not only did the success of pioneer placements belie the traditional excuses, but the public and the government were becoming more knowledgeable. New times de-

manded new rhetoric, if not new action. During the 1960's businessmen
began to show an increasing awareness of the underlying sociological reasons for the lack of qualified black workers—or at least they demonstrated
an increased sensitivity to sociological jargon.

By focusing on environmental rather than personal obstacles to Negro
advancement, businessmen seemed to imply that society could alter the
offending institutions, such as the educational system, and eliminate the
problem of economic discrimination. In fact, discrimination ceased to be
a subject of discussion. Business began to act as though discrimination had
disappeared and the only problem that remained was motivating and training blacks to take advantage of the myriad of opportunities that were now
open to them. So far as businessmen were concerned, the American Creed
was a reality and all they needed to do was to convince blacks that jobs
existed if only they would prepare themselves. Sponsors of an upgrading
seminar for employers held in Milwaukee in 1968, urged their colleagues
to prove that fair employment was a reality by promoting blacks. Seminar
leaders believed that such examples would motivate "other minority group
persons to seek employment, to stay employed, to aspire to better jobs,
and to take steps necessary to prepare themselves for better jobs."[53]

Increasing business emphasis on sociological explanations was an
attempt to shift the cause of unequal employment for blacks to the society
at large or even, by implication, to the blacks themselves. In 1966, Howard
C. Lockwood of Lockheed Aircraft noted, "Three or four years ago the
problems looming largest would have been how to eliminate discrimination
in employment and the acceptance of minority personnel in occupations
which formerly had been closed to them." Although Lockwood admitted
that "there is still much to be done," he felt that a more serious sociological problem had arisen. "Because of many years of discrimination and rejection," Lockwood said, "many minority individuals are very poorly prepared educationally and even psychologically to accept their new role."[54]
Two officials at a Georgia aircraft company took a similar view when they
told an interviewer that Negroes were not only unprepared for available
jobs but could not even qualify for company training programs. They believed that more emphasis should be placed upon motivation in the home,
urging parents to discipline their children to further study, [and] radical
changes in the school curriculum."[55]

Even hard-line southerners began to use sociological reasoning as a
facade to cover more traditionally racist viewpoints. Explaining his opposition to civil rights legislation in 1962, an officer of an Atlanta bank said
he felt it was economically and morally wrong to expect industry and provi-
dent people to care for the "shiftless and the chiselers." In itself, his was
the classic position of conservative businessmen, but he capped his argu-

ment with a more sophisticated sociological explanation when he admitted that "taken as a whole and disregarding the individual, thc Negro is not a second-class citizen but a third-class citizen," whose inferior socioeconomic position was due not to any racial traits but rather to "lack of cultural advantages, etc." He believed, however, that these shortcomings could not be overcome with civil rights legislation.[56] Charles B. Potter, personnel vice president to Burdine's one of the largest department stores in Miami, Florida, insisted that the race problem could not be attributed to businessmen. Potter cleary believed that the American Creed would be fulfilled by adherence to the Capitalist Ethic. Public antipathy toward black employees had vanished, and only blacks' lack of ambition and skills stood between them and good jobs. "The profit motive overlooks color; the dollar has no color," he explained. "The businessman isn't the obstacle. Our whole society has been the obstacle. The conditions society has imposed on the Negro's life have produced thousands of would-be workers without the skills or attitudes sought by employers." Potter called for remedial training to bring the black job seekers up to employers' standards. He warned however that "a simple expenditure for training is not going to do the job unless it includes the motivational, psychological factor. If the Negro is going to follow, as too many still do, the historical pattern —get paid on Friday and get drunk on Saturday—what is the training going to accomplish?"[57]

Although it is perhaps a bit clearer in Potter's comments than in those of other businessmen, a persistent trend developed during the sixties which used social science terminology not only to justify continued discrimination, but also to perpetuate racial stereotyping. The National Industrial Conference Board quoted an executive as saying large numbers of Negroes would never qualify for industrial employment because "they are illiterate or semi-illiterate, irresponsible, overly submissive or hostile, suspicious, resentful of white supervisors, and in other ways badly formed by their life experience."[58] It is a matter of some question whether the modifying phrase "formed by their life experience" is an honest attempt to express the problems of the black subculture as seen from the businessman's perspective or is merely a modern tag line on a time-honored string of racist generalities.

Employers became particularly fond of explaining the lack of qualified black applicants by alluding to the shortcomings of Negro family life. Some businessmen's discussions of black family patterns had obvious racist overtones. A Houston oil company executive whose company refused to take any community-level action to improve the conditions of the Negro, relieved himself, his children, and probably his grandchildren of any responsibility when he explained that "it will take several generations of

greatly improved education for Negro youth before any long strides can
be made; as the 'home atmosphere' of Negro children is not conducive to
intellectual attainment and advanced education, at least one generation of
educated parents is needed to lay the proper groundwork."[59] His words
were echoed by a New York employer who said, "Home life, as far as
parents are concerned, is probably not the best for colored people. The
momentum of parents is probably carried over into children. There must
be several generations yet before there will be any real change."[60]

Like the efficient-use-of-labor argument, the sociological argument was
a double-edged sword. Early proponents of fair employment had urged
employers to use blacks because Negroes were a readily available source
of trained manpower, only to have their argument turned against them
when the supply of trained blacks was exhausted. Conversely, the sociological objection to Negro employment was used mostly by opponents of
black employment, but could be used by problack forces as an argument
in favor of extra help for Negroes. Because the environment was subject
to change, the emphasis on the nonmiddle-class nature of many black
families led some employers to urge their colleagues to make a special
effort to bring blacks up to white par. Harold Mayfield, director of personnel relations for Owens-Illinois, called upon employers to "make allow-
ances . . . to see that a man may be qualifiable although not yet qualified;
we must make our selection of men on the basis of their teachability rather
than their present knowledge." This, Mayfield said, was because Negroes
"may not even have heard of these [technical] jobs nor of the tools we use
in them. They did not have chemistry sets as children; their parents and
friends did not talk about these matters; they are unprepared for this work
in a profound sense most of us cannot grasp because it is a subtle matter
of attitude more than simply a matter of facts."[61]

The "subtle matter of attitude" was the frequent target of employer
comments when they spoke of the environmentally caused shortcomings of
Negro workers. In another article Mayfield noted that people from "the
city slums, the rural backwoods, or an Indian tribe . . . are *truly* handicapped in performing business jobs and not all of them can or will make
the transition." Among the important qualities Mayfield believed these un-
fortunates lacked were an "acceptance of personal competition, respect for
authority, concern for the distant future, admiration of thrift, industrious-
ness, subordination of the personal good to the group welfare under certain circumstance, willingness to settle most personal disagreements peace-
ably, a complex code of ethics governing relations of one person to another,
and so on."[62]

The preoccupation of some businessmen with motivating Negroes
rather than with providing educational facilities could almost be viewed as

a sociological reincarnation of the stereotype of the lazy black. During the 1960's a large segment of the business community participated in a number of programs designed to counteract what the businessmen believed was the lack of motivation among black youth to seek the education and training necessary for successful employment. The youth-oriented motivation programs which sprang up in the wake of the riots of the mid-sixties could have very conservative sociopolitical overtones. For example, several businessmen in Racine, Wisconsin, arranged for ex-boxer Archie Moore to bring his ABC Club presentation to the high school students of that city. Although the businessmen wished to help motivate Racine's black youth, they did so by sponsoring an organization which actively campaigned against the activist thought prevalent in the black community at that time. Moore's club stressed self-discipline, education, and "a program that will inspire young people to walk away from trouble with courage and dignity and without cowardice." Moore was an outspoken opponent of urban violence and of the black power demonstration of John Carlos and Tommie Smith at the 1968 Olympic Games. Moore provided businessmen with a perfect opportunity to demonstrate their new-found sympathy with the American Creed without having to deviate a step from a fundamentalist interpretation of the Capitalist Ethic.[63]

The Indianapolis Chamber of Commerce established a more elaborate, but equally conservative, motivation project when it created the Committee for Employment Opportunity in 1965. From a number of sources, including business and industry, the committee recruited volunteers to counsel unemployed job seekers. While the Indianapolis project was not unique in its method of one-to-one individual counseling, committee supporters justified their activity in a way that clearly illustrated the conservative business interpretation of black sociological problems. Committee literature said that "on-the-spot research showed that the unskilled job seeker's frustration and lack of motivation to find work is caused primarily by poor job focus, personal problems, a history of poor interviews, and a resulting lack of self-confidence." The committee carefully explained that the root of the problem lay with the individual, not with the business community. The committee claimed that the unemployed worker's "lack of good work attitudes is caused by a poor understanding of his personal responsibilities to an employer, oversensitivity and defensiveness with supervisors, and a generalized hostility to business and industry whom he views incorrectly as the source of his troubles."[64]

The most concerted business attempt to deal with the problem of sociological disabilities related to employment was the Plans for Progress series of Youth Motivation Programs. The programs began in Cleveland in 1965 and consisted of sending minority employees into local schools to speak to the students as "living witnesses" that properly trained blacks could get nontraditional jobs. Linked with a national advertising campaign organized by the Vice President's Task Force on Youth Motivation, local Plans for Progress councils in sixteen cities sponsored programs in fifty-nine schools during the 1967-68 school year. While the program was basically an antidrop-out campaign, it was specially directed at minority students. The Youth Motivation Program recognized that many black youths needed both models and proof that education would indeed lead to jobs. Thus the program was a tacit admission that the business community had failed in the past to provide jobs to qualified blacks and was now trying to rectify the imbalance it had created. In the introduction to a booklet which contained hundreds of pictures of successful minority employees, Vice President Hubert H. Humphrey wrote, "There was a day when your choices might have been limited. But that day has now passed."[65]

To a limited extent the Vice President's words were accurate. By 1966, breakthroughs had been made into white-collar, supervisory, technical, professional, and even some managerial positions. Businessmen spoke out uniformly in favor of equal employment opportunity. While tokenism was undoubtedly still a problem, the lack of qualified black workers had supplanted the reluctance of business to hire Negroes as the chief difficulty facing the fair employment movement. During the mid-sixties pressure from the federal government and pressure from the black community finally forced business to begin living up to the pious expressions of equal employment which had been the formal position of most large national companies since World War II. In many cases the original policies of nondiscrimination had been instituted as the result of state FEPC laws, federal contracts, and, in some cases, pressure from industrial unions. It took the civil rights revolution to persuade businessmen, even those with formal policies of nondiscrimination, to stop taking the line of least resistance and instead face up to the implications of institutionalized racism.[66]

9

The Turning Point: Federal Pressure and the Civil Rights Movement

The combined forces of the federal government under the Kennedy and Johnson administrations and the direct action of the black community wrought a major change in the fundamentalist interpretation of the Capitalist Ethic and American Creed which had marked business attitudes towards blacks during the first fifteen years after the war. The state laws and tokenism of the forties and fifties had consolidated the position of blacks in semiskilled labor and had opened the possibility for Negro employment in higher level jobs. Many southern and border state firms and some northern companies as well continued to discriminate against blacks in production line work, and the black presence in white-collar jobs was statistically insignificant. Nevertheless, as a whole, the business community had come to accept black operatives, and to at least consider the possibility of Negro white-collar personnel.

Up through the beginning of the Kennedy administration business acceptance of black employees was predicated upon an extremely orthodox interpretation of the Capitalist Ethic. Blacks would be hired when there was no risk of excessive employee or public opposition and then only if the blacks could meet or exceed regular qualifications. The American Creed of equal opportunity was a reality only as long as there was no additional cost to the firm. It was this narrow economic interpretation of the American Creed which would fall by the boards under the onslaught of governmental and black demands during the 1960's.

Barely a month after he took office, President John F. Kennedy issued Executive Order 10925. From March 6, 1961, until it was superseded on October 24, 1965, by President Lyndon B. Johnson's Executive Order 11246, 10925 dominated the industrial race relations of the country's federal contractors. It established the President's Committee on Equal Employment Opportunity (PCEEO), which, unlike its predecessor, the Nixon Committee, had the power to initiate reviews of businessmen's compliance with their contracts and the authority to rectify any injustices it found. The Kennedy administration transformed an impotent coordinating and educational organization into a body with the power (if not the will) to search out discrimination in employment among federal contractors and to compel equal employment opportunity.

The new committee differed from the old in four significant respects. First, PCEEO created a definite timetable for dealing with complaints. The timetable applied both to the committee itself and to the contracting federal agency. While complaints could be filed and processed by either the agency or the committee, the committee had the power to review all cases and order compliance no matter what the findings of the contracting agency's compliance officer. This precluded possible deals between the agency and contractors at the expense of the complainant.

Second, PCEEO enlarged upon the review procedure begun by the Nixon Committee in its last several years. Unlike the Nixon Committee, which had to rely upon the contracting federal agencies to carry out reviews of compliance, PCEEO had the authority to conduct such investigations itself. These investigations were designed to dig deeply into potential problem areas revealed by the compliance reports which each employer was obliged to submit to the committee—also an innovation.[1]

Third, PCEEO rewrote the mandatory nondiscrimination clause which was a part of every government contract. Not only did the new clause contain the standard admonition, "The contractor will not discriminate against any employee or applicant for employment because of race, creed, color, or national origin," but it went on to require the contractor to "take affirmative action to ensure that applicants are employed, and that employees are treated during employment, without regard to their race, creed, color or national origin."[2]

Finally, the Kennedy committee had the authority to impose a variety of sanctions on noncooperating employers. Although the executive order urged that the committee act through informal means, such as "conference, conciliation, mediation, or persuasion," whenever possible, it did permit the committee to: 1) publicize the names of discriminatory contractors, 2) recommend injunctive or criminal action by the Department of Justice, 3) terminate contracts, and 4) prohibit further contracts until the contractor complied with the nondiscriminatory requirement.[3]

Compared to the Nixon Committee, PCEEO was a whirlwind of activity. It adjusted more complaints during its first year than the Nixon Committee had in seven years.[4] More importantly, it engaged in a series of highly publicized confrontations with contractors which gave it a reputation in the business community for toughness which in turn influenced many employers actively to recruit black workers in order to stave off similar difficulties.

During its first two years the committee forced the Lockheed Corporation to adopt the Plans for Progress which opened up a new era in affirmative racial personnel practices. PCEEO also placed five firms on the list of those prohibited from receiving further government contracts until they submitted acceptable compliance reports.[5] The committee's two most important moves were against Comet Rice Mills of Houston and Beaumont, Texas, and against the Danly Machine Company of Chicago. Danly, although it was located in an area with a large Negro population, did not have a single black worker among its more than 1,300 employees. Comet exhibited the typical pattern of segregation and discrimination that existed in many parts of the South. Its noncompliance included "racial separation of employees by department, racially discriminatory rates of pay, racially separate application forms, and separation of sanitary facilities by the designations, 'White,' 'Negro,' and 'Latin American.' "[6]

Early in 1962 PCEEO declared both companies ineligible to receive government contracts until they submitted plans for compliance with the nondiscriminatory clause. Within a month each company had submitted an acceptable plan to the committee. The plans were important not only because the companies agreed to eliminate the objectionable conditions, but because plans also specified the "affirmative action" steps each firm would pursue to insure equality of employment. Danly agreed to "establish contact with sources of minority group recruiting for referral of qualified minority group applicants," issue a policy statement, and set up methods to evaluate the success of its program. The company also "notified in writing all sources of recruitment that it expected referral without regard to race, creed, color, or national origin," and "it broadened the base of its advertising and recruitment activities to include periodicals reaching the minority group community and colleges with substantial minority enrollment."[7] Comet's affirmative actions were of a similar nature. In addition, Comet agreed to survey its minority employees to see if they had any skills which might qualify them for promotion. Before the committee's action Comet had not even provided space on its application blanks for blacks to indicate their educational experience.[8]

While the action against the five companies showed that the committee could get results when it was willing to use its muscle, PCEEO nevertheless operated very cautiously. One observer believed that the committee's caution sprang from its fear of being declared unconstitutional, at least until the passage of the Civil Rights Act of 1964.[9] Even though the publicity from the prosecution of offending firms gave the committee an important no-nonsense reputation in the business community, it was reluctant to engage in widespread public prosecution. According to vice chairman Jerry R. Holleman, the committee did most of its work in secret because, "we are seeking to avoid publicity. We're working through cooperation, not through compulsion or threats. We don't want to blacken [sic] anyone's name."[10]

While conciliation and informal pressure appear to have had some positive effect, particularly in the wake of the Danly and Comet cases, which lent an implicit threat to committee requests,[11] PCEEO clearly took a soft line. It was not trying to maximize the number of black job holders.[12] Despite its power to supersede government agencies, PCEEO, like its predecessor, continued to leave most of the enforcement up to the contracting agencies even though they were less than adamant in their demands for compliance. Although the committee had demanded and received affirmative action in recruitment from firms it threatened to prosecute, the head of compliance for the General Services Administration (along with the Defense Department, it was the largest purchaser in the federal government) said, "We don't tell companies that they have to go out on the street and hire Negroes, we just ask them to take applications and put everyone on an equal basis."[13] According to one trade magazine, PCEEO wished to achieve "more or less voluntary compliance. The theory is that the 'converted' are more likely to increase job opportunities for Negroes beyond a mere minimum than companies that are pushed hard and penalized."[14] It is difficult to distinguish between this concept of voluntary compliance and the supplicatory attitude of the Nixon Committee. The new committee was born with teeth. It tried them out a couple of times and apparently decided that it did not like the taste of red meat so it reverted to the gum beating that had characterized the previous Republican administration.[15]

Business generally reacted favorably to Executive Order 10925, perhaps because even such staunch conservatives as Barry Goldwater supported the government's right to demand nondiscrimination in its contracts.[16] Businessmen were concerned with the government's requirement for "affirmative action," but in comparison to some of the demands that were forthcoming from black protest organizations, the government's demands appeared reasonable, and businessmen sought to meet the new government standards. For example, several firms in Atlanta which held contracts with government agencies indicated they felt more pressure to act under Executive Order 10925 than they had under previous executive orders even though their contracts had obligated them to fair employment for as long as they had held them. In 1963, the Atlanta district manager of an office machines company said that the executive order had prompted him to "casually mention" the possibility of hiring Negroes and "to his satisfaction and some surprise lounge talk evidenced no unfavorable comment." He said, "It was almost as though thoughts of desegregation of the work force were in the air."[17]

The committee's power to deprive a company of its contracts, present and future, plus its threats to do so on a small number of occasions, created an atmosphere more conducive to employing blacks. Coupled with a rising tide of black antibusiness militancy, many contractors felt it prudent, if not imperative, to begin hiring more blacks in nontraditional positions.[18] The apparent willingness of white employees and public to accept blacks reduced the potential cost of integrating while the threat of contract cancellation clearly increased the cost of continued segregation. Under such circumstances there was obviously no conflict between the Capitalist Ethic and the American Creed.

The business community was singularly silent in opposition to civil rights legislation during the 1960's.[19] Public acceptance of the civil rights movement indicated a generally sympathetic attitude toward the American Creed, not only in theory but also in practice. Civil rights legislation was opposed by decreasing numbers of congressmen, and by opposing such legislation businessmen ran the risk of placing themselves outside the mainstream of national attitudes. Moreover, by the early 1960's most industrial states had FEPC laws and businessmen found they could live with them without incurring any additional costs. Of employers' organizations, only the Illinois Manufacturers' Association testified against proposed federal legislation, and even that occurred at the beginning of the decade.[20] The silence continued even after it became clear in 1964 that a civil rights bill of some sort was going to pass. With the single exception of the *Wall Street Journal,* which feared the law would open "the gates to new floods of bureaucracy and litigation" and would compel employers to hire unqualified workers,[21] open opposition to the civil rights bill came from nonbusiness conservatives, not from employers.[22]

On the other hand, on several occasions President Johnson called directly on businessmen to lend active support to the pending civil rights legislation.[23] But employers were no more willing to publicly support the legislation than to oppose it. Only a handful of employers spoke in favor of the bill.[24] Halward L. Homan, personnel manager of Friden, summed up the business position on the Civil Rights Act of 1964 when he wrote, "A few years ago I would have said there is only one way to handle the Fair Employment problem—voluntarily. I still feel that way, but we have done very little about it." Homan continued, "I am not particularly fond of legal coercion. I think that voluntary conduct is far better than legal force. But—where the rights of the individuals are not protected voluntarily, the law must step in."[25]

Title VII of the Civil Rights Act of 1964 prohibited employers from discriminating against employees in any facet of employment because of race, color, religion, sex, or national origin, and it established the Equal Employment Opportunity Commission (EEOC) to administer the law.[26] Congress passed the law as part of the memorial wave of legislation that followed President Kennedy's assassination. The period was also one of increasing antibusiness activity on the part of civil rights groups. Given this background, and the almost total absence of outspoken opposition to the law before it passed, it is hardly surprising that the business community accepted the new legislation calmly. The Mississippi Manufacturer's Association, for example, urged its members to accept the Civil Rights Act and pointed out that everyone in Mississippi would benefit "through gainful employment in a useful occupation in an expanding economy in which all citizens, all Mississippians have the equal opportunity to enjoy the fruits of their own individual labors."[27] A generally calm reception was not indicative of the disappearance of discrimination in employment. The work of EEOC made that abundantly clear. Rather, lack of opposition by employers indicated that the business community either accepted the new ideal, or at least was unwilling to speak out against the law of the land.

The apparent lack of animosity toward EEOC may have been due in part to the law's emphasis on conciliation. Upon investigation of a complaint, if EEOC found "reasonable cause" to believe that there had been discrimination, a conciliator contacted the complainant to determine what kind of remedy he would accept. The conciliator then presented this proposed remedy to the employer along with whatever other changes in policy EEOC believed were necessary to insure continued nondiscriminatory practice. The law did not bind the employer to sign the conciliation agreement. However, if EEOC found that the employer had not stopped his illegal behavior, it could recommend to the Attorney General that criminal charges be brought under Title VII of the Civil Rights Act.[28]

When the commission demonstrated a willingness to recommend legal action against uncooperative firms—and it initiated thirty-five such cases in fiscal 1967—it undoubtedly bolstered employer eagerness to sign conciliation agreements. EEOC officials reported that most businessmen they approached would comply both because they feared the legal and public relations impact of extended litigation and because direct approaches from the government gave the businessman someone else to take the blame for integrating his work force.[29]

Conciliation agreements with EEOC were designed to have a broad impact on the employment practices of the firm in question. Not only did the agreements include policy changes in areas not directly relevant to the specific complaint which initiated EEOC investigation, but the agreements also required the employer to take affirmative action, a continuation of the policy first developed by PCEEO.[30] Also like PCEEO, EEOC could initiate investigations into industries that appeared to widely underutilize minority workers. Unlike PCEEO, of course, EEOC was not limited to employers with government contracts. The policy of "confrontation and visitation" with firms in specified industries and geographic areas served the purpose of encouraging employers to hire more minority personnel both among those "confronted" and among those who wished to avoid awkward public hearings.[31]

The willingness of even southern firms to accede to the demands of the law without great bitterness or recrimination was a result of the Capitalist Ethic, which required the employer to do whatever was necessary to minimize disruption to normal business procedures, and it was obviously less disruptive to obey the law than to face the criminal consequences of maintaining blatant discrimination. The president of Hunt Foods said that his company would abide by its nondiscriminatory policy even if there were no Civil Rights Act, but he added, "I think governmental inspection of our plants and facilities is an asset. We all need some prodding."[32]

The state laws, the government contract compliance committees, and finally the Civil Rights Act of 1964, provided businessmen with a method of meeting the demands of black pressure groups and the liberal white community without having to deal with the protesters themselves. Given a choice, businessmen would undoubtedly have preferred no interference in their racial practices at all, but forced to decide between the demands of legislative bodies, with whom they had traditionally been friendly, and the demands of an aroused and angry black population, it is little wonder that they embraced the former.

While many businessmen felt that compliance with the law should have made them immune from attack by civil rights groups, the black groups did not share this point of view. The refusal of civil rights groups to depend on EEOC was probably well founded. A 1966 survey of 180 companies concluded, "Fair employment practices legislation is a necessary but not a sufficient cause in creating equality of opportunity." The report said that one or more of the following factors had to exist before a firm was likely to institute a fair employment policy: "A contract with government, a top company official imbued with the injustice of inequality, the organized awareness and resistance of the Negro community."[33]

Agitation for equal employment had originated in the black community years before any state or federal agency had even considered outlawing economic discrimination. There is no comprehensive study of black fair employment activity, but direct action by blacks took place at least as early as the 1920's. After white store owners had denied Negro requests to employ black salespeople in their Harlem establishments, black pickets forced the owners to change their policies.[34] A more concerted effort toward the same ends also took place in Harlem during the 1930's. The "Don't buy where you can't work" movement organized a boycott against offending proprietors and met with some success,[35] although some of its efforts at picketing were blocked by court injunctions.[36] And it was black activism in the form of the March on Washington Movement that forced President Roosevelt to issue Executive Order 8802, which opened the way for the modern fair employment campaigns.

To a limited extent during the 1940's and somewhat more widely during the 1950's, black action groups experimented with direct pressure techniques to open up more and better jobs for Negro workers. In 1943, a City-Wide Citizens' Committee on Harlem successfully continued the earlier pressure on uptown New York stores.[37] In 1946, when the Silvercup baking company in Chicago refused to hire Mrs. Mary Blake as an office worker because she was black, the co-op market in her neighborhood took Silvercup bread off its shelves. Silvercup claimed that a quarter of its workers were black and tried to convince the store manager to restock its bread by having some of the company's Negro employees testify as to the firm's fair employment policy. All the black workers, however, were in menial positions, and the boycott was not lifted until the company hired Mrs. Blake and other Negroes in nontraditional positions.[38] In 1952, NAACP picketing opened up job opportunities at a Philadelphia Philco plant, and in 1958, the combined efforts of NAACP and CORE convinced St. Louis retail store owners and a bread manufacturer that employing Negroes was less disruptive than picketing and boycotts.[39] While these local efforts clearly had an impact on the businessmen involved, the business community remained unconcerned about the possible effects of concerted black activity until the civil rights revolution began.

The civil rights revolution was manned and led by southern blacks, and quite naturally the first business reaction came from southern employers. The tragedy of Little Rock, Arkansas, became the number one exhibit in the moderate southern businessman's case for compromising with the civil rights movement. The tragedy, as far as the business community was concerned, was not that the governor of the state had used armed troops to prevent implementation of a Supreme Court ruling. The tragedy was that armed troops had enforced court-ordered desegregation, which in turn sparked riot and disorder on the part of whites. The head of the state's industrial commission, Winthrop Rockefeller (later to be governor), stated the business community's position bluntly when he said, "The industrial prospect doesn't give a hoot whether your schools are segregated or not, but he wants no part of disorder and violence."[40]

Although some businessmen who shared Rockefeller's observations reacted by urging caution and deferment of integration lest they "arouse resentment among white employees and violence 'on the nature of Little Rock,' "[41] many southern businessmen, particularly those in larger firms, supported moderation and peaceful progress. The 1957 disturbances in Little Rock severely retarded the city's economic development. During the five years preceding the integration crisis at Little Rock High School an average of five new plants a year moved to the city, providing a million dollars worth of investment and more than three hundred new jobs a year.[42] It was not until five years after the integration riots that any other important new industries moved into Little Rock.[43] There are clear indications that this hiatus in the city's growth was a direct result of the tension and turmoil that resulted from Governor Faubus' hard-line segregation policy.[44]

When Virginia's Governor J. Lindsay Almond, Jr., supported the Byrd machine's plan for "massive resistance" in order to protect Virginia children from "the livid stench of sadism, sex, immorality and juvenile pregnancy infesting the mixed schools of the District of Columbia and elsewhere," he met strong resistance from his state's business community.[45] Almond's state-wide policy forced the closing of several city and county school districts which otherwise would have had to desegregate under court orders. Virginia businessmen publicly opposed the school closings. They said it was hard enough to attract skilled technical and professional employees to the South without the additional obstacle of having no public school system.[46]

Business proponents of an industrial South placed growth ahead of segregation. Public pressure, including that from the business community, had a telling effect on Governor Almond, who changed his tune and began to warn against "those who would have Virginia abandon public education and thereby consign a generation of children to darkness and illiteracy, the pits of indolence and dependency and the dungeons of delinquency."[47] The legislature responded to the moderates' counterattack by repealing the massive resistance laws in a special session in 1959 and by instituting a local option plan in which each school dis-

trict could make its own decision on whether or not to integrate.[48] The
siren song of economic growth was sweet enough to insure at least *pro
forma* compliance with court orders in all school districts except Prince
Edward County. But even there, where the public schools remained closed
for five years, local businessmen formed the backbone of the proschool
forces.[49]

Under pressure from the courts to desegregate the schools in
Atlanta, Georgia, politicians considered following the Virginia pattern
of massive resistance. Once again the business community proved to be
the crucial force that prevented hard-line segregationists from permanently destroying the public school system of the state. Businessmen
were not in favor of integration, nor was their opposition to the hard-
liners a display of respect for the law; but if some businessmen cared
little for law, they cared mightily for order. Mills B. Lane, Jr., president
of the Citizens and Southern Bank, insisted, "I am just as much in disagreement with the Supreme Court decision as anyone, for I view it as
an invasion of state's right's."[50] Yet he, along with twenty-six other prominent businessmen, petitioned the state legislature in 1960 not to close
the schools.[51] In order to insure Georgia's attractiveness to new industry,
business maintained pressure to keep the schools open. The businessmen
were successful in convincing the legislature not to close the school system to escape court demands for what was, after all, only token integration.

It remained, however, for Dallas to provide the ultimate demonstration of the effect a highly organized business community could have in
bringing about peaceful racial integration, not only in the schools but in
other facets of civic life. While most businessmen were aware of the
power they wielded in their communities, few organized that power as
effectively as the business leadership of Dallas. The Dallas Citizens
Council (DCC) was an organization of 250 of the city's most powerful
business executives which was able to exert influence, if not absolute
control, over every aspect of city life with which it was concerned.[52] In
1960, DCC established a Committee for Desegregation. The committee,
in concert with a number of other civic groups, launched an extensive
year-long propaganda campaign to convince Dallasites that peaceful desegregation was in their best interests. Fear of the economic consequences
of racial violence apparently motivated the DCC, but the council tied its
public education program to civic pride, of which Dallas had an ample
amount, and to obedience to the law.[53]

The Dallas program was notable not only because it successfully
averted the violence which was endemic in desegregating southern cities
during the early 1960's, but also because it extended desegregation be-

yond the schoolroom. Under the leadership of DCC, with some prodding from the American Friends Service Committee, a number of firms promoted Negroes to previously all-white jobs. Negro policemen were put in uniform for the first time. The state fair was desegregated, and downtown eating places and hotels agreed to accept Negro patronage.[54]

Until 1963, the main thrust of the civil rights movement was for equal service rather than for equal employment. Since most northern, many border, and even some southern businesses had extended equal patronage privileges to blacks before 1960, the movement remained mostly southern and oriented toward retail establishments. Because the most important northern spokesmen for the business community were outside of the civil rights area of activity, most businesses attacked for not granting blacks equal service were left to work out their problems without the support of the national business community.

Once southern blacks discovered they could successfully demand equal service, they logically extended their demands to include equal employment.[55] As early as 1961 observers in Houston reported that after the city's schools and lunch counters were desegregated without overt trouble "employers began to shown awareness of the problem of discrimination in employment," and when blacks boycotted a Houston supermarket it began to employ black checkers.[56] In January, 1963, close observers of the equal employment scene in Atlanta said they had found "a significant change during the past year in objections raised in expressed reluctance to embark upon a policy of employment on merit." Formerly employers had said, "Atlanta is not ready yet," or "Personally I have no objections, but I must think of my customers, my staff," etc. By 1963, the observers reported, "We now more frequently hear, 'The Negroes don't apply,' or 'where are qualified Negroes.' This to us at least, implies a change in attitude that is difficult to describe but nevertheless apparent."[57]

Although most civil rights activists did not turn their attention to employment in northern firms until 1963, an important vanguard of the black equal employment movement emerged in the North during the early 1960's at the same time most attention was focused on the South. Early in 1961 a group of four hundred black ministers in Philadelphia organized a boycott of the Sun Oil Company.[58] Operating under the slogan "No more Sunoco till your preacher says so!" they drastically cut back consumption of the company's gasoline in Negro areas. The company had agreed to the Negro ministers' demand to hire thirty blacks in specific jobs but had been unable, or unwilling, to meet the thirty-day deadline which the ministers had imposed. The boycott ended only after the company hired the requisite number of blacks in the designated jobs.[59]

The Philadelphia boycott movement, or selective patronage program, was more or less led by the Rev. Leon Sullivan, who often acted as its spokesman. The description "more or less" is appropriate because participants feared legal retribution for taking part in a secondary boycott and, for safety, attempted to keep the leadership diffuse.[60] The boycott movement was astonishingly successful during the three years it operated. The selective patronage program took formal action against only two dozen firms, but it is difficult to estimate how many other companies opened additional jobs when they heard they were already on the ministers' list, or in an attempt to forego that dubious honor. The ministers claimed, and businessmen agreed, that more than four thousand jobs which whites had traditionally held were opened to Negroes as a direct result of the boycotts.[61]

The Philadelphia boycott movement erased the requirement of the American Creed that all applicants, white and black, receive absolutely impartial consideration, but the movement did not disturb the demand of the Capitalist Ethic that the employer need hire only men who met his standards. Although the ministers' demands for a specific number of new black workers in given jobs by a certain date were less flexible than the demands of any previous equal employment group, the ministerial alliance continued to accept one basic personnel concept—a company should be required to hire only qualified men. By demanding that companies hire black men the Philadelphia movement forced employers to give preference to qualified black men, but because the ministerial alliance accepted the premise that it could force employers to hire only qualified men, the movement quickly foundered on the rocks which emerged as business drained the shallow pool of qualified blacks.

By 1963 Sullivan had discovered that he could continue to force firms into opening up jobs to black candidates, but he could not find potential black workers who qualified for the proffered jobs. Rather than demanding that business undertake the responsibility for training the unemployables, simplify its jobs so less qualified people could work, or reevaluate job requirements, as later protest leaders did, Sullivan took upon himself the burden of supplying industry with appropriately trained and motivated personnel. With money from foundations and equipment donated by Philadelphia firms, including those which had been objects of "selective patronage," Sullivan opened the Opportunities Industrialization Center (oic) in late 1963. Essentially a private vocational school, oic received enthusiastic support from the business community and from government officials.

Whatever its other merits, and they appear to have been considerable, OIC provided the Philadelphia business community with a perfect "out."[62] Since Philadelphia employers did not object to hiring qualified blacks, and since the leader of the protest movement agreed that there was a shortage of skilled Negro workers, the business community remained immune from attacks by the black community as long as employers supported OIC and hired its trained graduates. Not only did the creation of OIC mark the end of the boycott movement, but Sullivan proved to be a man of essentially conservative values who helped reinforce the businessmen's own traditional beliefs. He worked against big government by operating independently of Washington, and to some extent in competition with established federal training programs. Nothing could be more satisfying to ideologically conservative businessmen than to help a "militant" leader who believed "that a man is like a balloon, that it's not a man's color that determines how high he can rise, but what he has inside of him."[63]

As the selective patronage campaign was being phased out in favor of OIC in Philadelphia, militant antibusiness activity began to appear in other cities throughout the nation.[64] At first equal employment activism followed the pattern set by the Philadelphia movement. The boycott was the primary weapon which the pressure groups used, and their targets were those firms most susceptible to consumer buying habits. The local nature of most of the boycotting organizations and their targets, and the minimum of public commotion which attended them (to say nothing of the reluctance of the press to publicize a boycott of their advertisers), make it impossible to know how many companies faced organized black consumer resistance. Although some poorly organized boycotts must have failed, businessmen appear to have met Negro demands for more jobs in the overwhelming majority of cases.[65]

In the South, from its inception in 1960, the civil rights movement had emphasized personal commitment and direct action. In the North, on the other hand, consumer boycotts had required a minimum of personal involvement and a maximum of organization. In the spring of 1963 the movement combined the passive boycott with the active street demonstration to demand more jobs for blacks and bring the Birmingham-style fair employment demonstration to the North. The Detroit Council for Human Relations held a "walk" in which more than a hundred thousand people marched for better jobs. The council, an all-black organization which rejected whites as members because they tended to be "gradualists," announced that it was going to conduct a series of boycotts starting with the A&P supermarkets and working up from there until they reached Detroit's pinnacle, General Motors. The leader of the council, the Rev. Albert B. Cleage, Jr., predicted that his boycott movement would spread, and when sufficient regional groups had been formed, he would institute nationwide boycotts.[66] Because of its size, GM was a natural target for the new activist mood. GM responded to the boycott threat by hiring additional blacks in all positions, but with an emphasis on technical and professional jobs since black workers already constituted between a quarter and a half of all GM production workers.[67] The automobile giant never suffered a formal boycott. NAACP led a day of nationwide demonstrations against the company in the spring of 1964, but the attacks and counterattacks in the GM battle remained a war of words.[68]

To a limited extent blacks continued the boycott movement after 1965, with a number of attempts to bring consumer pressure against companies on both the local and national levels.[69] However, the drama of direct confrontation increasingly overshadowed the boycott movement during the late 1960's. In its mildest form the confrontation consisted merely of picketing the offending establishment. Washington, D.C., ministerial groups had tried this technique against banks with mixed success as early as the spring of 1961.[70] The incidence of confrontation increased sharply as the civil rights movement concentrated more and more attention on the business community during the summer of 1963.[71] While picketing had always been an effective weapon against consumer-oriented firms, blacks discovered that even big industrial firms did not like to have people marching around in front of their doors and accusing them of discrimination. No matter what the public climate, when a consumer-oriented firm suffered from a boycott it had at least to weigh the costs of the boycott against possible public opposition. But during the 1960's, when people expected the business community to practice fair employment, picketing, even in the absence of a boycott, could have a negative impact on a firm's image and ultimately on its ability to do business. Even utility companies, which have both a monopoly and an inelastic product demand, nevertheless consulted with black groups in a number of cities after NAACP picketing. Because their monopoly positions subjected them to regulation by public bodies and made them particularly vulnerable to criticism, electrical, water, and gas companies throughout the nation agreed to review their hiring practices and to make a concerted effort to employ more Negroes in nontraditional positions in return for clear front sidewalks.[72]

Direct action against employers by black action groups reached a kind of climax in San Francisco during the winter and spring of 1964. Boycotts, and boycotts with picketing, may have been effective in the hands of large, widely respected groups such as NAACP or an *ad hoc* ministerial alliance, but the Congress of Racial Equality discovered that a small group of dedicated activists could be just as effective as a large group. Success demanded a new technique. Early in 1964, CORE decided to put pressure on San Francisco stores and banks in order to get them to hire more blacks.[73] In an alliance with the Baptist Union, an organization of Negro ministers, the demonstrators entered Bay Area Lucky super-markets, filled shopping carts, and then abandoned them at the checkout counters. This form of harassment continued daily for more than two weeks until bad publicity and disapproval from the Baptist ministers put a stop to the "shop-ins."[74] Mayor John F. Shelley mediated peace talks between CORE and Lucky which ended in an agreement to hire 45 to 75 additional black workers over a three-month period.[75]

A second wave of direct action occurred in San Francisco in March when the Ad-Hoc Committee to End Discrimination, a biracial group with some left-wing leadership, sat down in the lobby of the Sheraton-Palace Hotel. The group had been negotiating with the hotel for more jobs for blacks since December and had held a number of minor demonstrations for which the hotel had filed a $50,000 damage suit.[76] The hotel demonstrations reached their peak on March 6, when more than a thousand protesters jammed into the hotel lobby and sat down.[77] The San Francisco Hotel Association, representing the Sheraton-Palace and thirty-four other city hotels, met with the Ad-Hoc Committee in the mayor's office and through his mediation worked out a two-year pact. The hotels agreed that 15 to 20 percent of their new employees would be from minority groups, that they would make monthly reports to the civil rights group on their progress, and that they would not press charges against sit-in participants (although prosecutions took place nevertheless).[78]

As the Ad-Hoc Committee signed the agreement with the hotel association, NAACP began a new series of demonstrations in the city. On March 9, it threw a picket line around the General Motors Cadillac showroom on Van Ness Avenue to demand more jobs for blacks.[79] Five days later one hundred and ten protesters were arrested at a sit-in there.[80] Although GM took a tough public stand, saying that "no good purpose could be served by private discussion of allegations and unfounded charges made by unlawful demonstrators,"[81] it apparently initiated secret talks with NAACP.[82] The talks dragged on for a month until the protesters struck once again. On April 11, the police arrested more than 200 people who disrupted normal activity at four major auto firms on Van Ness Avenue.[83] The dealers balked at NAACP demands that they follow the lead of the hotel association and make periodic reports to the civil rights group on their progress in hiring blacks.

However, on April 17, one of the picketed dealers, not a member of the Motor Car Dealers Association, signed an agreement with NAACP which included a promise of a dealer-sponsored training program.[84] The next day the dealers' association announced it too had come to terms with NAACP. The new agreement did not go as far as the pact with the hotel association. The auto dealers acknowledged "the necessity for the acceleration of employment opportunities of minority group persons," but made no numerical or percentage commitments for actual hiring. Although the association promised to pursue a policy of minority re-cruitment and cooperation in training efforts, again the promises were general rather than specific. Finally, the agreement was worded in such a way that all commitments were made to the Mayor's Interim Com-mittee on Human Rights, which was led by businessman and ex-Secretary of Commerce James Mitchell, rather than to NAACP. It was the Mayor's Committee which would receive "such data or information as may be reasonably required to measure the fulfillment of all aspects of the fore-going pledge."[85]

In one sense all the activity of the winter and spring was prepara-tion for the assault on the final symbol of business power in California, the Bank of America. The nation's largest bank did not just sit and wait. Although none of the three organizations, CORE, NAACP, or the Ad-Hoc Committee, had approached the bank's executives, the bank ran a full-page advertisement in California newspapers. Bank management felt confident that it had a good record of hiring minorities and hoped to beat the demonstrators to the punch by taking its case to the public. The March 16, 1964, advertisement released the contents of a letter the bank president had sent to the chairman of the California Fair Employment Practice Commission.[86] Tough talk at the beginning and the end of the letter bracketed a number of voluntary concessions of major importance. The letter stated that the bank would refuse "to sign agreements and provide reports to non-government agencies such as the Ad-Hoc Com-mittee to End Discrimination. . . ." R. A. Peterson, the bank president, said that "as good Americans, we will not now or in the future capitulate to illegal pressures of the type prominent in San Francisco over the past weeks. . . ."[87] However, the Bank of America's public relations director conceded that if the firm hoped to get public support it had to "stand up and be counted on the urgent social problems posed by the fermenting unrest in the Negro community. . . ."[88] While saying it would never accede to the demands of race pressure groups, the bank disclosed that it was voluntarily setting up a program that incorporated all the points of the auto dealers' agreement and most of those of the hotel association pact. The bank promised to actively seek out minority applications for positions. The bank said that "because our experience has clearly shown that a large proportion of minority racial applicants have not completed high school and cannot pass simple clerical tests," it would not make any firm promises as to the numbers or percentage of minority people it would hire. However, it did pledge to periodically analyze the racial makeup of its employees and to report this information to the state FEPC.[89]

CORE responded to the bank's move by asking for a meeting with the bank management, to which it presented a list of demands. The bank had already implemented most of them in one form or another. The civil rights group did ask for more specifics in such areas as affirmative recruiting, but CORE's major substantive point of disagreement with the bank was the demand that CORE be designated the judge of the bank's minority hiring program. CORE asked the bank to turn over all statistics to it, that the bank clear all announcements with the civil rights group, and that the bank regularly meet with CORE to review employment progress.[90]

CORE broke off meetings with the Bank of America in May, accusing the firm of refusing to negotiate in good faith because it would not discuss CORE's demands that the bank turn over full statistics on minority employment.[91] CORE then began three months of picketing branches of the Bank of America all over California. CORE's tactics included "nickle and dime-ins" during which demonstrators clogged the bank's lines by changing bills into coins and then returning the change for bills. CORE refused offers of the governor to conciliate, and the bank refused CORE's offers to talk unless the civil rights group publicly announced it understood that the bank would not provide CORE with the information it demanded.[92]

In the meantime, the bank had been putting sharp pressure on all its branches to increase minority hiring. During the three months of the crisis the bank hired more than three hundred new black employees.[93] With this increase in nonwhite hiring safely in its pocket, the bank then announced on June 1 that executives had signed a memorandum of understanding with the California FEPC implementing the points of its March 12 open letter.[94] CORE continued to picket for the rest of the summer, but the bank held firm and eventually the demonstrations ceased.

The business community responded slowly but positively to the employment demonstrations of 1963 and 1964. When a firm found itself the object of public attack it almost invariably denied wrong doing, declared it would not be coerced, and then went ahead to meet the demands of the demonstrators, thus giving the lie to its original protestations of innocence. The need for immediate action to remedy employment injustice was the message that came through, even to those not specifically affected by the boycotts and demonstrations. Commenting on the San Francisco demonstrations, *Fortune* magazine advised its readers, "To achieve the kind of results Negroes are demanding business will have to move swiftly and aggressively."[95]

The militant action offended much of the white public. Among some employers there was enough fear of a white backlash to a strong equal employment position that they attempted to minimize publicity about any actions which they took to meet Negro demands.[96] While confrontation tactics may have offended much of the white public, consumers did not necessarily rally to the cause of a besieged firm. In the mid 1960's the public expected business to provide equal employment for blacks and it hurt a businessman's image to be branded discriminatory, which is why public relations firms were increasingly involved in business racial policies.[97] Moreover, businessmen recognized that the public had come to expect fair employment. A progressive hiring policy was good public relations, even if black pressure were the actual source of the move to employ Negroes.

The upsurge of civil rights protests in 1963 and 1964 alerted businessmen to the black community's increasing concern with employment problems, a concern which was burned into the minds of employers by the three years of urban disorders which followed. Mass violence with racial overtones is historically endemic in American cities. Until 1965, however, most businessmen ignored urban violence because it did not directly affect them. Only when the disorder approached the proportions of a spontaneous revolution did businessmen take an active hand in trying to deal with America's racism. Businessmen recognized immediately that unequal employment patterns for blacks was one of the underlying causes of the riots.[98]

The business community had not been totally blind to the possibly explosive consequences of unequal employment patterns.[99] With very few exceptions before 1965, however, businessmen feared the adverse effects of unequal employment would be political. For example, in 1964 William Miller, the president of Textron, warned, "Equal opportunity may be the most important issue that this nation faces for many decades . . . because the American system itself is being tested. Unless we assure equal rights and equal justice for all, our form of government will be in jeopardy."[100] In 1959 James C. Worthy, of Sears Roebuck, had suggested that discrimination was sowing the seeds of revolutionary change in the country. Worthy warned that if the Negro is "denied the white man's opportunities he may seek to take some of the white man's power away

from him." But Worthy was worried about political not violent revolution. His fear was the radical potential of legitimate black electoral
power tied "through heightened race consciousness, to demagogic appeals and boss control."[101]

The riots were thus a more severe reaction than even the most
pessimistic businessmen had predicted. It was not political extremists
that the businessmen feared, but violent street revolution. "It is no
longer solely a matter of justice and the principles of democracy," said
Henry Ford II. "After the tragic events of the past few summers we
must finally recognize—if we did not do so before—that our very national unity and the peace of our cities are at stake."[102] W. P. Gullander,
president of the National Association of Manufacturers, declared, "The
problem of Watts is not a Negro problem, it is our problem as a nation,"
and he went on to point out that "the fundamental cause of the Watts
riot was lack of jobs for Negroes."[103] Executive after executive echoed
Gullander's contention that the riots were a national problem which
business could help solve. Many admitted that they were spurred to
increased efforts by the spreading violence, and not a few implicitly
condoned the violence, like the California industrialist who commented,
"Perhaps riots help more at some stages in the evolution of this
thing than they hurt. How the devil do you get 200 million people to
wake up?"[104]

Three years of rioting left many businessmen with the belief that
the very foundations of society were under attack. It became mani-
festly clear, even to the most conservative businessmen, that something
had to be done to reestablish domestic peace. Rioting upset plans, and
long-range planning is the heart of rational business management. Some
employers continued to use many of the preriot economic justifications
for actively hiring Negroes. They spoke of making the Negro a purchaser
of goods rather than a consumer of taxes.[105] But they did so with the
clear implication that an increase in purchasing power would also lead
to a decrease in the propensity to riot. Stanley Marcus, head of Dallas'
Neiman-Marcus department store, commented on his own feelings by
observing that fellow retailer Joseph Hudson was head of a business
action movement in Detroit. "Once a man sees his investment in a community going up in smoke," said Marcus, "he is going to act."[106]

No man was more committed to the new cause than Henry Ford II.
Speaking to the Buffalo Area Chamber of Commerce, Ford remembered
that on a previous trip to Buffalo in 1950 "we were a complacent, self-
satisfied country. . . . Business executives and chamber officials in those
days were beginning to talk about social responsibilities or corporate
citizenship, but most of us had hardly begun to act." Ford sounded op-

timistic, however, when he told his audience, "More and more business-men are waking up to the fact that they must concern themselves in deeds as well as in words with the needs of their country and its cities."[107]

The riots climaxed six years of sharply increasing pressure on the business community. Beginning with President Kennedy's Executive Order 10925, businessmen had suffered a series of blows, the Civil Rights Act, the civil rights movement, and finally the uprisings in the nation's cities. There were businessmen who rebelled at the growing militancy in the black community and who refused to join in the breastbeating contest which followed the riots. A West Coast chamber of commerce official complained that despite "fundamental progress . . . in changing attitudes of businessmen in our city in the past five years," employers were beginning to "conclude that there is little chance of overcoming the trend toward anarchy in our major cities" and that it was "futile to seek an integrated labor force."[108] Most comment, however, was more along the lines of an American Telephone and Telegraph report which declared bluntly, "The question of whether or not a company participates in programs designed to provide job opportunities for Negroes is no longer appropriate. The question today is how it should participate."[109]

10

Beyond Equal Employment: The Revolution
in Personnel Policy

Increased federal pressure and the actions of the civil rights movement produced a series of profound changes in the attitudes of American businessmen toward Negro employment. Personnel policies which had their roots deep in the American Creed and in the Capitalist Ethic were torn up, and strange new doctrines were planted in their place. The ideal of equal employment opportunity gave way to affirmative action and compensatory practices. The law and the riots motivated businessmen to institute radically new policies of recruitment, selection, and training which went beyond anything even the most liberal fair employment supporter asked for in the 1950's. While the most extreme innovations were limited to the nation's largest corporations, their abandonment of the American Creed principle of color-blindness and of the Capitalist Ethic principle of hiring the best man for the job marked a fundamental new departure in employment attitudes.

In 1963 several hundred thousand demonstrators had marched on Washington demanding "Jobs now!" but it was to take civil turmoil in the nation's largest cities to actually get jobs *now*. The Watts riot of 1965 and the Chicago riot of 1966 gave rise to a handful of job programs,[1] but when more than two dozen cities experienced some sort of racial disorder during the summer of 1967, the nascent employment organizations engendered by the earlier troubles abandoned plans for slow, careful development and sought instant maturity. Businessmen in Dade County, Florida, for example, had joined with the government and various social welfare agencies in 1967 to form the Dade County Equal Employment Opportunity Task Force, which was to "conduct an effective action program to develop greater employment of minority group members residing in Dade County." After its founding in May, 1967, it took the task force almost two months to establish working committees. But Miami's businessmen had second thoughts about their measured pace on July 26—during the height of the Detroit riot. At an emergency meeting the organization's leaders decided they needed a crash program. It took them only two days to create a new emergency plan, and within the week they found two thousand jobs for minority group members.[2] The great crush to "do something" was on. By September the *New York Times* could comment that a list of the companies actively engaged in ghetto-oriented programs "would read much like a stock-market table and run just about as long."[3]

Demands made by civil rights organizations in the wake of the riots found an extraordinarily receptive audience in the business community. Businessmen who were not dependent on consumer purchases could afford to dicker over employing blacks when sit-ins, picketing, and boycotts were the ultimate weapons of the civil rights movement. But when the crackle of the flames and the sound of gunfire still echoed in the streets, civil rights groups could move businessmen, and move them fast, to hire immediately large numbers of Negroes who would have never even made it past the factory gate in more peaceful times. The way in which the black community in Rochester, New York, rioted and then used the threat of renewed violence to force that city's business community to make concessions provides a case study of the business response to the new black militancy.

The first postwar riot occurred in Harlem during the summer of 1964. Harlem is the capital of black America and traditionally has been the bellwether of the mood of black Americans. All the problems that beset Negroes converged in Harlem. Overcrowding, poor living conditions, high prices, friction with the police, poor schools, and high unemployment made the trouble in Harlem and in its sister ghetto, Bedford-Stuyvesant, understandable. But when blacks rioted in Rochester in late July, 1964, they shattered a number of illusions about the status of Negroes outside of the nationally known urban concentrations. The demand for labor in Rochester was high, but so was the unemployment rate among blacks. Many Rochester firms had long traditions of equal employment, and most of them also held government contracts. Rochester's leading industries— Kodak, Xerox, Bausch & Lomb, General Motors, and General Dynamics— employed black technical and professional personnel. But the very nature of the work that made the employment of technically trained blacks possible meant that there were fewer jobs for the unskilled who made up the bulk of Rochester's Negro population.[4]

Immediate business response to the riot was unimpressive,[5] but Rochester's Council of Churches reacted to the riot by inviting Saul Alinsky's Industrial Areas Foundation (IAF) to come to the city to organize the black community, and it was IAF that turned the riot into a weapon for better jobs. Funded by a hundred thousand dollars in church money and directed by IAF, the black community organized under the name FIGHT (Freedom, Integration, God, Honor—Today) in the spring of 1965. The Rev. Franklin Delano Roosevelt Florence (Minister Florence) led FIGHT in an attack on slum-lords, the United Fund, the antipoverty program, and local industry.[6]

FIGHT was successful in persuading the Xerox Corporation to expand its training program.[7] Then, in September, 1966, FIGHT turned its guns on Rochester's most important employer, the Eastman Kodak Company. FIGHT asked Kodak to hire six hundred hard-core unemployed whom FIGHT would recruit. Minister Florence said FIGHT wanted Kodak to train "the down and out, the man crushed by this evil system, the man emasculated, who can't make it on his own."[8]

Meetings between FIGHT and various representatives of Kodak continued for four months. FIGHT refused to back down on its figure of six hundred and the company refused to bind itself to a specific number because "jobs aren't something you turn out of a machine." Nevertheless, Kodak began to recruit blacks more actively and began to hire larger numbers of unskilled blacks by lowering its employment standards and undertaking a basic education program to equip new employees with educational fundamentals.[9]

On December 1 Kodak's new negotiator, assistant vice president John Mulder, signed an agreement commiting Kodak to hire the six hundred men over a two-year period. The next day Kodak's top management met and issued a statement declaring that Mulder had exceeded his instructions and nullified the agreement.[10] Minister Florence called Kodak "institutionally racist" for going back on its word and warned, "I see troubled times, grave times for the total community because of the dishonesty of Eastman Kodak."[11] FIGHT warned about a "long hot summer" and invited Stokely Carmichael to Rochester, where the militant black leader of SNCC and founder of the "black power" movement promised, "We're going to bring [Kodak] to their knees if it's the last thing we do."[12]

Fearing perhaps that their own creation had gotten away from them, the Council of Churches began preliminary action to set up a new committee to respond to the needs of black citizens. Meetings first expanded from Protestant church members to include other religious groups, then the business community, and finally organizations representing the poor. In April, 1967, these groups came together to form Rochester Jobs, Inc. (RJI).[13] RJI said its purpose was to mobilize "the resources of the Rochester area in order to develop a community-wide program that will make possible the hiring by participating business and industry of the unemployed in the Rochester community and provide motivation, counseling and training that will assist individuals in securing employment and remaining steadily on the job."[14] The twenty-man board of directors had ten representatives from business, commerce, and industry, seven from organizations directly involved with the poor, and three clergymen, one Protestant, one Catholic, and one Jew.[15]

Although RJI declared itself neutral in the FIGHT-Kodak dispute, it proposed a settlement that could give both sides a chance to settle their differences without losing face. RJI recommended that the business community establish centers to train the unemployed to fill the needs of local industry. RJI promised "to employ, educate and train fifteen hundred unemployed and underemployed, with emphasis on the hard core unemployed over the next eighteen months," through the use of quotas for participating firms.[16] Although Kodak had termed FIGHT's demands for hiring a specific number of Negroes "morally, legally and economically wrong,"[17] the company's executives apparently felt that similar quotas established by RJI were proper. Both FIGHT and Kodak agreed to work together under the umbrella of the new organization,[18] and the business community agreed to raise more than three hundred thousand dollars to finance the projected three-to-four-year program.[19]

Under the leadership of executive director Edward S. Croft, RJI members began hiring unemployed and recruiting in inner-city neighborhoods.[20] In the six months from the time it began operation, RJI filled thirty percent of its eighteen-month quota of fifteen hundred jobs.[21] In addition to finding jobs, RJI held an "educational seminar" in which it familiarized eight hundred people, most of them first-line foremen, with "the emotions and attitudes of the hard-core unemployed applicant and his plight to find and retain suitable employment."[22] RJI also helped finance two special programs: Teens on Patrol, a summer-time work program for unemployed minority youth, and Advancement Through Clerical Training, an on-the-job clerical training program run by the Urban League.[23]

Kodak not only supported the work of RJI but acted on its own to find and employ marginal black workers. Minister Florence succinctly summed up Kodak's motivation when he observed, "Kodak started its programs because they were kicked in the face."[24] Once kicked by the forces of the black revolution, Kodak did two things done by virtually every big company which tried to deal with the problem of militant black unrest. First, the company joined with other businessmen in a voluntary equal employment organization, and, second, it altered some of its fundamental approaches to personnel selection. It went from a simple policy of granting equal employment opportunity to one of actively recruiting, training, and hiring the marginal worker.

The civil rights movement created an atmosphere in which businessmen could act without serious fear of adverse public reaction. In fact, businessmen came to fear public disapproval for not having enough black workers rather than for hiring too many. As pressure for more Negro employment increased, the neat balance between the American Creed and the Capitalist Ethic began to deteriorate. No longer was it enough to apply the same criteria to both blacks and whites. Business had to make a positive and successful effort to get Negroes into the firm. The ideal of color blindness was left behind after 1965, as numbers of leading businessmen voluntarily initiated and participated in numerous affirmative-action programs in which they sought out, trained, and placed black workers.

The original impetus for affirmative action had come from the federal government. Under severe pressure in the spring of 1961 to meet the affirmative-action clause demanded by Executive Order 10925 in all federal contracts, the Lockheed Aircraft Corporation initiated a "voluntary" Plan for Progress in which it agreed to seek Negro workers for jobs at all levels and to promote employees without discrimination.[25] Lockheed's affirmative-action plan had little impact on companies without major government contracts until 1963, when Whitney M. Young, Jr., executive director of the National Urban League, called for a domestic Marshall Plan for Negroes. Young specifically denied that his plan was "preferential treatment, indemnification, special consideration, [or] compensatory activity." Young wanted special effort, not special privilege. He called for a "a planned effort to place *qualified* Negroes in all categories of employment at all levels of responsibility. This would mean that employers would consciously seek to hire qualified Negro citizens and would intensify apprenticeship and training programs to prepare new Negro employees and upgrade those already employed."[26] While Young did not ask for preferential treatment on the job, nor did he ask employers to lower their job requirements, he admitted he was requesting preferential hiring by suggesting that companies give "a time preference by actively seeking Negro applicants a week before opening the doors to others."[27]

Young's call for a special effort to hire Negroes was the formal presentation by a recognized national black leader of what civil rights groups had begun to demand through direct action.[28] In a widely discussed article, *Fortune* editor Charles E. Silberman used the Philadelphia boycotts as an example of militant black organizations that were demanding "business firms hire Negroes not because they were qualified but because they are Negroes." When Silberman quoted Young, the essential modifier "qualified" was nowhere to be seen. Silberman commended to his business audience Young's observation that "they must go further than fine impartiality. We must have, in fact, special consideration if we are to compensate for the scars left by three hundred years of deprivation. . . ."[29] By ignoring the term "qualified," Silberman was in effect saying that the employer had a special obligation to absorb the additional cost of employing a substandard worker. In one sense he was returning to the arguments of the pioneering employers of the 1940's who had urged equal employment even at the cost of alienating some employees or customers. But whereas the earlier proponents of Negro employment had demanded equal treatment for blacks and whites, Silberman was asking for "special consideration."

Although the federal government had been demanding that federal contractors actively recruit blacks since 1961, by 1963 the Labor Department had begun to encourage all employers, not only government contractors, to take affirmative action through personnel policy changes. Speaking to the Urban League in 1963, Secretary of Commerce Luther H. Hodges said that any company which wanted to make its equal employment opportunity program "truly effective" had to thoroughly reexamine its personnel policies. Hodges said, "A responsible management official personally commited to the program should supervise a review of seniority lists, recall lists, job descriptions and classifications, prerequisites for hiring, application forms, employment tests, the sources of applicants, and all aspects of employee recruiting."[30]

The Labor Department suggestions that nonfederal contractors consider policies of affirmative action took on new significance in 1964, when the Civil Rights Act established the U.S. Equal Employment Opportunity Commission (EEOC). EEOC had specific legislated power and could thus exert formal pressure for full fair employment on all employers. EEOC chairman, Franklin Delano Roosevelt, Jr., said, "We are asking management for more than fair hiring practices, we are suggesting creative recruitment policies that actually seek out qualified employees among minority groups." Although EEOC's concept of affirmative action still emphasized "qualified" applicants, the commission recommended that affirmative-action programs include: the adoption and communication of a strong fair employment policy to all company personnel; a broadening of recruitment sources to include those specifically designed to reach minority audiences; an active solicitation of minority participation in training programs; an auditing of skills of existing employees and promotion of those meriting it; and participation in community projects.[31] By 1967, state fair employment commissions and big city mayors had also begun to advocate affirmative action programs similar to that of the federal EEOC.[32]

Even in its mildest form, affirmative action required a special effort to recruit qualified blacks. More frequently it also entailed either lowering standards or bringing substandard recruits up to par. In any case, affirmative action required employers to undertake extra expenses in order to employ Negroes. Such costs could not be justified by the Capitalist Ethic, and there is some question as to whether affirmative action did not also violate the canons of the American Creed. It is ironic, but understandable, that no sooner had the business community accepted the American Creed as a guide for employment policy than external forces demanded that business move beyond equal employment into a program of compensatory action.

Until the late sixties, hiring the best man for the job had been a fundamental maxim of the selection and placement procedure. During the forties and fifties, most businesses based their objections to hiring Negroes on the assumption that while blacks might be technically able to perform the job, they had certain social liabilities which made them less than the best qualified candidate. Once pioneer placements had demonstrated that blacks could perform successfully, businessmen usually accepted the American Creed philosophy of impartiality expressed by Ivan Willis, the vice president of industrial relations for International Harvester and one of the early leaders in the field of equal employment. In 1952 Willis told a congressional committee, "We say that our policy is non-discrimination. To us that means not only 'no discrimination against' but also means 'no discrimination for.' We do not refuse to hire a man just because he is a Negro. Neither will we hire him just because he is a Negro."[33] By 1958 virtually all the employers interviewed in a study of Negro employment advocated a situation in which "Negro applicants are considered as a matter of course and Negro employees are given no additional attention or special consideration over other employees. . . ."[34] Thus by the late fifties and early sixties the business community had come to accept the ideal of equal employment. In thought at least, if not always in practice, the equal opportunity imperative of the American Creed had become a reality.

The demands for affirmative action during the mid-sixties presented the business community with a crisis of conscience. For years the business community had gone to great lengths to justify its failure to live up to the American Creed. Having finally accepted the ideal of fair employment, employers were reluctant to abandon so widely held a value for the apparently problack demands of affirmative action. Businessmen frequently voiced their resentment at what they considered governmental or civil rights pressure for "reverse discrimination."[35] Some employers claimed "the forces of free enterprise won't allow these special costs" of preferential treatment,[36] while others refused to engage in any compensatory effort because they "earnestly believed in the principle and practice of equal opportunity."[37]

While one segment of the business community was struggling to defend its so recently acquired principles of equal employment opportunity, a number of particularly progressive employers moved to accept the idea of affirmative action and to justify its supposedly undemocratic implications. In 1964, a vice president of American Airlines approvingly quoted Anatole France's remark, "The law in its majestic equality forbids both the rich and the poor to sleep under bridges," and went on to warn against falling "under the illusion that people are treated equally when no recognition is given to three hundred years of deprivation of opportunity."[38] This statement was remarkable not only for its candid support of compensatory action, but because it came from an airline official. Airlines had been among the most conservative of the service industries in their resistance to employing blacks in jobs in which they would have contact with the public.

The evolution of the racial personnel policies of Pitney-Bowes, manufacturers of postage meters and other office machines, provides an excellent example of the way in which business thought responded to changing public expectations. At any given time in the postwar period the Negro employment policy of Pitney-Bowes was representative of the most progressive thinking in the business community. The management of the company had a long tradition of community involvement, but like so many other firms, it was not until World War II that the company became concerned about discriminatory employment. As a regional director of the War Production Board, Walter H. Wheeler, Jr., Pitney-Bowes' chairman of the board, became acutely aware of the manpower shortage. Wheeler recognized that the black community represented an untapped labor source, and he ordered his personnel men to hire Negroes until blacks represented the same proportion of employees as they did in the company's home city of Stamford, Connecticut.[39] Company success with Negro production workers during the war encouraged the management to begin hiring black secretarial help in the postwar years.[40]

The firm began its Negro employment policy by skimming the cream off the black manpower pool. Although Wheeler expressed an initial desire to see that his company employed a percentage quota of the minority people in the community, a more "realistic" course prevailed during the late forties. Because Pitney-Bowes was a pioneering company in the field of minority employment, it took advantage of its position by selecting the few best qualified Negroes rather than hiring blacks widely. Not only did the early Negro employees have to pass the company's standard battery of preemployment tests, but they also had to have "intelligence, tact and diplomacy of a high degree." It was not enough that the black worker be able to perform his task. The company had to be sure "that each new employee was very well qualified from all standpoints and would create the highest possible impression of the race itself."[41] Once the pioneer placements were completed in the late forties, however, the firm pursued a straight, evenhanded equal employment policy.

Company spokesmen continued to be outspoken advocates of Negro employment through the 1950's,[42] but it was not until the mid-sixties that Pitney-Bowes took the next step forward. Whereas it had previously been color-blind, after an initial period of hiring overqualified blacks, starting in 1964 the firm began to seek out qualifiable Negroes and train them for available jobs. Pitney-Bowes president, John O. Nicklis, explained, "Equal opportunity is a fine principle, but it does not recognize the inability of many Negroes to compete equally, because of past discrimination in employment and education." The firm claimed that it trained blacks only for jobs for which there were no qualified white workers. "As long as we have to train someone, we'll train the Negro," said the director of employee and public relations, James Turrentine. Turrentine even implied that despite company statements, blacks were given actual preference over whites at lower job levels. He denied, however, that Negroes got any special consideration for management positions. "You cannot settle for a manager who is 20% less qualified for a task," Turrentine said, "but below the management level, we believe that we can justify the employment of persons who have a handicap— color—and who lack experience because of that handicap."[43]

Pitney-Bowes attempted to reconcile its hiring program with the traditional concept of fair play by explaining that because no whites were available, no qualified white worker was being cheated out of a job. But even if qualified white workers were available, there were some businessmen who advocated training and employing hard-core unemployed Negroes. Crown Zellerbach's senior vice president James P. Mitchell called upon businessmen to "hire what I would call 'qualifiable' Negroes and train them for jobs."[44] However, hiring "qualifiable" blacks when already qualified whites were available presented the businessman with an awkward problem for ideological justification.

During the forties and fifties employers with a strong personal commitment to solving the problems of Negroes placed their faith in the American Creed. They linked their own religious or ethical values to the American Creed and believed that evenhanded treatment of blacks and whites was the best solution to employment discrimination. It was clear by the late sixties, however, that color blindness had not significantly reduced black underemployment. It could be argued that the success of the American Creed could hardly be evaluated since the business community had accepted it for less than a decade, and then in an essentially token manner. But neither the government nor the black masses were willing to wait, and those employers whose commitment to the needs of the black people was preeminent had to begin to apply the concept of equal opportunity collectively rather than individually. Whereas traditionally concerned employers had applied the American Creed to individuals, by the late sixties they began to speak of equal opportunity for blacks as a group. Because historically whites had discriminated against blacks collectively, this new interpretation of equal opportunity discarded the American Creed and replaced it with an obligation to assist all blacks in achieving a better economic position.

Since there could be no reason in the American Creed for discriminating against the more qualified white, and since such a choice was clearly not in the immediate best economic interests of the firm, explanations for such action were usually based on personal values or long-run benefits. Employers who pointed to the black burden of three hundred years of discrimination to justify hiring blacks were in fact admitting they would shoulder the guilt and pay for the misdeeds of their fathers. On the other hand, businessmen who pointed to the riots were implying that the immediate costs of affirmative action were a form of insurance against the continued costs of social disorder—and that was an explanation which squared with the Capitalist Ethic. When the former president of the National Association of Manufacturers, H. C. McClellan, told the California Governor's Commission on the Los Angeles Riots that he was opposed to lowering the employment standards because "that, in itself, would be discrimination,"[45] he was taking a classical American Creed position. But when he said Negroes "should be given, perhaps, a bit of a priority in Watts because, in that area, unemployment presently is about four times that which prevails throughout the country,"[46] he was alluding to both a special obligation for reducing Negro unemployment and to a desire to prevent future riots.

The management of Owens-Illinois publicly and repeatedly took the final step in the philosophical justification for giving extra help to Negroes. The company's director of personnel, Harold S. Mayfield, told a meeting of insurance executives that while they might not have been able to cross the Delaware with George Washington, climb Mt. Everest, or go to the moon, "you are in the forefront of the fight to settle America's greatest internal problem of the Twentieth Century." Fairness was not enough, said Mayfield. Blacks were not starting off on a par with whites and could not be treated as though they were: "They need an extra boost because they have been injured." Mayfield admitted that he was calling for preferential treatment and for discrimination in reverse. For Mayfield expectations of fairness could be met by not discriminating against whites already employed by the firm. He pointed out that none of the employer's current employees would be hurt by a policy of recruiting and training unqualified Negroes, as long as they were fully trained. Implicit in Mayfield's argument was the understanding that a special training program for blacks might well be unfair to white job seekers, but that cost was necessary to compensate for generations of discrimination.[47]

By the mid-sixties many firms in the North, but not in the South, had developed a series of rather elaborate philosophical justifications for their departure from the narrow path of strict equal employment. Although not all firms that did so were willing to admit it, many companies had begun to give extra help to black applicants as pressure from the federal government and from the black community increased.[48] Most employers, however, were reluctant to go beyond a policy of "equal treatment regardless of race," and southern firms interviewed in a 1966 survey would not even profess simple nondiscrimination. Almost three-quarters of the southern businessmen stated they would "employ only enough Negroes to satisfy the government and the civil rights groups."[49]

Whether an employer was motivated to take affirmative action out of personal conviction or merely wanted to avoid governmental sanctions, he had to come to grips with the implications for personnel policy raised by the demands for affirmative action. The social and legal push for more black employment forced employers to reevaluate three areas of personnel management: recruiting, selection, and training.

Those firms which accepted the idea of affirmative action most commonly practiced it by giving extra attention to recruiting black workers. Until the beginnings of the civil rights revolution few if any firms included black-oriented sources, such as Negro colleges, in their regular recruiting activities. When an occasional employer conducted a special search for black workers in the forties and fifties he usually went to the Negro civil rights and welfare agencies, which, in the words of a personnel specialist of the late 1950's, "were of valuable assistance during the initial stages of Negro employment, for they generally referred the best qualified Negro applicants available."[50]

The legal and social pressure of the civil rights movement caused firms to change their recruiting policies for both high- and low-level jobs. At the upper end, the black colleges were the most obvious sources for black technical and professional workers. Southern black schools suddenly became regular stops in the corporation recruiter's rounds.[51] For lower-level jobs businessmen at first attempted to find black workers through traditional sources. Companies contacted the Negro civil rights and welfare organizations, advertised in the Negro press, and informed public and private employment agencies that the firm wanted black employees.[52] Recruiting through established channels may not have turned up many candidates, but, equally important from a public relations point of view, it created "the impression that the company was sincere in its solicitation of Negro applicants."[53] And, since at least part of the motivation for recruiting black workers was mollifying the black community, the appearance of active recruitment was sometimes as important as the actual rate of employment.

Employers quickly discovered that the traditional methods of recruitment were not producing the desired response from blacks. The problem became increasingly severe through the 1960's as excessive demand shrank the pool of qualified black job-seekers even for entry-level jobs and as the demands for firms to increase their hiring of Negroes grew. As the burden of contractual, legal, and social obligations to employ more blacks mounted, some businesses, particularly large companies with government contracts, discarded even the pretense of complying with the fair employment precept of the American Creed and began to aggressively recruit unemployed blacks.[54] Carl E. Haugen, a senior vice president of the Chase Manhattan Bank, admitted that his firm's recruitment of hard-core unemployed blacks was "a form of 'reverse discrimination'" and called it a "response to the change of emphasis by some civil rights leaders from 'color blindness' to 'color-consciousness.'"[55]

Having failed to attract sufficient numbers of black workers through traditional recruiting methods, businessmen attempted to use government antipoverty programs, job fairs, and company recruiting offices in the ghetto to reach the black community directly.[56] Job fairs, at which businessmen set up exhibits to show the black community the kind of employment available to blacks in their firms, were the least successful attempts of the business community to recruit directly from the black masses. Although the basic idea of bringing together all employers who desired to hire black workers was probably a good one, for the most part businessmen appear to have viewed the job fair as a public relations gimmick rather than as a chance to find new black workers. For example, during the summer of 1964, the Seattle Chamber of Commerce organized a job fair. But it did so only on the demand of CORE, which had been demonstrating in that city for a year. Moreover, Seattle was suffering from a high rate of general unemployment, and for the most part the company booths at the fair were intended more as an expression of concern for the black employment problem than as a commitment to do any on-the-spot hiring.[57] Because most job fairs were one-shot, or, at the most, annual attempts by the business community to show the flag in the ghetto, the publicity frequently overwhelmed the job placement purpose, turning the occasion into more of a carnival than a fair.

Even job fairs which found jobs for people could result in more frustration than satisfaction for the black community. A group of

Houston businessmen who planned a fair to get summer jobs for minority young people in 1967 discovered that two days before the opening they had 312 job openings for an estimated 7,000 young people who would attend the fair. Desperate last-minute pressure by civic and business leaders managed to raise that figure to a thousand—an achievement widely applauded by the press and federal government. But the fact remains that more than 80 percent of those who came to the highly publicized fair went away as unemployed as they had arrived.[58]

A number of job clearinghouses or placement centers supported by voluntary groups were both more permanent than the transitory job fairs and somewhat more successful in finding places for Negro job-seekers.[59] Job placement centers, which employers operated outside of regular private employment agencies or state employment services, existed in numerous cities including Boston, Omaha, St. Paul, Newark, and Columbus.[60] Some of them provided a place where businessmen could find qualified job applicants—in other words doing what the Urban League had been doing for many years. Others concentrated on finding work for the so-called hard-core unemployed, whom the traditional placement services would normally screen out.

Until the riots in the years after 1965, job placement centers usually concentrated on finding and placing qualified blacks. However, the numerous job placement centers which employers created in the wake of the riots sought work for the unskilled hard-core unemployed who were assumed to be the major component among the rioters. Unlike most of the previous recruiting efforts, the employment drives in 1967-68 were geared toward giving the maximum number of jobs to the maximum number of blacks, even if this meant lowering employment standards. The National Alliance of Businessmen (NAB) organized much of the postriot wave of recruiting which sought the hard-core unemployed.[61] The genuine depth of the initial business commitment to hire the hard-core unemployed expressed itself in the willingness of some big corporations to forego the safety of the herd and strike out into the ghettos on their own. Instead of joining collective efforts to find the hard-core unemployed, the companies sent their own recruiters into the inner city or, in some cases, set up employment offices in black neighborhoods.[62] Most major firms, however, were reluctant to recruit the hard-core unemployed. Only twenty-five of four hundred companies contacted by the White House in 1968 agreed to participate in NAB's hard-core recruitment program.[63]

The Ford Motor Company ran the most publicized and probably the most successful of the recruiting programs which aggressively sought out the hard-core unemployed. Chairman of the board Henry Ford II was the head of NAB and a leader in the New Detroit Committee, two business organizations which business leaders had formed in response to the riots of 1967. Declaring that "management should be willing to go directly into the city, to seek out the unemployed, to make sure that hiring standards are not unnecessarily or unrealistically restrictive," Ford directed his company to open inner-city recruiting offices which hired men who met minimum physical standards for employment regardless of police records and other normally disqualifying factors.[64] In one year Ford claimed to have hired five thousand hard-core unemployed.[65]

The extent to which an employer would modify his recruitment policies depended on whether or not he believed affirmative action required him to lower employment standards. Those firms sticking closest to the traditional interpretation of the American Creed took affirmative action by merely seeking blacks without altering their standards. For example, a southern-oriented textile journal advocated recruitment of black workers, but cautioned employers against relaxing standards which "would damage the best interests of both the employer and the minority group." The journal even suggested raising standards in order to select Negroes with potential for advancement.[66] More unorthodox were managers like Alcoa's employment director, R. C. Becker, who recommended against lowering standards but who qualified his position by calling for a review of the standards with a conscious attempt to get away from "middle class bias."[67] Most removed from the American Creed were those special programs designed to get jobs for the so-called hard-core unemployed which asked employers to "waive all normal standards" including high school diplomas, police records, and aptitude tests.[68]

Even employers who agreed that standards should be lowered for black applicants disagreed on the actual method by which they would ease entry for the Negro worker. Employers could reevaluate job requirements to eliminate those not germane to actual job performance. They could lower standards and hire applicants with deficiencies which the worker would remedy in a training program. Or the employer could, and this was never advocated although it was occasionally practiced, lower his employment standards so that blacks who were not up to par with available white workers would be hired and retained.

Traditionally companies had set standards higher for the black applicant than for the white. In the late 1940's, a Negro personnel assistant said, "I am very careful in the selection of our girls. It is generally agreed that the Negro girls working here are of a higher type than the white girls."[69] Superselectivity continued in varying degrees through the mid-1960's.[70] It remained particularly prominent as a feature of pioneer placement, and as long as there were large numbers of firms which had not hired their first black employees, overqualified applicants continued to be in demand.

Demand for higher qualifications for blacks was particularly evident in the South. In 1964 the management of the Atlanta branch of a national mail order house with less than a glowing reputation as an equal opportunity employer had to have its executives pull a number out of a hat to determine who would get the company's first Negro secretary. Even though this was a southern branch of a go-slow firm, all the executives wanted the new black secretary because they knew she would have to be superior to the average white girl.[71] But management's overcautious approach to pioneer placement and extreme, if not discriminatory, care in selecting subsequent Negro employees could not withstand the pressure for increased black employment of the late 1960's. Clearly an employer could not maintain traditional standards and at the same time hire the hard-core unemployed.

The demands for aggressive recruitment had a profound impact on one of the personnel officer's most cherished selection devices, the test. Scientifically rational, and free from the prejudices of personality, equal employment proponents had long advocated objective testing procedures as a way of complying with the American Creed and of eliminating racial discrimination in employment.[72]

The legitimacy of tests as a selection device remained unchallenged until the early 1960's. Even then many, probably most, employers continued to depend on tests to protect themselves from accusations of discrimination. A 1967 survey of seventy-four Los Angeles firms found that 85 percent of them used employment tests, and 78 percent of the using group observed the same cut-off scores for both Negro and white applicants.[73] If the Los Angeles employers counted on the tests to prove their fair employment practice, they were on solid legal ground. During the war and up through the 1950's, government agencies advocated testing as a means of insuring unbiased selection.[74] As late as 1966, the vice chairman of the Equal Employment Opportunity Commission told southern businessmen, "The commission doesn't intend—or want—to lower employment standards. . . . Testing programs which help determine a qualified employee are permissible under the law."[75]

The discriminatory nature of employment testing was not widely recognized until 1964, when an examiner of the Illinois Fair Employment Practices found the Motorola company guilty of an unfair practice for refusing to hire a Negro applicant who had "failed" a short general intelligence test. Late the same year, the examiner ordered Motorola to hire the applicant and to cease using the test. The examiner was partially overruled by the full commission. While the commission did not demand the employment of the complainant or ban the further use of the employment test, it confused the issue by ordering Motorola to pay the complainant a thousand dollars for the expense and embarrassment which the incident had caused him, and it ordered the company to cease unfair practices. A court subsequently threw out the award but sustained the ban on unfair practices. Because of legal technicalities dealing with the way charges were brought against the company, neither the courts nor the commission ruled directly on the propriety of preemployment testing, but they succeeded in opening up a wide-ranging debate that forced employers to question both selection methods and selection criteria.[76]

Because the federal EEOC deferred to state commissions, businessmen had to worry about state FEPC interpretations of employment testing such as that in the Motorola case, but as far as the federal commission was concerned business fears were unfounded. Section 703(h) of the Civil Rights Act of 1964 specifically permitted the use of "any professionally developed ability test provided that such test, its administration or action upon the results is not designed, intended or used to discriminate because of race, color, religion, sex or national origin." As a matter of fact evidence indicates that many firms interpreted this section of the act to mean that valid employment tests could be used as a defense against charges of discrimination and thus began using them for the first time.[77] While the federal commission accepted the concept of testing, it cautioned employers to be sure that their tests did not inadvertently discriminate. In 1966, USEEOC issued a set of guidelines to help management develop acceptable test procedures. The commission suggested six steps, all of which boiled down to insuring that the tests were valid. If a firm could demonstrate that its objectively administered tests differentiated between applicants who would succeed on a given job and those who would fail, it was operating within the law.[78]

Legally, no employer was obligated to give special treatment to Negro test takers; in fact, however, some did. In a number of firms the acceptable passing scores were lowered in order to include larger numbers of blacks in the work force,[79] and in other companies the cut-off point for black applicants was set below that for whites.[80] When the KLH corporation discovered that no one without a high school education could pass the Wonderlic test (a standard, short general intelligence test), the company attempted to validate the test by administering it to some of the firm's best Negro supervisors. When they failed to pass, KLH eliminated the high school education requirement and the use of the test.[81]

Some highly progressive firms like KLH said, "The hell with the Wonderlic,"[82] but by and large employers were reluctant to do away with employment tests that were a "product of at least a half century of exploring and disproving alternative approaches."[83] However, all employers seemed willing to accept, at least in theory, the need for more rigorous attention to the validity of testing. Large numbers of companies began to re-evaluate both their job requirements and their tests.[84] Having determined the actual minimum skill necessary to perform a given task, business began to look for tests which measured only those skills and did "not depend upon the applicants having been born and raised in a particular cultural environment and having been exposed to a specified educational system."[85]

The impact of the civil rights revolution affected each firm's selection procedure differently. Some companies introduced employment testing for the first time, others threw out testing for some jobs, and still others attempted to find out what their tests were testing and whether it was relevant to the job. Although the techniques adopted could be diametrically opposed, the purpose was actually the same: to increase the number of Negro employees until there were "enough," but how many was that?

In the halcyon days before 1960, the equal employment opportunity movement never seriously considered the idea of quotas except as objectionable devices contrary to the spirit of the American Creed used by employers to limit the number of minority workers in their firms. Arguing in favor of FEPC in 1945, Malcolm Ross called the idea that FEPC would require positive quotas "obvious nonsense. The whole idea of quotas indicates discrimination." He continued, "FEPC has repeatedly condemned racial quotas, and insists merely that employers shall hire the best qualified person for a specific job."[86] American Friends Service Committee field workers told employers in 1950 not to pay attention to quotas or percentages but merely to hire and promote the best qualified people.[87] When employers did maintain quotas they used them for the most part as devices to prevent Negroes from becoming overrepresented in any job category, including that of janitor. But while quotas set a maximum number of black employees, they seldom set a minimum and so could only work against black job seekers.[88]

Prior to 1960 quotas were regarded as restrictive devices (although the Urban League occasionally advocated them as a way to insure a minimum number of jobs for blacks) that fair employment forces opposed, not only for practical reasons, but because they believed hiring blacks in proportion to their percentage in the population was "discriminatory, since it is based not on the individual's particular capacities but on his ethnic group identity."[89] But when in the 1960's militant black leaders began advocating benign quotas, it was the businessmen who appealed to the classic fair employment ideal of employing the best man for the job as a reason for not hiring specific numbers of black workers. In its equal employment policy the Babcock and Wilcox Company stated that it would not "foster unsound practices such as: . . . offering of employment opportunities without regard to individual classifications of ability, for the purpose of achieving correlation between the company's employee population and the population of the community on a racial, religious, or other basis."[90]

Section 703(j) of the Civil Rights Act of 1964 clearly stated that the law could not be interpreted to require hiring to correct "an imbalance which may exist with respect to the total number or percentage of persons of any race. . . ." Thus employers were entirely within their legal rights to reject calls for quotas. But reality was more complex than the letter of the law. President Johnson's Secretary of Labor, Willard Wirtz, continually reiterated the government's position that "there will be neither passing nor acceptance of the idea of quotas as far as the administration and government is concerned, and as far as the President's Committee is concerned and as far as Plans for Progress is concerned."[91] But Wirtz's pious adherence to the fair-play ideal of the American Creed did not square with the observations of more impartial students of the black employment scene. In 1965 Ray Marshall said, "Federal agencies sometimes have [implicitly] sanctioned quota systems and have at least left the impression that Government contractors are expected to give preferential treatment to minorities."[92] According to one account, affirmative action as called for by Executive Order 10925 required the employer to have "minority representation . . . [that] is significantly representative of the population ratio of white to minority in the community location of the facility." This proportional representation was to be carried out "in all divisions of the work force" and in the income of minority employees.[93]

In part as a response to the demands of the civil rights groups and of the government, and in part because they wanted some guideline to insure fair employment, firms began to accept the idea of establishing racial quotas. In some cases, the quota was seen as a minimum. For example, two northern companies stated that their Negro employment goals were "to employ at least one Negro sales clerk at all times," and "to hire Negroes in all major job categories."[94] The Bekins Van and Storage Company placed the minimum in strict percentage terms. It told its district managers, "Our goal is a minimum of ten percent this year. Any office with ten or more salaried personnel should have at least one. Operations crews should have a minimum of ten percent."[95] Some of the more outspoken advocates of black employment defended this kind of strict minimum quota system. Although they acknowledged its inherently undemocratic nature, they contended it was the only way of insuring fair employment.[96]

In most instances businessmen rejected strict numbers or percentages, but were willing to accept the idea of a guideline or hiring target. A personnel director whose department split over the question of a numerical target "decided that no specific number should be spelled out—it might be misconstrued as another form of discrimination—but, informally, we are reviewing exactly how many Negroes are in how many jobs, which jobs, and at what pay, and are stressing the necessity for getting closer to racial balance."[97]

The civil rights revolution forced new methods of recruitment and selection on the business community. Where such affirmative action was limited to finding additional qualified black workers, the employer faced no new problem in placing black workers on the job. Where, however, standards were altered or relaxed in order to increase the number of acceptable Negro applicants, companies had to alter their training methods in order to accommodate the new employees.

One of the main thrusts of the new interest in training Negroes was an increased business concern with the quality of vocational education available to blacks. When blacks served only in menial capacities, businessmen paid little attention to Negro schooling,[98] but as circumstances forced them to begin hiring more blacks at higher levels, the business community began to pay increasing attention to the public school system. Inland Steel's vice president William Caples thought that industry's first job was to "convince Negro youth that business is a realizable, satisfying and rewarding career." Once having motivated young blacks, Caples urged that business "take a continuing interest and involve itself in public education, general, technical and vocational at the primary and secondary level."[99]

Businessmen had a long history of involvement with some aspects of public vocational training, particularly through participation in "cooperative education" programs which enabled students to work part-time during school hours in order to give them experience and to demonstrate to them the applicability of academic subjects. Once employers began hiring Negroes into the kind of jobs taught in high school vocational classes, it was logical to extend cooperative education programs to minority students. While the traditional cooperative programs enriched the regular school curriculum of the average student, the new programs directed their attention to the drop-out or potential drop-out. The antidrop-out cooperative programs were not limited to Negro students, but they included large numbers of minorities since minorities constituted a disproportionately large segment of drop-outs.

The nature of the plans varied widely. Some were actually counseling or tutoring programs, not strictly cooperative programs. Rather than giving the students jobs, managerial personnel donated their time as big-brothers who would give advice about vocational, educational, and personal problems. Most plans, however, followed the pattern of Carson Pirie Scott and Company's "Double E" program. Carson's had been one of the first of the major Chicago department stores to hire minority workers, and store president C. Virgil Martin admitted that he was thus able to hire the best black workers available. Carson's created the Double E program to help what Martin called "the 'other' Negroes—those who, because of youth and lack of education and training and cultural deprivation, were hardly equipped to compete for *any* job,"[100] In the name of morality and good business, Martin demanded that businessmen stop "skimming the cream of high school and college graduates . . . allowing the under- privileged and mediocre to find what they can."[101] Carson Pirie Scott be- gan its Double E (Education and Employment) program in August, 1961. With money from the Ford Foundation (for the initial experiment) and with teachers from the Chicago school system, Carson's provided class- room space and jobs for high school drop-outs who wanted another chance.[102]

Businessmen also helped school systems by assisting them in their vocational education programs. Because acting as an adviser required less commitment than participating in a cooperative program, the advisory approach to helping schools was extremely popular among businessmen. In some cases a school and a particular firm had an understanding that the school could call on the company for information about jobs, for speakers, and for career guidance conferences with the students. As early as 1963 General Electric had such an arrangement with Benjamin Franklin High School in Philadelphia.[103] The use of employers as vocational program advisers spread, and after the riots of 1967, a number of firms in Michi- gan "adopted" schools to which they gave time, manpower, and material aid in order to strengthen the schools' programs.[104]

The most widely adopted business-school plans were the vocational guidance programs which industry ran for high school counselors. While such programs existed prior to the establishment of the Plans for Pro- gress,[105] it was not until Plans for Progress introduced its Vocational Guidance Institutes that the idea became widespread. The first institute was held at Wayne State University in Detroit in the summer of 1964. Ac- cording to the official description, the three-week institute for high school guidance counselors was designed to "increase the counselor's knowledge about changing employment conditions and opportunities for Negro and other minority groups." The institute's planners also hoped to set up con- tinuing communication between schools and businesses; to educate the counselors about the "attitudes which disadvantaged youths have toward such matters as employment, education, family life, their place in society, and the world beyond their experience"; and "to provide opportunities for youth by making employers and schools aware of matching potential to job demands."[106]

The wide acceptance of the institutes by counselors, spurred no doubt by the academic credits and stipends which some early participants received, led to a proliferation of institutes during the summers of 1967 and 1968. Both the business participants themselves and outside evaluators agreed that the Vocational Guidance Institutes performed a valuable service. Hugh L. Gordon of Lockheed believed the most important thing businessmen learned from the institutes was "how uninformed are the counselors of these young people as to business opportunities, and how the public school systems in general are so unprepared to provide career counseling to our youth and how much they need the assistance of the business community."[107] Theo Volsky, who evaluated the first institutes, concluded that "no other organized segment of society has the kind of commitment and organizational ability that business has to lend to education in its efforts to prepare youth to enter into society and the job market."[108]

But, just as businessmen had never depended totally on the public schools to train their white workers, they did not limit their educational activity to public education when it came to training black workers. As firms began to desegregate their job classifications, they also stopped discriminating against blacks in company job training programs. In training, as in recruitment and selection, merely granting blacks equal access was not enough. Members of the Plans for Progress were expected to take affirmative action in the area of training primarily by encouraging minority employees to take advantage of company training and apprentice programs.[109]

Special training programs for adult minority workers do not appear to have been at all widespread until after the urban disorders of 1967 and the creation of the National Alliance of Businessmen.[110] Until the riots most companies were preoccupied with taking affirmative action in recruiting. Businessmen were busy finding the qualified black worker or, at most modifying job requirements so that they could hire the black candidates they found. In either case Negroes did not need special training programs. Firms could place the new black employees in the same training programs in which they placed new white employees.

Through the early 1960's special training programs for Negroes were usually *ad hoc* courses designed to bring a particular individual up to par so the company could hire him. Such programs were used only by firms which wanted to increase their black work force but which could not find qualified blacks.[111] But for the most part, unless a company made a practice of hiring large numbers of unskilled Negroes, companies had no special training programs for blacks.

Secretarial training was the one area in which there was a concerted business effort to prepare unqualified blacks for employment. Business suffered from a chronic shortage of secretarial help, and special programs for the training of minority women appeared to be the solution for a number of firms. Some companies, like Aetna Life & Casualty, operated their own courses which taught typing, shorthand, and remedial English.[112] New York University ran a similar course with the support of several large New York City firms. The companies recruited for the training sessions through the Urban League, and in at least one case partial funding came from an outside foundation.[113] Although these courses successfully trained competent secretaries, they also proved to be expensive, and similar programs for other skills did not appear until the riots, government pressure, and government financing of 1967.

The civil rights revolution of the 1960's had a profound impact on management personnel policies in the area of Negro employment. Pressure from the government and from the streets forced business to abandon its recently achieved ideological integrity. For a few years in the late fifties the business community could be true to both the American Creed and the Capitalist Ethic, but an integrated philosophical system was a far cry from an integrated economic system, and employers bent to the demands for increased Negro employment even if it meant renewed ideological inconsistency. Businessmen were most willing to accept affirmative action in the area of recruiting already qualified blacks. They were more reluctant, however, to modify their overall employment standards, to modify their standards for Negroes in particular, or to give time, effort, and money to bring substandard workers up to an employable level. Although the number of blacks employed as a result of the growing acceptance of affirmative action was still not enough to significantly diminish the vast sea of underemployed blacks, the change was, nevertheless, a revolution in management's thinking and even a revolution in management's action when compared to the inactivity of the 1950's.

11

Voluntarism as a Rear-Guard Action

During the early 1950's businessmen in several cities formed voluntary equal employment councils in order to head off state FEPC legislation. Employers reasoned that if they could practice fair employment without legal compulsion the legislators might spare them the burden of an additional regulatory law, while at the same time the business community would be demonstrating its commitment to the American Creed.[1] The voluntarist approach to the Negro employment problem remained popular through the Eisenhower years, although businessmen did not organize and coordinate their individual efforts into councils until the Kennedy administration. Like the voluntary fair employment councils of the 1950's, the voluntary efforts of the 1960's were a response to the threat of legislative sanctions, but unlike the earlier period, the voluntary equal employment activity of the 1960's came after, not before, the enactment of compulsory legislation. In addition, the extra-legal inducement of urban racial violence spurred the formation of voluntary merit employment councils during the mid-sixties.

As Ray Marshall has observed, "There is something about the threat of prosecution that seems to make voluntary programs work much better."[2] The threat of prosecution began in 1961 with President Kennedy's Executive Order 10925, which demanded affirmative action from government contractors, and the threat increased sharply after the passage of the Civil Rights Act of 1964. The number of voluntary programs increased steadily through the 1960's to reach a climax with the establishment of the National Alliance of Businessmen (NAB) in late 1967. NAB, a national voluntary organization of businessmen, was the ultimate voluntary response to the ultimate act of pressure—rioting.

A variety of factors influenced the growth of voluntary fair employment efforts during the Kennedy administration. In addition to the pressure from the government and the civil rights movement, business organizations began to urge employers to help solve the problems be-

181

setting society. The business community acted partly in the spirit of the New Frontier, doing what it could for its country, but also out of the more traditional fear of what its government might do instead. Both the National Association of Manufacturers and the Chamber of Commerce of the United States lent their support to the voluntary equal employment effort. NAM president W. P. Gullander warned that business was "letting government take too big a role in leadership." NAM believed that thirty years of federal action had failed to solve social and employment problems, but "in hundreds of communities throughout America those same 'unsolvable problems' have been effectively and successfully solved by local action groups dealing with problems of local dimensions."[3] In 1964, NAM began to act as a clearinghouse for local voluntary programs that dealt with problems of high school drop-outs, training, and employment. NAM called its program Solutions to Employment Problems (STEP) and published more than seventy studies of successful local voluntary efforts to solve employment problems and distributed hundreds of thousands of copies to interested businessmen.[4]

Although numerous firms responded to the growing demands for more black employment by individually adopting affirmative-action personnel policies, the dominant trend during the 1960's was toward collective action. Rather than merely acting alone, businessmen organized councils through which they could pool their resources (or, at least, behind which they could hide their individual responsibility) to work to improve the economic conditions of blacks. In 1966, the Task Force on Economic Growth and Opportunity of the Chamber of Commerce of the United States issued a report which, among other things, recommended that "local chambers of commerce and individual businessmen should initiate full employment programs tailored to the needs of their communities."[5] The report gave no rationale for this suggestion other than a classical Capitalist Ethic call for an "effective use of all our resources,"[6] but an earlier report by the New York Chamber of Commerce shed additional light on the thinking of organized business groups. The New York report noted that legal redress through FEPC had reached the point of diminishing returns, which explained why black groups were exerting pressure directly on the business community. The report concluded that businessmen could not escape the problem of black employment. But neither should businessmen want to escape because the business community could "best organize and administer job training programs designed to qualify Negroes for better jobs. The business community can set the tone and style of a new acceptance of the Negro on all levels of life."[7]

The composition and activity of voluntary equal employment associations which grew up after 1961 varied widely. Some were composed only of businessmen, and, within this group, some only of federal contractors. Others were more community-oriented and contained representatives from labor and civil rights organizations in addition to employers.

The history of the Milwaukee Voluntary Equal Employment Opportunity Council (MVEEOC) provides an excellent case study of the activity and motivation of local voluntary fair employment groups prior to Plans for Progress becoming a national organization in 1966. "We Milwaukeeans"—an informal group of white businessmen and Negro community leaders formed to facilitate intergroup communications—first discussed the idea of a voluntary council in 1963.[8] Although many of MVEEOC's charter firms were individual members of Plans for Progress and held government contracts, government pressure does not appear to have provided the primary impetus for the council's formation.[9] In both private correspondence and public announcements MVEEOC's founders justified their organization as good for the economy and excellent for continued civic peace. Emphasizing the element of the Capitalist Ethic which stressed long-run rather than immediate benefits, MVEEOC argued that employing blacks would save the urban taxpayer money. "It is a fact," said R. A. Burns, one of MVEEOC's founding fathers, "that a low economic status of seven percent of our population tends to lower the strength of the entire community, reflects a higher than necessary cost for unemployment compensation, welfare costs and social agencies."[10] Burns noted that cities experiencing racial incidents had their "public and industrial images" adversely affected.[11] "In many locations," he continued, "prearranged major industrial installations have been cancelled because the sponsor believed he could not wittingly become part of a community which could not, or would not, take affirmative control of its civil rights responsibilities." Burns congratulated the city for avoiding incidents but warned, "Fires are smoldering."[12]

Although a desire to prevent racial demonstrations apparently motivated some of MVEEOC's founders, the council's official pronouncements never cited black activism as one of the reasons for its existence. Even a comprehensive discussion of business attitudes by a MVEEOC founder, which included virtually every other possible reason for creating a voluntary council from manpower utilization and morality to Plans for Progress and "the world-wide ideological struggle," failed to mention threats or demonstrations or riots.[13] No single event precipitated the formation of MVEEOC in December, 1963, but there can be little doubt that the civil rights movement which had moved north and begun to focus its guns on business was a major contributing factor. Businessmen formed the council in response to a changing national mood. It represented the business sector's participation in the spirit of the New Frontier, a spirit which dictated understanding rather than opposition to the black revolution.

In its first official prospectus MVEEOC listed five objectives: 1) to eliminate employment discrimination, 2) to persuade employers to affirm this purpose and openly support it, 3) to communicate this policy to the Negro community, 4) to encourage Negroes to get education and training in order to qualify for jobs, and 5) to gather statistical data to measure the progress of the first four objectives.[14] By becoming a member of MVEEOC a company agreed to subscribe to the council's objectives and to take several steps toward implementing them. All MVEEOC members were to adopt a formal written policy of nondiscrimination and to "impress upon employment and supervisory personnel the responsibility of insuring compliance. . . ." Members agreed to advertise as "equal opportunity employers" and to use black media and organizations for recruitment of minority personnel. In a final catch-all promise, member firms agreed to "participate in other programs and activities designed to promote minority group knowledge of the Milwaukee business community and employment opportunities—such as plant tours, school career days, school co-op, and summer employment programs.[15] It is clear that MVEEOC knew what attitudes individual members should have, and generally what actions they should take to implement them, but was rather hazy about what its own role as an organization should be.

Two months after its founding, MVEEOC moved to establish its first practical program. It set up a one-day seminar for industrial relations and personnel directors. Assuming that the personnel men might be reluctant to take even the first step toward integrating, the workshop sought to convince them that voluntary equal employment was a good idea. In his introductory remarks Elmer Winter, president of Manpower, Inc., and chairman of the MVEEOC governing board, urged the participants to "put up the 'Welcome' sign" and tell Negro applicants, "We will work with you on upgrading your skills and qualifications so that you may be better prepared to meet the challenges of the future." And Winter reminded the executives that they had an opportunity to say to Congress, "We do not need the sanctions of Federal legislation to force us into fair employment practices. We are prepared to meet our responsibilities fairly and with dignity."[16]

Speaking at the same meeting Peter G. Scotese, a vice president of Federated Department Stores (the Boston Store) and a mainstay of MVEEOC, urged businessmen to support MVEEOC as a way of countering radical black politics. Scotese observed that the "distinctions between 'morals' and 'economics' " were becoming blurred, and that what once had been do-good humanitarianism was now essential for maintenance of the system. Scotese pointed out that "within 10 years the dominant group in most large American cities will be Negro." The one-man one-vote ruling of the Supreme Court meant that "the largest single bloc of votes in the House will be controlled by the Negro voter." Scotese observed that this bloc had been so alienated, so deprived, that "relying on the common ground of mutual interest with mutual goodwill that has tended to unite us in even the most violent political arguments will be risky." Having raised the specter of black consciousness, Scotese went on to explain how it could be destroyed. This "potentially dangerous bloc" had to be prevented from "developing either physically or psychologically." This could be done by the "combination of economic opportunity and physical mobility that broke up the other ethnic blocs which have from time to time exerted a powerful force on America politically." Integration was no longer a humanitarian ideal; it had become an essential act of sociopolitical co-option. With perhaps more prescience than he realized in that year before Watts and "black power," Scotese warned his audience, "In order to have the free enterprise system, opportunities for the Negro citizen must be found, so that this 10% of our population will not oppose the system he cannot participate in."[17]

MVEEOC concentrated much of its early energy on black education problems. Although the council rejected recommendations that it establish scholarships to assist poor minority students, it did develop several other educational programs. Council leaders recognized that city high schools aimed their "career days" at middle-class white students and that these vocational programs had little meaning for black students. An investigating committee recommended that members of the council and the school board meet to plan a wholly new program of career information and motivation as well as to explore all other work-related aspects of academic and vocational education.[18] But before they could plan for activities for the school year of 1965, a number of MVEEOC members felt that the council should face the challenge of unemployment for ghetto youth during the summer of 1964. Winter suggested that council members offer jobs that would give black students an opportunity to experience meaningful, interesting work.[19] The advisory committee sent letters to all MVEEOC members requesting summer positions for disadvantaged students. This was the first real test of member commitment. The committee asked council members to voluntarily participate in a program that would serve the dual purpose of giving students jobs and an insight into the business world and of showing the Milwaukee community that the business sector was willing to help the problems of the black unemployed. Of the more than one hundred members of MVEEOC only ten companies offered any jobs. In all, companies offered fewer than one hundred jobs, more than half of which were in the telephone company. Given the unwillingness of MVEEOC members to participate in the council's job program, it is not surprising that when the publisher of the *Milwaukee Journal* began a general campaign to find summer work for Milwaukee youth, the advisory committee refused to support the drive because it did not "fall within the scope of the activities of the MVEEOC since it is not directed at the problem of racial discrimination in employment."[20]

Unable to get any support from the council advisory committee for a summer employment program, Elmer Winter launched his own venture. Winter's company, Manpower, Inc., created and sponsored Youthpower, Inc. to find jobs for black young people. Volunteers staffed the Youthpower offices, which successfully served as special employment centers for students seeking summer work. Manpower, Inc., offices in many other cities copied the Milwaukee Youthpower idea, frequently with the support and cosponsorship of other organizations.[21]

Aside from two seminars (a second seminar was held on May 9, 1964) and an active speakers bureau, MVEEOC entered its first summer, and seventh month, with very little to show beyond its press clippings.[22] By generating wide publicity and expectations, and at the same time doing nothing concrete, MVEEOC was setting itself up for a nasty fall. Without programs in the community which blacks could see and appreciate, MVEEOC was taking on the appearance of a publicity stunt. As one MVEEOC leader noted, "The council has received much favorable publicity for its activities, and this in itself has stimulated many questions as to the impact on minority employment. Ultimately we will have to measure our performance or lose our effectiveness in the Negro community."[23]

The original charter called for gathering information to measure effective progress, but the advisory council had been reluctant to ask its members for a minority head count. Their reluctance was based upon the fear that member companies would refuse to cooperate, first because divulging such information would be in violation of company sovereignty and second because if such information fell into their hands, civil rights groups might use it against the individual firm. The advisory committee devised a plan that avoided these pitfalls by having members report statistics to an independent auditor who released only cumulative figures. The survey was supposed to demonstrate progress in black hiring, and "for companies plagued by demands for employment information from militant civil rights groups, participation in this program will offer an additional reason to not comply."[24] Despite advisory committee support and guaranteed anonymity, the membership responded very slowly to the request for information. Only ten of the more than one hundred members reported figures for 1964.[25] The refusal of council members to cooperate voluntarily with the advisory committee prevented the council from gathering the statistics it would need when the organization was attacked as ineffectual.

Although in March, 1964, the advisory committee had stated, "[Education] should not be a significant function of this committee,"[26] within a year MVEEOC expanded its educational activity well beyond the original intentions of its founders. Beginning in the summer of 1964, council members cooperated with the Milwaukee public schools in a work-study program which gave sixty students on-the-job experience during school time.[27] In early 1965, the heads of MVEEOC's advisory sub-committee met with principals and guidance counselors to determine how the business community could participate in career guidance.[28] The council and the school board established a "buddy" system between executives and vocational counselors at inner-core schools. Each executive "agreed to work with the counselors at two schools on a regular and continuing basis for the purpose of assisting counselors in doing a more realistic and effective job and to be available to these individuals when they wish to discuss their plans, problems and programs with the industry representative."[29]

MVEEOC found the buddy system of counselor advising so successful that when Plans for Progress approached Milwaukee Plans for Progress members to set up vocational guidance institutes, the advisory committee turned down the idea as unnecessary. Of course, the fact that Plans for Progress seminars would have cost members five hundred to a thousand dollars each and the buddy system cost practically nothing might have had something to do with the decision, but monetary considerations aside, the council believed it was getting an equal product for a lower price.[30]

Besides the two personnel seminars and the school counselor program, MVEEOC was the sponsor of only one other project, the "man-marketing clinic." The genesis of the clinics is unclear, particularly in light of the insistence of many council founders that training was not properly within the council's purview. The idea probably came originally from the "man-marketing clinics" that had been held in New York City since 1933 to assist unemployed executives find new jobs,[31] but why MVEEOC tried to use a management device for blue-collar workers remains a mystery. The clinics did not train an individual in a new skill, but taught him how best to utilize the skills he had—how to market himself. Volunteer instructors from fifteen member companies conducted the council clinics. Both MVEEOC and the instructors considered the clinics a success, and they were continued through 1966 as the "How to Get a Job Program."[32] However, there was never any objective measurement of the usefulness of the sessions.[33]

During 1965, MVEEOC moved the clinics into the core-area schools. Having already established close contact with the school counselors, participating companies were able to integrate the How to Get a Job Program and the counselor-adviser program into a total approach to vocational information and motivation. Like the original clinics, the school How to Get a Job Program contained two sessions. The first meeting consisted of an assembly presentation during which businessmen gave the students tips on how to dress and act during an employment interview. The second part of the program took place in the classroom, where the businessmen distributed sample applications, explained how to use the classified ads, and answered any questions the students had.[34] Originated in five core-area schools, the program proved so popular with school administrators that in the spring of 1966 MVEEOC expanded it to twelve other schools, including a number of predominantly white schools.[35] While the council basked in the glory of such an obviously successful program, none of its members mentioned that holding such programs in white schools certainly exceeded the original purposes of the council.

MVEEOC's glory was not merely local. The Wisconsin Industrial Commission lauded "this educative, information, direct action program. . . ." A federal commissioner from the United States Equal Employment Opportunity Council reported MVEEOC was doing "the outstanding job in the country." The plan received national press coverage, and Winter presented the Milwaukee program to six hundred members of the Plans for Progress. Although he obviously realized its shortcomings, Elmer Winter was not reticent about describing the program and its accomplishments. He traveled to Washington several times to collect official accolades and to explain the council's program to businessmen from across the nation.[36] Toward the end of 1965, Winter apparently began to have second thoughts about the extensive publicity. At a meeting of the advisory committee he "reported the MVEEOC is receiving nationwide recognition, perhaps to a greater extent than deserved." But his doubts were not strong enough to prevent his continued proselytizing.[37]

There were signs that the black community was getting fed up with what appeared to be MVEEOC's meaningless and self-serving projects. Privately, Negro leaders told the advisory committee that MVEEOC responded only when the government brought pressure, and that blacks were tired of programs like the man-marketing clinic which were all talk. Such projects did not provide jobs and they did not bring money into empty pockets.[38] Finally on January 15, 1966, Negro resentment broke into the open. The *Milwaukee Star,* a black newspaper, printed an article by Walter Jones which observed that the emperor's clothes were not nearly as resplendent as the reports out of Washington would lead one to believe. The paper noted that all the pledges and clinics and educational programs were so much "ballyhoo" without producing jobs. Jones accused MVEEOC employers of continuing to discriminate against blacks by saying that they were not qualified for the available jobs. The paper pointed out that the job openings advertised in its pages were for technicians, keypunch operators, auditors, programmers, statisticians, etc., jobs for which most blacks had no training. Jones demanded that council members move beyond simple equal opportunity and begin to practice affirmative action. "The real solution," said Jones, "is to seek out the unemployed and the unemployable Negro and to teach him a skill." The paper then called for programs of vocational training, remedial education, job counseling, realistic employment standards, and more entrance jobs.[39]

Much to the council's discomfort, the state Industrial Commission, which had previously praised MVEEOC, decided that maybe the council was not so great after all. Joseph C. Fagan, chairman of the state commission, accused some members of the council of hiding behind the announced policy of the organization. As a result of a survey of minority employment conducted by the Industrial Commission, Fagan concluded that some council members "have been sitting on their haunches . . . because they joined they feel they don't have any more duties or obligations."[40]

MVEEOC responded to these attacks with less than total candor. The chairman of the advisory committee called the Industrial Commission report inaccurate and inconclusive and refused to comment further on the charges.[41] Internal reaction, however, was both more forceful and more honest. The chairman reported to Winter that while there were statistical problems with the commission's report, "unless some startling corrections occur we definitely will not look very good as an organization." He concluded that MVEEOC was on a "hot spot which requires some prompt and effective concrete action on our part."[42] The chairman noted that the Wisconsin State Employment Service and the Urban League had over a thousand names of unemployed men in their files, most of whom could not qualify for existing openings. He suggested a crash employment program, with all members of MVEEOC pledging to hire at least one unqualified man for on-the-job training. Employers would hire blacks on the spot at an inner-core location. The chairman believed that he could obtain "a substantial number of commitments from employers," and the resulting employment would redeem MVEEOC's tarnished reputation.[43]

At the same time Milwaukee CORE charged the council with hypocrisy for running a How to Get a Job Program and then having no jobs to get. CORE called MVEEOC's approach ten years too late and said it was time for the business council "to put up or shut up." Disturbed by these attacks, Winter wrote a circular letter strongly urging member companies to examine their personnel practices to insure that they fairly recruited, hired, and promoted minority workers. However, lest they feel too guilty about their role in the employment problem, Winter assured the executives that he had talked "to many Milwaukee Negroes who tell me to disregard the complaints of the few." Thus, Winter implied, by *not* ignoring the complaints of the "few" the businessmen could once more demonstrate their progressive and humanitarian concern.[44]

The adverse publicity the council suffered as a result of the *Star* article did not produce any significant changes in council activity. Rather it forced council members to recognize that MVEEOC was not the final answer to racial employment problems in Milwaukee. The black community was dissatisfied, and if MVEEOC could not be the great black hope, it could not be the great white hope either. But rather than spurring increased activity, the criticism merely generated a brief surge of good intentions which died in the planning stages.

During the summer of 1966, Plans for Progress companies throughout the country began to join local employers' councils designed to coordinate the activities of member concerns. The employers' councils also planned to participate in community programs of training, motivation, and placement. In other words, national Plans for Progress councils said they would embark on the trail MVEEOC had blazed, but MVEEOC was at the point of admitting that it had lost its way in the woods.

MVEEOC modified its purely voluntary nature somewhat when members hired a permanent staff in the spring of 1967—about the same time that Father James Groppi and the NAACP Youth Council were beginning to stir things up in Milwaukee with their demonstrations. When Milwaukee civic leaders became aware of widespread unrest during the early part of the summer, they initiated a program to employ inner-city youth for the month of August. While in 1965, MVEEOC had refused to cooperate with a general drive for summer jobs and had responded weakly to a spring 1967 drive for employment of inner-core youth, now under the pressure of daily marches, the members of MVEEOC not only came up with as many jobs in July as they had during the earlier drive (which took place during the period of regular summer hiring), but companies which no longer had openings donated almost seven thousand dollars to pay the wages of youths to work for the city.[45]

By the end of 1967 MVEEOC had settled down into a fairly unobtrusive position. Although it continued to participate in various programs initiated by CORE, the Board of Education, and the Milwaukee Chamber of Commerce, the pioneering spirit which had permeated MVEEOC in its early days could not be revived even by Milwaukee's first riot. The proliferation of problems simply overwhelmed this precursor of voluntary collective business action, and the growth of similar councils throughout the nation stole MVEEOC's thunder.

Two other business councils, the Business and Industrial Coordinating Committee of Newark, New Jersey, and the Association of Huntsville Area Companies of Huntsville, Alabama, began in almost the same month as MVEEOC and demonstrate the diverse nature of voluntary business organizations, both geographically and in terms of their structures and programs. During the summer of 1963, civil rights groups in Newark picketed the building site of the city's new $5,000,000 Barringer High School. The complaints about discrimination at the high school sparked general dissatisfaction, and the civil rights groups began to discuss picketing downtown department stores—which were not directly related in any way to the construction project. The senior vice president of Bamberger's, one of the department stores, recalled that "while there had been no violence up to this point, there was a belief that the Negro community could erupt at any time." He was afraid that a failure to "proceed along the road of an open door policy of hiring nonwhites . . . would probably bring economic and social chaos to the city."[46]

Led by the department stores, the business community of Newark formed the Business and Industrial Coordinating Committee (BICC) in the fall of 1963. Membership was open to civil rights groups, government agencies, private welfare agencies, and labor unions as well as to businesses. Perhaps because they previously had been so out of touch with the problems of the black community, the businessmen seemed most impressed by the communications aspect of the new organization. The first objective of BICC was "to take positive action in a forum where open communications will be available at all times between business, industry, labor and civil rights organizations to openly discuss problems of mutual interest."[47] In a more immediately practical vein BICC also pledged to train, place, and promote unemployed and underemployed Negroes and Puerto Ricans.[48]

Member firms began to list job openings with the Urban League and actively recruit minority applicants.[49] BICC placed approximately five thousand applicants in full-time jobs during its first four years.[50] However, four thousand of these applicants received their jobs during the first year.[51] The radical drop-off in the placement rate may have resulted from either a declining interest in the program[52] or from a quick drying up of the underutilized skilled manpower pool. Prior to the BICC drive underutilization of black skills may very well have been widespread.

Western Electric, for example, reported that it found "Negroes with college degrees were working at menial jobs; many others were under-employed and over-qualified for the jobs they held" in its Newark operation.[53]

During its first year, BICC members adhered to a strict Capitalist Ethic interpretation of the American Creed and turned away applicants who failed "to meet specific job requirements because of educational deficiencies, environmental background gaps, inadequacies in vocational training and possible discrimination."[54] Subsequently, BICC took a more affirmative-action approach and launched projects to get members to reevaluate their testing procedures and job requirements and sponsored a number of crash courses to help marginal workers bring their skills up to an employable level. Industry financed thirteen training courses and BICC cooperated with federal agencies to finance other programs to train minority workers.[55]

Late in 1966, one of BICC's founders, Charles Garrison, attributed the falling off of Negro attendance at BICC's monthly meetings partly to the improved job situation for blacks. "With more and more Negroes finding full time employment," said Garrison, "their concern and free time for civil rights activity is lessening."[56] But all the BICC's programs were a pathetically small gesture when contrasted to the widespread unemployment and other kinds of economic, social, and political exploitation suffered by Newark's black community. In the summer of 1967, the "economic and social chaos" that the founders of BICC were trying to head off erupted in Newark. Fear of riots and the threat of picketing had been enough to get the business community moving, but a job placement rate of fewer than a thousand people a year in a city with more than two hundred thousand black people could not stem the angry tide.

Voluntary groups in Rochester, Milwaukee, and Newark all grew up independently of the forces of the federal government. They were responses to direct or indirect pressures from the civil rights movement. Their purposes and programs, while uninspired, were local in origin and designed to meet what the business community in each city saw as its unique problems. During the fall of 1963, at the same time that the Milwaukee Voluntary Equal Employment Opportunity Council and Newark's Business and Industry Coordinating Committee were emerging, the business community in Huntsville, Alabama, created a third association which was to have the widest impact on the national scene.

Sixteen federal contractors formed the Association of Huntsville Area Contractors (AHAC—the final word was later changed to "companies") in the Alabama missile town which had grown from thirty thousand to one hundred and fifty thousand population in fewer than twenty years. Firms such as Chrysler, IBM, Lockheed, General Dynamics, Douglas, Boeing, Sperry Rand, and Xerox joined together to bring pressure on the community to improve the environment so that they in turn could benefit from larger numbers of qualified black workers. All of the companies held government contracts, were members of Plans for Progress, and claimed they did not discriminate against Negroes. However, they were located in the heart of the Deep South and they were under federal pressure to show an increase in minority employment. Qualified Negroes from the other parts of the country were less than enthusiastic about moving to Alabama, and local facilities had not been geared toward producing highly trained black workers.[57]

AHAC referred to itself as a "community resources development association" and in this respect departed somewhat from the standard business council concerned solely with Negro employment. Most of AHAC's efforts were directed at various training and educational programs which would directly contribute to the alleviation of the manpower shortage, although the association also became involved in improving Negro housing, in working to end discrimination and segregation in public facilities, and in improving social welfare. AHAC itself actually ran very few programs. It called itself a "catalyst for community action for the disadvantaged" and either relied on existing local agencies, private and governmental, or, if such agencies did not exist, tried to see to it that the community created them.[58] Since AHAC sought to be a coordinator and initiator rather than implementer, it is difficult to judge the association's effect. AHAC appears to have spent most of its time "cooperating with" or "assisting" local, state, and federal programs to improve education, housing, and employment for blacks.[59] However, given the importance of AHAC's members to the Huntsville area, it seems safe to assume that their expressed interest in a particular program was of considerable help to its eventual success.

More so than most employer groups, AHAC had objectives directed at the basic needs of the community. In no uncertain or equivocating terms, it proposed to act for the "relief of the poor, the distressed and the underprivileged; to improve the housing and standard of living of disadvantaged groups; to lessen neighborhood tensions, to eliminate prejudice and discrimination; to promote the availability of public and community facilities for disadvantaged groups; and [to advance] education, job training and apprenticeship programs for disadvantaged groups."[60]

The federal contractors in Huntsville formed their first Plans for Progress community council in 1963, during the period when the civil rights movement was beginning to turn its attention to the problem of employment discrimination against blacks, but the idea did not spread to other cities until 1966, when the national Plans for Progress Advisory Council began encouraging the formation of community "merit employment councils." The national Plans for Progress Advisory Council assumed that the nature of local unemployment differed widely from area to area, and that local, rather than national, direction would be most effective in coping with the problems of unemployment among minorities. In 1966, there were seventeen local councils affiliated with Plans for Progress; by early 1968 this number had grown to more than eighty.[61] Although Plans for Progress advocated local councils as a way of introducing a flexible response to unique local employment problems, in fact most of the councils appear to have been little more than paper organizations created along lines laid out by the national Plans for Progress.

As the first local council composed of Plans for Progress companies, newly formed Plans for Progress groups frequently looked to AHAC for guidance in establishing structure and programs, and AHAC was more than pleased to assist. As a result of its paramount position AHAC's philosophy dominated numerous local councils, many of which adopted whole-cloth a "Suggested Constitution and Bylaws" that the Huntsville association published. As the local council's first objective the "suggested constitution" called for an "organized, orderly and reasoned approach" to "achieve a community climate necessary for growth and development," which would be headed by business leaders who were "uniquely equipped to assist citizens in a community in an enlightened approach to community progress." Having tied fair employment to economic development and to the aggrandizement of business leadership, the suggested constitution went on to explain what the council would do to achieve these worthy ends. It would support training and recruiting of "bypassed disadvantaged" people on the nondiscriminatory basis of "individual qualifications and merit." Not only would the council work with community groups but it would also communicate to the community the "willingness and sincerity" of the businessmen to live up to the objectives of the council.[62]

Most Plans for Progress councils elected not to adopt AHAC's suggested rationale, although they did accept its five basic objectives. It would seem that after 1966, outside of the Deep South, the ideal of economic equality for Negroes was widely enough accepted not to require an apologia. The basic objectives of the standard voluntary council were to:[63]

1. Make certain that there is no employment discrimination in the community on account of race, color, religion, or national origin.

2. Persuade all area employers to affirm this purpose and to openly support the principle and practice of nondiscriminatory hiring, promotion,

training, and compensation of employees on the basis of individual qualification and merit.

3. Convincingly communicate to the Negro community and other
minority groups the willingness of employers to hire qualified Negro and
other minority group applicants and the availability of jobs, and thus
establish a community knowledge that attaining of essential qualifications
leads directly to equal employment opportunity.

4. Directly encourage Negroes and members of other minority groups
to obtain necessary education and training to qualify for existing and
future jobs and to aspire to upgraded employment status.

5. Establish a systematic method of assembling and disseminating
data and information among area employers relating to minority group
employment and progress made in achieving plan objectives. Encourage
individual employees to evaluate, on a continuing basis, the level of minority group employment within their own firms in order to ascertain whether
the aims of the plan are being met.

The failure of most merit employment councils to develop either
original rationales or original programs was symptomatic of both the basic
lack of commitment on the part of most employers and of the powerful
influence of the "fad" mentality which gripped the business community
searching for an answer to the racial upheaval of the late 1960's. One
observer noted that community programs were more likely to succeed
than individual plans because "employers feel freer to take affirmative
action when they are part of a concerted movement. No employer feels he
is taking an individual risk."[64] Businessmen believed that merit employment councils impressed the minority community and involved no individual risk, which is another way to say they involved no individual
responsibility.

The mushroom growth of merit employment councils attested to the
business community's sensitivity to the demands of society. The black
community, the white community (the press), and the government all
expected businessmen to demonstrate their commitment to the problem
of urban black unemployment. Membership in merit employment councils
admirably served that purpose. The lack of meaningful activity on the
part of most firms and councils indicated the shallowness of the business
commitment and the hope that the councils could talk the problem away.
Reluctance to accept individual responsibility for solving black employment problems could on occasion take extreme forms. In 1965, Cincinnati
businessmen along with representatives of local civil rights groups formed
a Committee of 28. Its members included the heads of the city's most
important businesses. No one could accuse the Cincinnati business community of producing publicity instead of jobs, for the Committee of 28

created neither. It met in secret for two and a half years without doing anything. When black leaders asked for jobs and training programs for the unemployed, a committee member responded in pure Capitalist Ethic terms by saying, "Business is not going to create temporary jobs for those who are unqualified, and business is not going to lower its standards; if anyone does that it will have to be government on a WPA basis."[65] According to another businessman the purpose of the committee was not to take action, "but to change attitudes"—of the Negroes.[66]

The Chicago Association of Commerce and Industry ran a merit employment program which went a step beyond the Cincinnati approach. Like Cincinnati the Chicago group did not attempt to do anything, but unlike the Committee of 28, the Chicago Merit Employment Committee prided itself on its efforts. In 1964 the Chicago Association of Commerce and Industry's Committee on Full Employment was in charge of the association's equal employment activity. The Committee on Full Employment published a "Merit Employment Manual" and conducted a voluntary survey of its members to ascertain the state of black employment in Chicago.[67] The survey disclosed that "as a laggard in providing job opportunities for the Negro" the nation's Second City was second to none.[68]

To meet the challenge of Negro underemployment the association formed the Chicago Merit Employment Committee (CMEC) in June, 1965. CMEC took over the task of equal employment action from the Committee on Full Employment. CMEC met the challenge of black underemployment squarely by denying that it existed. CMEC claimed, "Most businessmen are convinced that merit employment is good business—and are practicing it." Having thus disposed of the major obstacle to full fair employment the committee defined its job as having "to communicate this knowledge to minority groups to motivate them to prepare themselves."[69] Perceiving its job as propaganda production, CMEC bent its efforts to telling the black community—through newspaper features, radio spots, a school Youth Motivation Program, and lectures to black service organizations—about the success of Negroes employed by CMEC members. The depth of business commitment to the program was best summed up in CMEC's own words, "There are no required dues or other costs for Merit Committee members. Nor is any personal or company involvement in Committee activities required."[70]

John D. deButts, chairman of CMEC and president of Illinois Bell Telephone Co., explained that while CMEC members did not have to do anything, membership had some definite advantages. Members signed a Statement of Merit Employment which deButts said was "considered a sign of good faith by minority group leaders. Government agencies too have taken the position that if an employer is *on record* for equal opportunity employment, they will assume that he *is* as he represents himself to be."[71]

The Chicago Association of Commerce and Industry believed that its Merit Employment Committee "made gigantic strides in meeting the needs of the unemployed and the under-employed among the city's minority groups." It received awards from the Chicago Commission on Human Relations, Plans for Progress, and the Federal Equal Employment Opportunities Commission, which "cited the Committee's work as the outstanding local voluntary program in the nation."[72] That CMEC should receive these accolades was indicative of the uninspired nature of the programs sponsored by most other local voluntary merit employment councils.

Just as most local councils accepted a standard set of objectives, they also stuck pretty closely to the prepackaged, low-risk, easy-to-present programs, most of which came from national Plans for Progress advisory committee. The key words in most councils' statements of objectives were "persuade," "communicate," and "encourage." In other words, Plans for Progress councils were talkers rather than doers. Responsibility for specific action rested with the individual company, while the council usually limited its activities to seminars, conferences, institutes, and motivation programs, all of which may have proved valuable in educating both management and minority youth but did not directly provide employment for anyone. In the following summary of the different kinds of programs Plans for Progress councils sponsored in 1968, only 2, 3, 11, and 18 placed blacks in jobs, and the vast majority of councils concentrated their efforts on the other fifteen kinds of programs.[73]

1. Vocational Guidance Institutes—instruction of high school guidance counselors in the needs of business.

2. Work-study and co-op programs for high school students in which they worked part-time and went to school part-time.

3. Job fairs—mostly for graduating seniors.

4. Liaison with high school teachers to let them know what industry expected from students.

5. Coordination of minority employment programs in the community.

6. Speakers' bureaus.

7. Career days to introduce high school students to the kinds of work available in industry.

8. Youth motivation programs—including speakers, panels, skits, and instruction in how to apply for and keep a job.

9. Scholarships for minority students going on to college or advanced vocational training.

10. Publicizing available training opportunities conducted by both private and public agencies.

11. Jobs Now program—a placement program for the hard-core unemployed originated by the National Alliance of Businessmen.

12. Local research on community problems.

13. Sponsoring local chapters of the Opportunities Industrialization Center, the vocational training program started in Philadelphia by the Rev. Leon Sullivan.

14. Developing a roster of organizations which offer services to minorities.

15. Preschool kindergarten programs (run with Ford Foundation funds) to allow black women to work.

16. Open forums to allow minority groups to present grievances to the government and the business community.

17. Veterans' transition program.

18. Placement of graduates from local training programs.

19. Adopting schools with disadvantaged students.

The Greater Cleveland Plans for Progress Council was fairly typical of Plans for Progress councils in its emphasis on propaganda rather than on job placement.[74] Formed in September, 1965, the Cleveland council pioneered in a student motivation program in which black employees of council member firms spoke to assemblies in city high schools. These talks tied in with a national Plans for Progress advertising campaign based on the theme, "Things are changing." The speakers explained their jobs and encouraged students to stay in school so that they too could succeed. In addition the Cleveland council supplied speakers to individual classes, civic groups, churches, and other organizations which asked for them.

With similar emphasis on talk rather than action, the Cleveland council held a "manpower development seminar" to "inform employers of the various federally assisted educational and training programs to help disadvantaged persons to prepare for jobs." And, like many other councils, the Cleveland group sponsored vocational guidance institutes to inform high school teachers and counselors about the availability and nature of jobs open to black students. It was only after the Hough riot of 1966 that the council directly participated in a program to find jobs for blacks. It sponsored an emergency job hiring center in the riot area. Thirty-one companies interviewed applicants for jobs in this one-shot response to the trouble.[75]

There were, of course, scores of councils, and in specific cases some of them, especially non-Plans for Progress councils, deviated from the general pattern of talk rather than job placement. Indianapolis, for example, had a unique program in which businessmen not only found jobs for the unemployed but went door to door looking for them. The Indianapolis business community also provided individual counselors for new black employees for several months to help work out personal and job-related problems which might otherwise have led to a high job turnover among program participants.[76] The Businessmen's Interracial Committee on Community Affairs in Cleveland also went beyond the ordinary. It procured special federal and private foundation grants to prepare and place the hard-core unemployed, worked closely with the local school system on a number of problems, and became involved in the area of minority housing.[77]

Although the Plans for Progress councils all declared that the elimination of discrimination in hiring was one of their major objectives, very few of them actually became directly involved in recruiting or placing black workers. Employment is a highly individual process, and the voluntary nature of the merit employment councils meant that they were not in a position to dictate employment policy to member firms. Those councils which were created in response to a riot in the local community were usually much more sensitive to employment problems than were those which merely jumped on the Plans for Progress bandwagon. Black activism played a major role in persuading merit employment councils in Rochester and Newark to begin to find jobs for blacks. Black pressure also played a significant role in getting jobs, rather than propaganda, from the councils in Cleveland and Miami, and the "threat of a flare-up over a police incident" in Buffalo, New York, in 1966 transformed that city's Job Opportunities Council from a do-nothing group into a catalyst and coordinator of federally financed training projects for a thousand jobs offered by Buffalo firms.[78] Similarly in Los Angeles before 1965 a number of businessmen had been discussing the value of coordinating efforts for fair employment, but it took the Watts riot of August, 1965, to transform a number of loosely organized groups into a single Los Angeles Management Council for Merit Employment, Training and Research.[79] Originally the Plans for Progress section of the council had run a standard educational rather than action program.[80] But after the riot, under the leadership of H. C. McClellan LAMEC placed unusual emphasis on the employment and job-training aspects of the program and, according to one report, placed almost five thousand blacks on jobs in the six months following the Watts riot.[81]

Having died out after an initial attempt to stop state FEPC legislation in the 1950's, voluntary employment councils reemerged in the 1960's in response to the pressures of the civil rights movement, government contract requirements for affirmative action, and the Civil Rights Act of 1964. With only a few exceptions, however, the councils were mainly propaganda agencies which allowed members to avoid individual responsibility by hiding in the collective security of the community council. Whereas the voluntary councils of the 1950's had attempted to blunt the impact of the fair employment movement by seeking to prevent FEPC legislation, the voluntary business efforts of the 1960's sought to blunt the impact of the FEPC legislation once it had passed and to cool the anger of the black community once it had been aroused.

12

Voluntarism: Centralization and Doubt

The changing attitudes, policies, and actions of the business community during the 1960's produced a proliferation of voluntary plans and associations designed to assist businessmen in coping with growing demands of the government and the civil rights organizations. As one voluntary employers' organization observed in its "General Statement," "Management, as well as the entire country, has been made more aware of the problem by government decree and by concerted action from those victims of the problem."[1] The heavy hand of federal coercion was behind practically every step the business community took to improve employment opportunities for blacks. The federal government forced Lockheed to develop the first Plan for Progress in 1961, which set the pattern for company affirmative-action personnel policy for a decade. The federal government encouraged its other contractors to draft their own Plans for Progress and then suggested that Plans for Progress firms combine locally into Plans for Progress councils. Finally, the federal government created the National Alliance of Businessmen to coordinate business urban reform activity after the riots of 1967. A nationwide voluntary organization of socially concerned businessmen, NAB was the culmination of organized business response to the needs of black workers.

Since businessmen created almost all of the voluntary associations of the 1960's in order to facilitate compliance with the demands of the government, there is a sadly comic aspect to that small school of businessmen who insisted on maintaining the fiction that voluntarism was good because it was a way to preclude government interference in business affairs. It might have made some sense for Sara Southall to warn in 1950, "If organized business is unwilling to provide economic opportunity for qualified individuals, it cannot expect freedom from government interference."[2] But Executive Order 10925 in 1961 and the Civil Rights Act of 1964 should have put an end to exaggerated warnings

201

about the threats of government interference and the saving grace of voluntary business action. Employers continued to praise voluntarism as an alternative to government control, however, because voluntarism provided a valuable theoretical vehicle with which businessmen could justify their participation in such dubiously "voluntary" programs as the Plans for Progress, the Plans for Progress councils, and NAB. Thus, even after the passage of the Civil Rights Act, G. A. McLellan, administrative director of the Advisory Council of Plans for Progress, could say, "There is the feeling that solutions can be found better by private enterprise than by government."[3]

Plans for Progress (PFP) was the program behind all the publicity, and some of the progress, in equal employment prior to the Civil Rights Act of 1964. PFP saved a billion dollar contract for the Lockheed corporation and became the prototype of voluntary compliance plans for all government contractors. At the beginning of World War II Lockheed employed no Negroes in its California production facilities. "Not that the late chairman or his brother . . . had any prejudice against using Negro workmen," as one writer delicately put it, "it was simply that aircraft building had never been on a mass production basis and that the skill requirements were far beyond the ability and training of the few Negro applicants."[4] Either because of streamlined mass production techniques or because of Roosevelt's wartime FEPC, the firm did begin to employ black workers after 1941.[5]

In 1951 the Lockheed corporation opened a gigantic facility in Marietta, Georgia. Whatever its employment policies in California, Lockheed had no intentions of upsetting local customs in Georgia. Lockheed's director of industrial relations, E. G. Mattison, explained, "If we were not careful in gaining community acceptance, we might have some unpleasant incidents and unfavorable publicity with which to contend." With unwarranted moderation Mattison noted, "We went about [integration] very quietly and slowly; not timidly, but wisely."[6] Presumably as part of this "wise" policy, J. P. Lydon, director of administration, said in 1957, "We just don't feel we can push Negroes into higher jobs just for the sake of doing it. I dread sudden moves, particularly now when emotional tension is so high throughout the community."[7] Apparently there was some token hiring of blacks in nontraditional positions before 1961,[8] but according to NAACP meaningful numbers of blacks were hired only in unskilled and semiskilled positions. In addition, Lockheed barred blacks from the firm's apprenticeship program, blacks were made to use separate rest rooms and dining rooms, and blacks were members of a segregated union.[9]

Although Negroes had filed complaints against Lockheed since 1956, investigations by the Nixon Committee "found the company to be complying with existing regulations."[10] One week after President Kennedy issued Executive Order 10925, despite Lockheed's segregated facilities, segregated union, and long history of charges of employment discrimination, the Defense Department announced it was awarding a billion dollar contract to the firm to build the C-141 cargo plane.[11] On the day the Executive Order took effect, April 7, 1961, NAACP filed a complaint with the President's Committee on Equal Employment Opportunity charging Lockheed with flagrant violations of the executive order. Jerry R. Holleman, vice chairman of PCEEO told NAACP that if, after investigation, the company were found in violation of the executive order the committee would recommend cancellation of the contract.[12]

This was the situation which prompted the company to introduce what a Lockheed executive later called "a voluntary program" rather than to submit to "forced" integration under the executive order.[13] This, of course, was an inaccurate interpretation on the part of the company official since the committee had no power to force the firm to do anything but could merely recommend cancellation of the contract if the company failed to live up to its contractual obligations, one of which was complying with Executive Order 10925. On May 25 Lockheed announced that it had signed an agreement with the government, the first Plan for Progress, in which it promised to undertake a "company-wide program to expand and strengthen its efforts to promote equal employment opportunity."[14] As a start the company eliminated its segregated facilities. On some, like the rest rooms, it removed the signs. On others, like the cafeterias and the drinking fountains, Lockheed eliminated the segregation by eliminating the facility. Mobile hot food carts were substituted for the cafeterias, and the company replaced the fountains with taps and paper cups—according to one report at the rate of 63,000 cups a day.[15]

In addition to eliminating the gross forms of discrimination Lockheed agreed to:

1) disseminate its policy widely and emphasize the need for implementing it at all levels,

2) "aggressively seek out more qualified minority group candidates" and make sure that its sources of manpower were informed of its nondiscriminatory policy,

3) "re-analyze its openings for salaried jobs to be certain that all eligible minority group employees have been considered for placement and upgrading" and attempt to hire more minority teachers for summer

jobs and otherwise inform the school system of the opportunities for
blacks in the firm,

4) "support," "secure," "encourage," and "make certain" that
minority workers participated in the company's various training programs at all levels,

5) desegregate all facilities and institute periodic checks to insure
that the policy was being implemented.[16]

The impact of the Plan for Progress on Lockheed's hiring appears
to have been significant. Segregation in the plant disappeared. Negroes
were actively recruited and promoted, and the company extended its
activity into the community, working closely with local black secondary
schools and colleges. But the immediate implementation of the Plan for
Progress in Lockheed plants was not nearly as important as the impact
the Plan for Progress had on the business community in general. By
pressing other federal contractors to establish Plans for Progress, the
Kennedy administration was able to enhance its image in the black
community. At the same time, the "voluntary" nature of the Plans for
Progress strengthened the administration's position with the business
community as being reasonable and not antibusiness. For the participating
businessmen, the Plans for Progress had the admirable quality of giving
them a glowing equal employment image, with reams of free publicity,
while legally not binding them to do anything.

In the six months following Lockheed's Plan for Progress, four more
aerospace contractors, Boeing, North American, Douglas, and Martin,
plus the Radio Corporation of America, all signed Plans for Progress.[17]
Then, in February, 1962, Vice President Lyndon B. Johnson announced
that an additional thirty-one defense contractors would come to the
White House to participate in a mass signing of Plans for Progress. Only
one contractor demurred from the public baptism, indicating that he
preferred to "avoid the hoopla."[18] The number of companies that joined
Plans for Progress continued to grow. In 1963 Plans for Progress formed
an advisory council to coordinate individual efforts, and the advisory
council promoted the formation of local voluntary community councils.
By the end of 1967, there were more than four hundred member firms.[19]
While some company plans, like that of General Electric, were "unspe-
cific and little more than a polite response to the panel's invitation to
cooperate,"[20] most adhered to the form of Lockheed's original plan.[21]

The 1963 Plans for Progress formal statement of purpose neatly
summed up all the justifications that businessmen had used to defend equal
employment for the previous twenty years:

1) morality: "Enriching our free society by advancing human rights,"

2) the American Creed: "Providing equal job rights for all Americans,"

3) long-run economic benefits: "Developing the full potential of our nation's human resources,"

"Reducing the costs to the nation of unemployment, underdevelopment, health and welfare programs, increasing crime and delinquency rates, and deterioration of urban areas,"

"Improving the economic conditions necessary for continuing prosperity, thus increasing the gross national product by many billions of dollars and raising the standard of living,"

4) community citizenship: "Promoting better community conditions in order to provide an environment for dignity and tranquility in our daily lives,"

5) voluntary action: "Contributing through private endeavors toward solutions of a major national problem."[22]

Significantly the simple Capitalist Ethic justification of the short-run economic benefits is missing from the list. In 1963 most businessmen were not about to admit they wanted to make a buck on black employment—but perhaps more to the point, there was no way such an argument could be formulated. While it may have been great public relations, hiring blacks was not necesarily good economics. Joining Plans for Progress, however, allowed firms to have their cake and eat it too. Through membership in PFP employers could reap the rewards of being socially conscious while actually doing nothing. H. W. Wittenborn, personnel vice president of Cook Electric Co., urged members of the American Management Association to become members of Plans for Progress. He contended that industry had been willing to let the "sleeping dog" of economic discrimination "lie while the community customs remained static or changed slowly. But now," he warned his listeners, "community customs are changing and changing fast. The business executive is faced with a dilemma. More and more he is feeling the squeeze between the external pressures (the government, racial groups, interracial groups, and the community) demanding change and internal structured customs within his organization demanding status quo." According to Wittenborn one way to resolve the conflict was to "seize the initiative" and join the Plans for Progress as "evidence of their affirmative action."[23]

The business community enjoyed taking the credit for participating in PFP and for the great advances in black employment that businessmen claimed would result from PFP activity. A Lockheed official commented that Plans for Progress was a "public declaration by the heads of companies who are not accustomed to failing or half-heartedly pursuing their objectives."[24] In fact, however, many businessmen appeared much more interested in posturing for the press than in actively participating in the program. Most firms viewed the plan as protection against the President's Committee on Equal Employment Opportunity which enforced Executive Order 10925. A contemporary observer suggested that "the signing of the Plans by the president or the chief executive officer usually received enough publicity in national, state, local, and company press to make it abundantly clear that the organization's executives were fully committed."[25] Although PFP firms were supposed to periodically review their progress and all government contractors had to report to the PCEEO, there is evidence that many firms viewed joining Plans for Progress as an end in itself. A majority of steel companies interviewed by one student of industrial racial policies believed that simply by joining PFP they had instituted an effective equal employment policy and had proven they were not discriminating.[26] Another study found that companies which claimed they had taken affirmative action to assist blacks, including joining Plans for Progress, were actually attempting "to give an impression of having more employment integration than actually existed."[27] Thus it is not surprising that companies which had signed Plans for Progress used them as a defense against black protest groups who demanded increased minority employment.[28]

There is no reason to assume that black protest groups were impressed by a firm's membership in Plans for Progress, since Negro groups had been suspicious of the program from the beginning. Initially blacks feared that the government was using Plans for Progress as a substitute for a strong civil rights bill.[29] Herbert Hill, NAACP labor secretary and the most persistent critic of the Plans for Progress, charged that PFP companies were more interested in "publicity than progress," and that many companies that signed the plans regarded them as "a way of securing immunity from real compliance with the anti-discrimination provisions of their Government contracts."[30] Hill condemned Plans for Progress as "simply a euphemism for what a previous Administration called voluntary compliance."[31]

Robert A. Troutman, an Atlanta lawyer, friend of President Kennedy, member of PCEEO, and the man credited with originating the idea of Plans for Progress, was a special target of critics of the program. Hill claimed that Troutman was "an avowed Southern segregationist" and was very closely involved with "two of the leading racists in the United States Senate," Richard B. Russell and Herman E. Talmadge, both from Troutman's home state of Georgia.[32] Troutman was head of a PCEEO subcommittee concerned with Plans for Progress, and his strong emphasis on the voluntary nature of Plans for Progress did nothing to enhance his reputation with the critics.[33] Because most members of Plans for Progress were government contractors, although others were permitted to join, they were under pressure not only to give their word, but to live up to it. Perhaps to eliminate even this subtle form of compulsion, Troutman recommended that the Plans for Progress be "severed from the committee [PCEEO] and operated as a private organization supported by private funds."[34]

There was a running debate on the actual effectiveness of the Plans for Progress. Its supporters were able to prdouce figures of individual PFP companies that showed significant increases in the proportional representation of Negroes in their work forces after signing a plan.[35] On a national basis there was an impressive increase in the number of white-collar Negroes employed by all Plans for Progress companies, and a corresponding decrease in the proportional number of blacks being hired into traditional black jobs between May, 1961, and January, 1963.[36]

In fact, some firms hired substantially more Negroes in nontraditional positions than the Plans for Progress cumulative figures indicated because southern Plans for Progress companies virtually ignored their commitment. A survey of PFP companies in the Atlanta area undertaken by the Southern Regional Council in 1962 found that of twenty-four member firms only seven had taken affirmative action and of these only three, Lockheed, Western Electric, and Goodyear, demonstrated what the council called "a vigorous desire to create job opportunities."[37] Most of the Atlanta-based managers who were even aware that their firms had signed Plans for Progress believed that the sales and service offices that they ran were exempt from the Plan's provisions. It was their understanding that the Plan was designed for production facilities only. Implicit in this was the belief that integration was acceptable only in low-status, blue-collar production jobs.[38] For example, at the Atlanta office of PFP member Continental Motors, an official assured investigators that they allowed "no discrimination whatsoever." He went on to explain that three of his twenty-six employees were black. "Back in the back, where we work these three Negroes, there are eight whites," said the official. He then went on to describe the firm's nondiscriminatory practices: "One of the Negroes is a porter and general helper. . . . The other two are engine teardown and cleanup men. We term them 'mechanic's helpers.' Their restroom is called the 'janitor's room.' They're not told to go anywhere; they just go where they want to go."[39]

A follow-up of the Southern Regional Council report by the contracting agencies, the Army, Navy, and Air Force, did not support the council's full findings. The armed services investigators claimed that there were no companies unaware of their obligations under Plans for Progress (perhaps because they all had been previously visited by the council), and furthermore that those that were in violation of the agreement were usually deficient on technicalities such as posting equal employment signs.[40] The armed forces report did not significantly undercut the council findings since the definition of affirmative action was somewhat open to interpretation and the armed forces did find that the firms were ignoring black community resources for recruiting workers. Moreover, the council had taken the companies to task for not living up to the Plans for Progress, while the government was merely investigating compliance with the executive order, a less demanding document.

The Plans for Progress, Eisenhoweresque emphasis on voluntarism, education, and cooperation between government and business not only continued the discredited philosophy of the Nixon Committee but conditioned both business and government to expect conciliation rather than forced compliance from the Civil Rights Act of 1964. While Plans for Progress continued to add firms to its list of members, it ceased to be a central element in the federal fair employment enforcement scene after the passage of the Civil Rights Act. Since many businessmen had viewed their membership in Plans for Progress as a way of softening the impact of Executive Order 10925, which had required affirmative action from government contractors, one corporate vice president concluded that once "the Civil Rights Act had been passed, he didn't see any need for the Plans for Progress Program."[41]

Between the passage of the Civil Rights Act in 1964 and the riots of the summer of 1967 the business community took no significant national action to further the employment of black workers. However, the riots of 1967 set off a chain of business and government responses leading to the formation of the National Alliance of Businessmen, which marked the culmination of formal business involvement in minority employment problems during the postwar period. Somewhat paradoxically, the riots also gave rise to the Urban Coalition, an organization with strong business support, which called for increased government intervention in the problems of the cities, the first such concerted business support for federal action in twenty years.

The Detroit riot of late July, 1967, prompted Detroit businessmen to found the New Detroit Committee (NDC). But rather than remain merely another local merit employment council, NDC provided the model and leadership for a national merit employment council, the National Alliance of Businessmen. To a large extent industry in Detroit meant automobiles, and with the exception of Ford, auto employment policies were less than enlightened prior to 1967.[42] Because many other major cities had riots prior to 1967 while Detroit remained calm, some of its business leaders were a little too quick to praise their own limited equal employment activity. In 1964, Richard E. Cross, chairman of the board of American Motors, said Detroit had avoided racial disorders because top management had taken an affirmative attitude toward the problem of Negro employment and had maintained good communications with the black community.[43] Arjay Miller, president of Ford, echoed these sentiments the following year, praising Detroit for the (unspecified) steps it had taken and lauding the federal government for its war on poverty. However Miller covered himself by warning that past peace was no guarantee of future calm.[44] Douglas Fraser, head of the United Auto Workers' Chrysler department, said after the July, 1967, riot, "Everybody was so cocky, including myself, that a riot could not happen here, because we had probably done more than other cities."[45]

As had been the case in cities where blacks had rioted previously, Detroit responded to the violence by creating a community council. Despairing of additional federal help, Governor George Romney and Mayor Jerome P. Cavanagh appointed a citizens' committee "to mobilize the public and private resources" of Detroit.[46] Along with fourteen businessmen the New Detroit Committee consisted of labor leaders and representatives from the black community, including three strong black nationalists.[47]

Neither NDC nor its program was radically different from the merit employment councils that had sprung up around the country during the previous four years, except that NDC followed one of the worst of the urban riots and contained some of the most powerful industrial leaders in the country, including the heads of the three major automobile companies. Similar to the Association of Huntsville Area Companies, NDC did not intend to operate any programs itself but rather was "oriented to helping the community utilize its existing agencies more effectively in both the private and the public sector."[48] The committee believed that action was needed to improve communications, to improve community service including health, welfare, and police protection, to improve education, employment and job training, to clean up after the riot, and to build new housing for Negroes.[49] The most immediately successful of the programs was NDC's plan to find ten thousand jobs for the hard-core unemployed in two months. Working with the Greater Detroit Board of Commerce, NDC persuaded many employers, especially the automobile companies, to lower, or virtually eliminate, normal hiring standards and to actively recruit in the inner city.[50] By the beginning of 1968, General Motors and Ford together had hired almost ten thousand Negroes, many of them, according to the companies, hard-core unemployed.[51] Their success was temporary and, even then, unique in all the nation.

Within half a year of its founding, dissension was tearing NDC apart. First, moderate Negro members of the committee complained that NDC leader Joseph Hudson was working too closely with the radicals, and they threatened to boycott his department store.[52] Then the black nationalists pulled out of the group and accused the businessmen of not allowing them to formulate their own programs.[53] An evaluation report in the spring of

1968 concluded that the committee's achievements, except in the field of employment, were "woefully inadequate" to meet the city's needs.[54] For all the good they did, the businessmen concluded that the private sector could not cope with the manifold problems of the cities, and that "unless vast sums of money are made available to the cities by the federal government, which alone possesses the necessary taxing and distributive power, and unless central planning and guidance are provided to assure consistency and to prevent offsetting effects, there is little hope for arresting the growth of inner city hopelessness and despair."[55]

The idea that the government should assist business in assisting the blacks became an increasingly common contrapuntal theme to the standard business contention that private voluntary activity was the best way to solve black employment problems. As long as employing blacks was a problem that had to be settled between the businessman and government agencies, or between businessmen and local black protest groups, the business community could afford to insist that the problem might be solved through voluntary action. But when the riots demonstrated that unemployment was merely one symptom of the complex syndrome of urban decay, and that to solve even that one problem would require truly extensive employer commitment, the business community began to moderate its grandiose claims about the power of voluntary action and looked to government for support.

After the riots businessmen recognized that solving the black employment problem meant hiring large numbers of hard-core unemployed. This meant increased costs, which in turn meant lower profits, and very few employers were willing to commit themselves to a program which would eat into their profits.[56] Thus, when they were confronted with the full economic implications of relieving the economic plight of black workers, the Capitalist Ethic once more stopped businessman from hiring blacks. Unlike the forties and fifties, when costs due to racism were the source of rejection, the economic bar to blacks during the sixties lay with the inability of many blacks to meet traditional employment standards. As they had during the Great Depression, businessmen began to turn to the government to rescue them from the trap of their own making. William G. Caples, vice president of Inland Steel, believed that industry would "accept some of the hard-core burdens," but he felt it was "naive to expect that industry can accept large numbers of individuals for hard-core employment without subsidy and incentive when the responsibility of business management is to wisely use capital and produce profit."[57]

During 1967, the federal government launched two programs which took tentative steps toward meeting these demands. Through the Concentrated Employment Program (CEP) the government attempted to centralize the various federal programs that dealt with the hard-core unemployed. CEP spent most of its first year trying to decide who the hard-core unemployed were and where and how they lived.[58] The second program was an experimental one designed to encourage business to move into the ghetto and to provide training for the "seriously disadvantaged." By making it easier for such firms to land government contracts and by assuming the full cost of training and bonding hard-core employees, the experimental program hoped to mitigate some of the economic disadvantages associated with inner-city operations.[59] But, as the *New York Times* pointed out editorially, the program merely made it easier to do a difficult job. It did not guarantee a profit. For the long term, the *Times* called for "substantial tax incentives."[60]

Other representatives of the business community continued to call for making social responsibility more profitable and therefore compatible with the Capitalist Ethic. *Fortune* magazine not only suggested tax incentives but in effect called for a kind of new National Recovery Administration by which the government would suspend antitrust action against all companies "engaged in 'public service operations' from the same competitive base."[61] The Advisory Panel on Private Enterprise to the National Advisory Commission on Civil Disorder picked up and elaborated the tax incentive idea. The advisory panel, which was made up of the heads of Litton Industries, North American Rockwell, General Mills, the Bank of America, and the National Industrial Conference Board, declared that statements supporting business involvement with urban problems were "more than mere rhetoric." If for no other reason, the panel believed that business would voluntarily enter the fields of job training and employment, housing, economic development, Negro enterpreneurship, education, and attitudinal change "because they recognized that the price of inaction may well be continued tension and disorder and the ultimate breakdown of the tranquility which underlies our entire social fabric and economic growth."[62] The panel's justification was the long-run benefit interpretation of the Capitalist Ethic, which held that what was good for society was good for business. Becoming somewhat more realistic, however, the panel added, "But we believe that a truly massive number of companies could be induced to participate only if appropriate monetary incentives are provided by the federal government to defray the unusual costs of participation."[63] The panel then went on to detail the kind of income tax write-off that it thought would best help both business and the hard-core unemployed.[64]

On January 24, 1968, President Lyndon Johnson delivered a special message to Congress which proposed legislation to combine monetary incentives and the voluntary programs that the Plans for Progress companies had developed. The President called for an increase in the scope of the

Concentrated Employment Program, but more importantly he announced that Henry Ford II had agreed to head a new National Alliance of Businessmen (NAB). NAB was to administer a program known as JOBS (Job Opportunities in the Business Sector), which would attempt to persuade companies to employ 100,000 hard-core unemployed by June, 1969, and 500,000 by June, 1971.

Based on a successful experiment the government conducted in five cities in 1967, the President believed that business would participate in the NAB-JOBS program, given certain economic encouragement. The President foresaw business and government working in a partnership in which "the Government will identify and locate the unemployed. The company will train them, and offer them jobs. The company will bear the normal cost of training, as it would for any of its new employees."[65] The economic incentive came with the government's agreement to compensate business for the cost differential between the normal expenses of training and the additional effort required for the hard-core unemployed.[66]

In each of the fifty cities where NAB chapters were initially established, local firms loaned managerial staff who worked with Department of Labor personnel to find jobs for the hard-core unemployed.[67] Once NAB obtained business commitments the Labor Department was supposed to find job seekers vocationally unqualified enough to be eligible for the special programs which would be financed by federal funds.[68]

The JOBS program fell between two stools. It did not provide a genuine profit incentive which would attract large numbers of business participants, and it placed enough restrictions on its reimbursements to alienate employers who feared government scrutiny. The payment for extra costs incurred did not meet the demands of those businessmen who believed that real commitment would come only with guaranteed profit.[69] If the NAB program could not provide positive incentives for hiring and training the hard core, it at least tried to assure business that it would not suffer any unusual financial burden by working for black economic equality, but businessmen did not participate in the reimbursement program. Only between 20 and 25 percent of the companies which hired hard-core unemployed under the JOBS program signed contracts with the federal government for reimbursement of training costs. Some employers steered away from federal involvement because they feared government interference. According to one NAB official, "Employers do not like the rigid guidelines of a Government contract or do not want people looking over their shoulders, or do not like filling out government forms."[70] The JOBS program employers may not have wanted anyone looking over their shoulders, however they may also have been shy about accepting money because many of them were training busboys, porters, maids, parking lot attendants, housekeepers, laborers, and baggagemen, jobs which, contrary to the purpose of the program, did not offer much promise of promotion.[71]

Nevertheless, private efforts at training the hard-core unemployed did increase after the formation of NAB. By late 1969, more than seventeen thousand companies had signed training contracts with the Labor Department. Coupled with firms which trained hard-core unemployed without a contract, this represented a degree of business participation well above pre-riot proportions.[72]

Although the idea for NAB had originated with the federal government and impetus had come from the riots, many businessmen tended to see the JOBS program as an abdication of government responsibility and an example of their own leadership ability.[73] William F. Raven, vice president of Pan American World Airways and chairman of the JOBS program in Miami, Florida, observed, "The government tried to do the job but with no spectacular success. So President Johnson, in effect tossed the ball to the private sector of business."[74] To some businessmen the spectacle of government coming to industry for help looked like a last chance for the business community to retain control over minority employment. Gerald L. Phillippe, chairman of the board of General Electric, told the National Association of Manufacturers that "the price of not acting now in this crisis, of not contributing in concert all of the business skills we can muster, will be to abdicate our position as leaders."[75]

The actual success of the NAB-JOBS program was open to question even before the 1970 recession, when firms openly stopped hiring the hard-core unemployed.[76] Because NAB wished the JOBS program to appear successful, the alliance placed great emphasis on numerical goals in hiring the hard-core unemployed. "It's a numbers game we all play," said one NAB official. "We play it because that's what businessmen understand more so than talking to them about social problems or reminding them of their social responsibilities."[77] The fact that local NAB groups established quotas, albeit voluntary quotas, apparently had a negative effect on some businessmen who adhered to the American Creed, calling quotas "antithetical to the ideal of equal employment."[78] The stress on numerical goals led to the counting of normal hiring of blacks as "hard-core," multiple counting in high turnover positions, and other statistical devices which rendered NAB's figures unreliable.[79]

While the extent of hiring-policy change brought about by the JOBS program may not have been very great, the fact that hundreds of firms from all over the country were willing publicly to commit themselves to hiring the hard-core unemployed demonstrates that positive action in favor of Negroes had become the acceptable norm. As a national voluntary program dedicated to finding and hiring people whom businessmen had traditionally viewed as unemployable, the NAB-JOBS program climaxed the post-war fair employment movement. Whereas in the late forties businessmen feared public reaction if they hired any blacks at all, by the late sixties employers sought public acclaim by joining a nationwide movement which required businessmen to break with the Capitalist Ethic by hiring the least qualified workers, and to break with the American Creed by giving those workers special consideration.

The National Alliance of Businessmen's drive to hire the hard-core un-employed represented the business community's new attitude toward the employment of blacks. But NAB was the result of twenty years of mounting pressure for more black employment that had finally exploded in the riots of 1967. The riots exposed not only the extent of the black unemployment problem, but also the multitude of other economic and social diseases afflicting the inner city. The business community responded to the non-employment urban problems by supporting the Urban Coalition (UC), a national organization which sought to mobilize both the public and private sectors to fight the deterioration of city life.

UC both lacked a clear rationale and a consistent method of operation, which was indicative of the businessman's own loss of bearings in the late 1960's. For twenty years employers had claimed that economic problems could be best solved by allowing the private sector to handle things in its own way. Even when moved to act by government pressure, employers argued that the actual technique of working out a problem was best left to businessmen. The riots, however, undermined the business community's faith in the absolute efficacy of voluntarism; yet employers were not sure they were willing to leave the field of social action entirely to the govern-ment. The ambiguity of the business position emerged clearly in the com-ments of Henry Ford II, who was a founder of both NAB and UC. At the same time Ford seemed to feel both that businessmen could save the coun-try and that only increased government action could solve urban problems. When Henry Ford II introduced the NAB program he said that business would have to take the burden of "bringing these disadvantaged people out of the ghettos and into the mainstream of the American economy."[80] How-ever, Ford was contradicting a stand he had taken just five months earlier. As one of the members of a thirty-two-man steering committee which for-mulated UC's "Statement of Principles," Ford had presumably committed himself to the concept that "when the private sector is unable to provide employment to those who are both able and willing to work, then in a free society the government must of necessity assume the responsibility and act as the employer of last resort or must assure adequate income levels for those who are unable to work."[81]

Except for a kind of interlocking directorate typified by Ford's membership in both groups, UC and NAB were independent organizations. An emergency coalition of mayors and business, labor, church, and civil rights leaders created UC in August, 1967. Whereas NAB limited its membership to businessmen and dealt exclusively with the problems of minority hard-core unemployment, local UC units had a broader base and were supposed to be concerned with the whole spectrum of urban ills. In addition to attacking unemployment, UC called upon the nation "to provide a decent home and suitable living environment for every American family with guarantees of equal access to all housing, new and existing," and to "create educational programs that will equip all young Americans for full and productive participation in our society to the full potential of their abilities."[82]

Given the increasingly favorable public attitude toward business social responsibility, especially in regard to minority employment, UC was almost a reflex reaction to the riots of 1967. It extended to the national level the kind of local coalitions that had begun to appear in individual communities over the previous five years. The coalition was new only in the sense that it represented the first such national-level coalition of "liberal" business, government, and private groups since the National Civic Federation of the Progressive Era.

The UC was formed explicitly in response to the rioting of the summer of 1967. Its statement of principles started with a litany of the urban violence since 1965 (with the usual condemnations). It went on to advocate action "directed to the deep-rooted and historic problems of the cities."[83] The first UC chairman, John W. Gardner, expressed the underlying fears of the men who founded the coalition when he said, "We believe that the private sector of America must directly and vigorously involve itself in the crisis of the cities by a commitment to investment, job training, and hiring, and all that is necessary to the full enjoyment of the free enterprise system and *also its survival.*"[84]

Gardner's comments accentuated the dichotomy which permeated the voluntary action movement in the business community in the late 1960's. The original "Statement of Principles" adopted by the emergency coalition had placed its major stress on a call for the federal government to act. It seemed to call for more and bigger programs along the lines of President Johnson's "Great Society."[85] On the other hand, as chairman, Gardner appeared to place increased emphasis on the voluntary element of the program. The *New York Times* commented that many of the coalition's staff members, like Gardner himself, were ex-public officials who had "transferred their hope for a better society from the public to the private sector."[86] Gardner did not officially abandon the idea that the federal government should deal with the problem. He outlined the three purposes of the coalition as: 1) lobbying, 2) problem solving, that is, generating new ideas to solve urban problems, and 3) familiarizing the businessmen with the needs of the city because, Gardner said, "The closer business people get to the problem the more they see the need for new and more effective federal legislation."[87]

The original "Statement of Principles" of the emergency coalition also reflected the tension between what the government and the private sector should do. The first section called upon the government to provide an emergency work program to give socially useful jobs to everyone who wanted to work. The statement also called for government-financed training programs to insure upward mobility among the marginally skilled. It then outlined the action corporations should take to help solve urban problems. Some of the suggestions amounted to asking industry to participate in proposed new government programs. Others were a reiteration of the kinds of affirmative action that Plans for Progress companies had presumably been taking for seven years and which would subsequently be reemphasized by NAB. These included recruiting in the inner cities, youth motivation, special training, and development of black-owned businesses.[88]

Because many of the UC local units were actually preexisting councils of one kind or another, the activities which they undertook tended to emphasize the local voluntary effort rather than the grandiose federal programs envisioned in the original meeting.[89] The New York Coalition, for example, by applying for Internal Revenue Service tax-exempt status, which legally precluded lobbying, explicitly rejected the national UC's call for the business community to exercise its political influence.[90]

The formation of the National Alliance of Businessmen and the Urban Coalition were the culmination of twenty years of slowly developing commitment to the problems of the black worker. Both organizations emphasized voluntarism as a means of solving the problems so forcefully spotlighted by the riots. Their voluntarism was consistent with the conservative antigovernment ideology traditionally held by American businessmen. The fact remains however that the National Alliance of Businessmen was created in response to government pressure, and the Urban Coalition, although born within the business community, called upon the government to participate more actively in solving social problems. The two organizations were a somewhat unsuccessful attempt to salvage the businessman's image of himself as a leader by tying the voluntarist forms of the past to the obvious need for government action in the future.

13

Conclusion

Business attitudes toward the employment of Negroes underwent a revolution in the twenty-five years which followed World War II. At the beginning of the war Negroes received only dangerous, arduous, or unpleasant unskilled jobs no matter what their education, training, or ability—when businessmen would employ them at all. By the end of the 1960's employers were actively recruiting and hiring blacks who were unqualified for employment by traditional standards.

Like all human beings, businessmen have a fundamental need to maintain a degree of consistency between what they do and what they believe. When circumstances force an individual to alter his actions, he must absorb his new activity into his established set of reasons for doing things—his values. He could, of course, reject his traditional values and adopt a new ideological framework in which to operate, but such a revolution in personal beliefs is infinitely more difficult than trying somehow to fit the new actions into the old values. The explanations which employers used to justify their radical change in black employment policy are an illustration of the rationalization process which men go through to reconcile their values with their actions.

The American businessman operates under two theoretically complementary set of values, the American Creed and the Capitalist Ethic. The American Creed promises the individual equality of opportunity. It is the fundamental belief that all Americans are entitled to "life, liberty, and the pursuit of happiness," unencumbered by artificial barriers. The idea of individual freedom contained in the American Creed directly contributes to the Capitalist Ethic. In the Capitalist Ethic the idea of individual freedom is translated into entrepreneurial freedom. With "happiness" economically defined as long-run profitability, the businessman is able to cite the American Creed as justification in his pursuit of long-run profits.

But however complementary the American Creed and the Capitalist

Ethic are in theory, they have not always been mutually inclusive in practice. There were three distinct sets of business attitudes toward the employment of blacks after World War II, and the two value systems were compatible in only one of them. In the first period, between the war and 1954, aversion to black workers was so strong that businessmen did not dare apply the American Creed to employment practices. They feared that the costs to their businesses would be too high, and the Capitalist Ethic, i.e., profitability, took precedence over the American Creed. During the second period, 1954 to 1963, public acceptance of blacks in nontraditional positions had moderated sufficiently to allow businessmen to begin employing Negroes in token numbers. Moreover, there were enough well qualified black workers in the labor pool to make this change in employment policy profitable for the firm. Thus there was no necessary conflict between the American Creed and the Capitalist Ethic during this period. Finally, after 1963 pressure from the civil rights movement and the government forced employers once more to abandon the American Creed, but this time in the direction of actively assisting black job seekers rather than in the direction of discriminating against them. In particular the riots of the mid-sixties convinced the business community that it must act to save the system. In this instance the Capitalist Ethic demanded that business absorb certain short-run costs of hiring the hard-core unemployed rather than risk the long-run dangers of economic and social upheaval.

To say that businessmen became increasingly willing to hire blacks in the postwar period is to say that Negro employment became an accepted form of social responsibility. Although rejected by some ideological conservatives, throughout American history businessmen have widely accepted the concept of social responsibility. The idea that businessmen should accept some responsibility for the general welfare of society reflected four needs felt by most businessmen: first, businessmen wished to be leaders; second, they wanted to exercise power; third, they wanted society to accept them; and fourth, they wanted to do what was morally right. Social responsibility was thus a process through which the businessman achieved status in the community, and by definition acts which were contrary to popular expectations could not be socially responsible.

Until 1954 progress in hiring blacks in nontraditional jobs was slow and limited to rare instances of tokenism. In the period before the Eisenhower administration, the Capitalist Ethic worked against the employment of Negroes. Businessmen believed that the risks of employing blacks were so high that sound business practice required discrimination against Negroes. Many employers were personally biased against blacks and accepted stereotypes which characterized Negroes as racially incapable of succeeding in nontraditional jobs. Even those employers who did not harbor personal racism believed that their white employees and their customers would object to Negro workers and, therefore, they could hire blacks only at the cost of harmonious personnel relations and sales.

The unwillingness of most businessmen to assume leadership in the employment of blacks before 1954 reflected the generally negative attitude which the public held toward black employees. Obviously businessmen could not have led in the field of Negro employment until there were people willing to follow—followers are what separate leaders from eccentrics. But when we discuss the followers of businessmen we are talking about two distinct groups, the general community and the business community. At no point in the postwar era were businessmen leading society in general. Broad social expectations, as reflected in governmental action, always preceded business activity in the field of fair employment. However, there had to be some businessmen who led the way in employing blacks within the business community, and these men were in a very real, if limited, sense leaders of their peers.

Although the drive for a permanent federal fair employment practice law failed after the end of World War II, several states and cities did pass such legislation. These early successes in the equal employment movement, while they did not represent a flood tide of popular support for black employment, did indicate that some change in public sentiment had taken place. These straws in the winds of change were enough to prompt a few pioneering businessmen to hire their first black workers in nontraditional jobs. Those businessmen who participated in voluntary fair employment programs to forestall state or local FEPC action hired blacks not out of a sense of leadership but rather to prevent the government from eroding their power to employ whom they pleased. However, some pioneering businessmen were motivated by a desire to do good. The business community was not the employers' sole point of reference. For many pioneering businessmen their roles as church members were as important as their membership in the business community. Religiously committed employers found that the combination of their belief in a religious code of ethics and in the American Creed was stronger than the Capitalist Ethic which dictated no Negro employment when there might be extraordinary costs to the firm. It should, however, be remembered that religious morality did not widely influence business practice until the public had begun to show preliminary signs of accepting fair employment practice.

The level of pioneer placement increased after 1954 as the Eisenhower administration lent its support to voluntary fair employment policies. The Nixon Committee's emphasis on educating businessmen and the public in the values of equal employment made it easier for businessmen to begin to accept black employment as a form of social responsibility. With the imprimatur of a conservative Republican administration, businessmen could pursue voluntary equal employment with a fair certainty that their efforts would be rewarded with public acceptance. And since, during at least the mid-fifties, there was an available supply of qualified blacks, the American Creed and the Capitalist Ethic combined into a fully integrated set of values.

President Kennedy's Executive Order 10925 accelerated the rate of Negro employment that had begun voluntarily during the Eisenhower administration. The Kennedy order called upon government contractors to go beyond mere equal employment. The federal government asked them to take affirmative action to find and employ black workers. Although it asked employers to look for black workers, the government did not demand that businessmen lower their employment standards for Negroes. This request may have bent the equal opportunity meaning of the American Creed but it did not break it. Numerous voluntary fair employment practice councils sprang up in the wake of the federal action and the beginnings of the civil rights movement. These groups did help place blacks in pioneering positions, particularly in technical, professional, and managerial jobs. However, the voluntary fair employment councils mostly produced propaganda. That in itself was a clear sign that black employment had become a totally accepted form of social responsibility. Whatever their actual employment practices, businessmen worked actively and collectively to convince the public that they were equal opportunity employers.

The Civil Rights Act of 1964 and the formation of the Equal Employment Opportunity Commission sanctified with law the concept of fair employment which the business community had come to accept over the previous decade. But beginning in 1963 and continuing through 1967, the black community began pushing for a more radical interpretation of fair employment. Sound personnel policy and the Capitalist Ethic demanded that the employer hire only the best qualified workers and this rule was not seriously challenged until mid-decade. The combination of the Capitalist Ethic and the American Creed which prompted some businessmen to start hiring Negroes in the late fifties had the ironic effect of giving other employers an excuse not to hire blacks during the early sixties. Whereas before 1954 employers simply ignored the American Creed when they excluded blacks from their firms, by the sixties they could claim that the American Creed demanded equal treatment for all applicants, and since most blacks were unqualified by traditional standards, they could not be hired. Recognizing that businessmen were using the concept of equal employment opportunity to reject unqualified black workers, the civil rights movement put pressure on employers to hire the so-called unemployables. Blacks, and to some extent the federal government, called upon business to move beyond the American Creed by changing the nature of jobs, lowering standards, or providing training for unqualified blacks.

Aside from a handful of unusually dedicated individuals, businessmen rejected the demands for unequal treatment of black and white applicants. Employers may have been willing to go out and look for black workers, but they were unwilling to lower their standards to hire them. Not only were black demands a clear violation of the American Creed, but the costs involved were in direct conflict with the Capitalist Ethic. The riots of the mid-sixties provided the impetus necessary to move the business community to an acceptance of extra help for the hard-core unemployed. The National Alliance of Businessmen and the Urban Coalition both advocated going the extra mile. Employing the hard-core unemployed would burden the firm with additional costs, and normally these expenses would have been considered a violation of the Capitalist Ethic. Businessmen, however, suddenly recognized that unless they were willing to assume some short-run costs, they might find themselves in a long-run period of social and economic chaos that would be far more expensive. The American Creed was forgotten once again, but this time in order to employ rather than reject blacks.

For all their hopeful statements about the way business would solve the urban crisis, NAB and UC began to see that voluntarism was not going to cure the problem. Businessmen found in NAB and UC all the elements which defined social responsibility—leadership, power, acceptance, and morality—but no solution to the problem of Negro unemployment. In twenty years voluntarism had come full circle. In the 1940's businessmen had attempted to prevent FEPC laws by forming organizations which would voluntarily provide jobs for Negroes. Those groups served only to demonstrate the real need for legislation. In the 1960's businessmen formed organizations to provide jobs for unemployed blacks. Like their predecessors the latest groups proved unable to deal with the fundamental problem and served primarily to highlight the need for a legislative remedy.

The creation of NAB and UC was the climax of twenty-five years of postwar business thinking. The end of the sixties not only witnessed the bankruptcy of voluntarism as a solution to the black employment problem, but it also saw the end of economic expansion, escalating black pressure, and growing federal fair employment activity. The election of

Richard Nixon in 1968, the reduction of black violence after the riots of 1968, and the beginning of a recession the following year all contributed to a relaxation of pressure for increased black employment. Although the Equal Employment Opportunity Commission and other federal agencies continued their affirmative action policies of the 1960's, the sense of immediacy was gone, and the economic downturn which lasted through 1972 made it increasingly difficult to hire hard-core unemployed blacks while regular workers were laid off. In the end the Capitalist Ethic remained the dominant force in determining personnel policy.

Notes

Introduction

1.   Dale L. Hiestand, *Economic Growth and Employment Opportunities for Minorities* (New York: Columbia University Press, 1964), 118.

2.   Nathan Wright, Jr., "Economics of Race," *American Journal of Economics and Sociology,* XXVI (Jan., 1967), 1–12.

3.   Arthur M. Ross, "The Negro in the American Economy," in Arthur M. Ross and Herbert Hill, eds., *Employment, Race and Poverty* (New York: Harcourt, Brace & World, 1967), 35–47.

4.   Arjay Miller, "Address to Detroit Roundtable of Catholics, Jews and Protestants," Dec. 12, 1965.

Chapter 1

1.   Gunnar Myrdal, *An American Dilemma* (New York: Harper & Bros., 1944), 8–12.

2.   Jack Blicksilver, "Social Responsibilties of Businessmen, Parts I and II," *Atlanta Economic Review* (Mar.-Apr., 1966), 3–4.

3.   Ernst Troeltsch, *The Social Teaching of the Christian Churches,* Vol. I (New York: Harper Torchbooks, 1960), 128.

4.   Bernard Bailyn, ed., *The Apologia of Robert Keayne* (New York: Harper Torchbooks, 1965), viii.

5.   Foster Rhea Dulles, *Labor in America* (New York: Thomas Y. Crowell Co., 1966), 73–5; Morrell Heald, *The Social Responsibility of Business* (Cleveland: The Press of Case-Western Reserve University, 1970), 3–5.

6.   H. M. Gitelman, "The Waltham System and the Coming of the Irish," *Labor History,* VIII (Fall, 1967), 227–253.

7.   Blicksilver, *Atlanta Economic Review* (Mar.-Apr., 1966), 5.

8.   *Ibid.*

9.   Morrell Heald, "Management's Responsibility to Society: The Growth of an Idea," in William T. Greenwood, ed., *Issues in Business and Society* (Boston: Houghton Mifflin, 1964), 476–8.

10.   Heald, *Social Responsibility,* 30, 49–52.

11.   *Ibid.,* 93.

12.   Arthur M. Schlesinger, Jr., *The Crisis of the Old Order, 1919–1933* (Boston: Houghton Mifflin Co., 1957), 179.

13.   Howard R. Bowen, *Social Responsibilities of the Businessman* (New York: Harper and Bros., 1953), 45.

14.   Heald, *Social Responsibility,* 117–147.

15.   *Ibid.,* 193–198.

16.   William H. Whyte, Jr., *Is Anybody Listening?* (New York: Simon and Schuster, 1952), 1–45.

17.   Earl F. Cheit, "The New Place of Business," in Earl F. Cheit, ed., *The Business Establishment* (New York: Wiley, 1964), 153–155; Arthur Larson, *Eisenhower: The President Nobody Knew* (New York: Popular Library, 1968), 127.

18.   Erwin D. Canham, ed., *The Disadvantaged Poor: Education and Employment Task Force on Economic Growth and Opportunity, Third Report* (Washington, D.C.: Chamber of Commerce of the United States of America, 1966).

19.   *Esquire,* "A Report on Corporate Involvement in the Youth of Today," an advertising prospectus, summer, 1968.

20.   Grace J. Finely, "Business Defines its Social Responsibilities," *Conference Board Record,* IV (Nov., 1967), 9–10.

21.   *Ibid.,* 10.

22.   Bettye K. Eidson, "Major Employers and Their Manpower Policies," in *Supplemental Studies for the National Advisory Commission on Civil Disorders* (Washington: GPO, July, 1968), 115–123.

23.   Thomas A. Petit, *The Moral Crisis in Management* (New York: McGraw Book Co., 1967), 37.

24.   *Ibid.*

25.   Richard Eells, *The Meaning of Modern Business* (New York: Columbia University Press, 1960), 44–46.

26.   *Ibid.,* 46.

27.   "What the Kodak Fracas Means," *Business Week* (May 6, 1967), 192.

28.   H. L. Hunt in an interview on the CBS television show *Sixty Minutes,* July 22, 1969.

29.   Francis X. Sutton, Seymour E. Harris, Carl Kaysen, and James Tobin, *The American Business Creed* (Cambridge, Mass.: Harvard University Press, 1956), 351.

30.   Letter, Sept. 20, 1968, in files of *Esquire.*

31.   Theodore Levitt, "The Dangers of Social Responsibility," *Harvard Business Review,* XXXVI (Sept.-Oct., 1958), 48.

32.   Sutton, *The American Business Creed,* 353.

33.   *New York Times,* April 28, 1968, IV, 1.

34.   Levitt, *Harvard Business Review* (Sept.-Oct., 1958), 48.

35.   James C. Worthy, *Big Business and Free Men* (New York: Harper, 1959), 28–29.

36.   The [University of Wisconsin—Madison] *Daily Cardinal,* Oct. 31, 1968, 10.

37.   R. V. Hansberger, "The Incredible Credibility Gap," an address to the National Association of Purchasing Agents, San Francisco, May 21, 1968, emphasis added.

38.   Richard A. Cloward and Frances Fox Piven, "Corporate Imperialism for the Poor," *The Nation,* CCV (Oct. 16, 1967), 355 ff.; Peter Wiley and Beverly Leman, "Crisis in the Cities, Part One, the Business of Urban Reform, *Leviathan,* I (March, 1969), 11 ff.; Michael Harrington, "Can Private Industry Abolish Slums?", *Dissent,* XV (Jan.-Feb., 1968), 5.

39.   *New York Times,* Feb. 10, 1969, 38:4.

40.   *Ibid.,* Sept. 7, 1967, 34:1.

41.   *Ibid.,* Jan. 24, 1953, 8.

42.   Editorial, "What Business Can Do for the Cities," *Fortune,* LXXVII (Jan., 1968), 128; Richard Eells, "Social Responsibility: Can Business Survive the Challenge?", *Business Horizons,* II (Winter, 1959), 41; Clarence C. Walton, "The Changing Face of a Business Corporation's Responsibilities," *Economic and Business Bulletin* [of Temple University], XVII (September, 1964), 13.

43.   John D. Harper, "The Public Responsibilties of Private Enterprise," *Looking Ahead,* XV (Apr., 1967), 20.

44.   Henry Ford II, address to the annual stockholders meeting of the Ford Motor Company, Detroit, May 23, 1968, press release.

45. Donald J. Gaudion, address to annual stockholders meeting of the Ritter-Pfaudler Corp., New York, Apr. 25, 1968.

46. James K. Dent, "Organizational Correlates of the Goals of Business Management," in William T. Greenwood, *Issues in Business and Society* (Boston: Houghton Mifflin, 1964), 404; John Kenneth Galbraith, *The New Industrial State* (Boston: Houghton Mifflin Co., 1967), 176–177.

47. Eli Goldston, "New Prospects for American Business," *Daedalus*, XCVIII (Winter, 1969), 80–81; ideally, a study such as this should examine the impact on social responsibility of many other variables besides size: organizational structure, profitability, plant history, nature of product and type of customers, just to mention a few. Unfortunately such information is impossible to obtain about the past. However, the Equal Employment Opportunity Commission has been collecting some of the data, as it relates to minority employment, since 1964, and future historians may be able to provide answers to these questions.

48. Eells, *Meaning of Modern Business,* 125–133.

49. Bert E. Elwert, "A New Look at the Soulful Corporation," *Business and Economic Dimensions,* III (Nov., 1967), 5–6.

50. Eidson, "Major Employers," *Supplemental Studies,* 115–123.

51. Keith Davis, "Can Business Afford to Ignore Social Responsibilities?", in Greenwood, *Issues in Business,* 488–489.

52. Keith Davis, "Understanding the Social Responsibility Puzzle," *Business Horizons,* X (Winter, 1967), 49.

53. Arjay Miller, address to University of Illinois symposium, Chicago Circle Campus, April 21, 1967.

54. Bowen, *Social Responsibilities,* 118.

55. Mead Johnson et al., "Consultation: Are Profits and Social Responsibility Compatible?" *Business Horizons,* II (Summer, 1959), 56.

56. Eells, *Meaning of Modern Business,* 126.

57. For a discussion of the role of individual morality in business, see Alvin O. Elbing and Carol J. Elbing, *The Value Issue of Business* (New York: McGraw-Hill, 1967), 48–50.

58. *Wall Street Journal,* June 14, 1968, 1:6.

59. F. S. Connell, letter to the editors, *Harvard Business Review,* XXXVII (Jan.-Feb., 1959), 22.

60. William C. Frederick, "The Growing Concern Over Business Responsibility," *California Management Review,* II (Summer, 1960), 58.

61. Eli Goldston, address to graduating class of the Program for Management Development, Harvard Business School, May 16, 1968.

62. Quoted in *Action Report,* I (Winter, 1968), 3.

63. Robert N. Hilkert, "The Responsibility of Business and Industry for Social Welfare in Today's World," *Federal Reserve Philadelphia* (July, 1966), 3–9.

Chapter 2

1. Arthur M. Ross, "The Negro in the American Economy," in Arthur M. Ross and Herbert Hill, eds., *Employment, Race and Poverty* (New York: Harcourt, Brace & World, 1967), 15.

2. Herbert Garfinkel, *When Negroes March* (New York: Atheneum, 1959).

3. S. L. Wolfbein, "War and Post-War Trends in Employment of Negroes," *Monthly Labor Review,* LX (Jan., 1945), 1–3.

4. *Ibid.,* 4–5; Robert C. Weaver, *Negro Labor: A National Problem* (New York Harcourt, Brace & Co., 1946), 80.

5. Wolfbein, *Monthly Labor Review* (Jan., 1945), 1–4; Norval D. Glenn, "Changes in the American Occupational Structure and Occupational Gains of Negroes During the 1940's," *Social Forces,* XLI (Dec., 1962), 191.

6. Weaver, *Negro Labor,* 32–33.

7.   Glenn, *Social Forces* (Dec., 1962), 188–195.

8.   Minnesota Governor's Interracial Commission, *The Negro Worker in Minnesota: A Report to Governor Edward J. Thye* (St. Paul, 1945), 11.

9.   Weaver, *Negro Labor,* 32–40.

10.   U.S. Committee on Fair Employment Practice, *First Report, July 1943-December 1944* (Washington: GPO, 1945), 63–75.

11.   Herbert R. Northrup, *The Negro in the Automobile Industry,* Report No. 1, *The Racial Policies of American Industry* (Philadelphia: Industrial Research Unit, Department of Industry, Wharton School of Finance and Commerce, University of Pennsylvania, 1968), 12–15, 20.

12.   D. M. Powell, "Negro Worker in Chicago Industry," *Journal of Business of the University of Chicago,* XX (Jan., 1947), 21–32.

13.   Weaver, *Negro Labor,* 80.

14.   Herbert R. Northrup, *The Negro in the Rubber Tire Industry,* Report No. 6, *The Racial Policies of American Industry* (Philadelphia: Industrial Research Unit, Department of Industry, Wharton School of Finance and Commerce, University of Pennsylvania, 1969), 38.

15.   Weaver, *Negro Labor,* 21–25.

16.   *Ibid.,* 17, 38.

17.   *Ibid.,* 63–66; Northrup, *The Negro in the Automobile Industry,* 18–21.

18.   Weaver, *Negro Labor,* 109.

19.   Louis C. Kesselman, *The Social Politics of FEPC* (Chapel Hill: The University of North Carolina Press, 1948), 7.

20.   Herbert R. Northrup, *The Negro in the Aerospace Industry,* Report No. 2, *The Racial Policies of American Industry* (Philadelphia: Industrial Research Unit, Department of Industry, Wharton School of Finance and Commerce, University of Pennsylvania, 1968), 19–20.

21.   Louis Ruchames, *Race, Jobs and Politics: The Story of FEPC* (New York: Columbia University Press, 1953), 32.

22.   *United States Code of Federal Regulations, Title 3—The President,* 1938-1943 Compilation (Washington: Office of the Federal Register, GPO, 1968), 957.

23.   C. E. Yount, "Anti-Discrimination in Industry," *Conference Board Management Record,* VII (October, 1945), 289.

24.   *Ibid.*

25.   *Ibid.,* 288–289; Ruchames, *Race, Jobs and Politics,* 31–33.

26.   Donald Dewey, "Four Studies of Negro Employment in the Upper South," in National Planning Association, Committee of the South, *Selected Studies of Negro Employment in the South* (Washington: National Planning Association, 1955), 175.

27.   Julius A. Thomas, "War-time Changes in the Occupational Status of Negro Workers," *Occupations,* XXIII (Apr., 1945), 403.

28.   S. C. Johnson and Preston Valien, "The Status of Negro Labor," in *Labor in Postwar America,* Vol. II (Brooklyn: Remsen Press, 1949), 555.

29.   J. A. Davis and M. M. Lawson, "Postwar Employment and the Negro Worker," *Common Ground,* III (Spring, 1946), 5.

30.   *Ibid.,* 7–11, 14–15; Herbert T. Northrup, *Will Negroes Get Jobs Now?,* pamphlet No. 110 (New York: Public Affairs Committee, Inc., 1945), 8–14.

31.   Davis, *Common Ground* (Spring, 1946), 12–15.

32.   John Williamson, "Defend and Extend the Rights of Negro Workers," *Political Affairs* (June, 1949), 28–29.

33.   S. L. Wolfbein, *Monthly Labor Review* (Dec., 1947), 664–665.

34.   For a fuller discussion see Garfinkel, *When Negroes March,* 154–170.

35.   Alex Elson and Leonard Schanfield, "Local Regulation of Discriminatory Employment Practices," *Yale Law Journal,* LVI (Feb., 1947), 431–454; for state laws see Michael I. Sovern, *Legal Restraints on Racial Discrimination in Employment* (New York: Twentieth Century Fund, 1966), 19–20.

36. Malcolm Ross, "Should the U.S. Permanently Ban Racial and Religious Discrimination in Jobs?", *Modern Industry* (April 5, 1945), 119–121.

37. *New York Times*, Aug. 2, 1952, 17:1.

38. American Friends Service Committee, press release, April 13, 1947.

39. U.S. Congress, Senate, Committee on Labor and Public Welfare, Subcommittee on Civil Rights, Hearings, *Anti-discrimination in Employment,* 83 Cong., 2nd Sess., Feb. 23-Mar. 3, 1954, testimony of Richard K. Barnett, national secretary, community relations, AFSC, 163.

40. *New York Times*, Feb. 1, 1945, 15:1.

41. Kesselman, *The Social Politics of FEPC,* 117, f.n. 9.

42. W. R. Thomas, "Problems Under FEPC," *Personnel Journal,* XXX (May, 1951), 14–18.

43. U.S. Congress, Senate, Subcommittee of the Committee on Labor and Public Welfare, Hearings, *Anti-discrimination in Employment: Hearings,* 80 Cong., 1st Sess., June 11-July 18, 1947, testimony of F. A. Virkus, representing the Conference of American Small Business Organizations, 792–793.

44. U.S. Congress, House, Committee on Education and Labor, *Hearings, to Prohibit Discrimination in Employment,* 81 Cong., 1st Sess., May 10-26, 1949, testimony of H. McAllister Griffith, vice president, National Economic Council, 570.

45. Donald R. Richberg, "Fair Employment Practices Scheme," *Public Utilities Fortnightly,* XLI (Apr. 22, 1948), 541–542.

46. Senate, Subcommittee of the Committee on Labor, *Anti-discrimination,* 1947, testimony of Charles Hollman, district governor, Employment Agencies Protective Association, 550, emphasis added.

47. L. M. Evans, "Freedom or Regimentation: Fair Employment Practices Act," *Vital Speeches,* XIII (June 15, 1947), 541–543.

48. Senate, Subcommittee of the Committee on Labor, *Anti-discrimination,* 1947, testimony of Mrs. Edwin Selvin, chairman, Women of the Pacific, 780.

49. House, Committee on Education, *Hearings,* 1949, testimony of Griffith, 568.

50. Senate, Subcommittee of the Committee on Labor, *Anti-discrimination,* 1947, testimony of Tyre Taylor, general council, Southern States Industrial Council, 754.

51. *New York Times*, Feb. 12, 1945, 32:1.

52. George H. Fisher, "Fair Employment Practice," *Manufacturers Record* (Jan., 1946), 120.

53. Senate, Subcommittee of the Committee on Labor, *Anti-discrimination,* testimony of Taylor, 754.

54. R. Van Nostrand, "Against FEPC," *Personnel Journal,* XXX (Apr., 1952), 427.

55. For example see J. H. Burma, "Can FEPC Work?", *American Mercury,* LXX (June, 1950), 657; A. Forster, "In Favor of FEPC," *Personnel Journal,* XXX (Jan., 1952), 298–303.

56. Ross, *Modern Industry* (Apr., 1945), 122; Forster, *Personnel Journal* (Jan., 1952), 299.

57. Ross, *Modern Industry* (Apr., 1945), 122; Burma, *American Mercury* (June, 1950), 657–658.

58. *Ibid.,* 659–660; *Special Report on Employment Opportunities in Illinois* (n.p.: Illinois Interracial Commission, 1948), 97–98.

59. Forster, *Personnel Journal* (Jan., 1952), 303.

Chapter 3

1. A. A. Liveright, "The Community and Race Relations," *The Annals of the American Academy of Political and Social Science,* CCXLIV (Mar., 1946), 106–110.

2. Interview, Columbus, Ohio, Sept. 4, 1952, American Friends Service Committee archives (AFSC), Columbus Visits Book, a-h.

3. "Attack on Bias," *Business Week* (April 30, 1949), 106.

4.   J. A. Davis, "Negro Employment: A Progress Report," *Fortune*, XLVI (July, 1952), 103.

5.   *Ibid.*

6.   Davis, *Fortune* (July, 1952), 103; private sources suggest that total expenditure may have been as high as $80,000 but there is no indication how this figure was arrived at, interview, n.p., June 2, 1950, AFSC, Community Relations Visits Book, 1950–1951.

7.   "Attack on Bias," *Business Week* (Apr. 30, 1949), 106–108; J. J. Bambrick and Harold Stieflitz, "Negro Hiring: Some Case Studies," *Conference Board Management Record*, XI (Dec., 1949), 520 ff.

8.   "Bias Issue Persists," *Business Week* (Sept. 3, 1949), 81.

9.   *Cleveland Press*, Jan. 31, 1950, quoted in U.S. Congress, House, Committee on Labor, Hearings, *Discrimination and Full Utilization of Manpower Resources*, 82 Cong., 2nd Sess., Apr. 7-May 6, 1952, testimony of Frank W. Baldau, executive director, Community Relations Board, Cleveland, Ohio, 199.

10.   Davis, *Fortune* (July, 1952), 103, 158.

11.   Quoted in House, Committee on Labor, *Discrimination*, 1952, testimony of Baldau, 206.

12.   *Ibid.*, 202–203; H. R. Northrup, "Progress Without Federal Compulsion," *Commentary*, XIV (Sept., 1952), 211.

13.   Malcolm H. Ross, *All Manner of Men* (New York: Reynal and Hitchcock, 1948), 172.

14.   St. Clair Drake and Horace R. Cayton, *Black Metropolis*, Vol. I (New York: Harper and Row, Torchbook Edition, 1945), xliv-xlv.

15.   Interview, Apr. 19, 1950, AFSC, Job Opportunities Program (JOP), Chicago.

16.   Interview, Apr. 7, 1950, AFSC, JOP, Chicago; interview, Apr. 14, 1950, AFSC, JOP, Chicago; interview, June 1, 1950, AFSC, JOP, Chicago.

17.   Interview, May 24, 1950, AFSC, JOP, Chicago; interview, Apr. 19, 1950, AFSC, JOP, Chicago.

18.   Interview, Aug. 1, 1950, AFSC, JOP, Chicago.

19.   Ibid.; "It's Good Business," *Business Week* (Mar. 31, 1951), 39–40.

20.   *Ibid.*, 39.

21.   Interview, Oct. 5, 1950, AFSC, JOP, Chicago.

22.   Ibid.; "It's Good Business," *Business Week* (Mar. 31, 1951), 39.

23.   Northrup, *Commentary* (Sept., 1952), 211; W. C. Leland, Jr., "We Believe in Employment on Merit, but—," *Minnesota Law Review*, XXXVII (Mar., 1953), 266.

24.   Interview, New York, Aug. 3, 1954, AFSC, Letter Book, Community Relations, a-z.

25.   Script for the television show, "You Be the Judge," shown on WFBN-TV, Indiapanolis, July 18, 1952, comments of William Bok, AFSC, Indianapolis Visits Book, a-l.

26.   *New York Times*, June 16, 1956, 8:3.

27.   Earl Conrad, "Exploring Jobs in the News Field," *Opportunity*, XXIV (April, 1946), 64–65.

28.   "Jobs Becoming More Available for Negro Grads," *Editor and Publisher*, LXXXII (July 2, 1949), 35.

29.   Conrad, *Opportunity* (April, 1946), 64.

30.   Henry G. Stetler, *Minority Group Integration by Labor and Management* (Hartford: Connecticut Commission on Civil Rights, 1953), 35.

31.   Theodore F. Malm, "Hiring Procedures and Selection Standards in the San Francisco Bay Area," *Industrial and Labor Relations Review* (Jan., 1955), 246.

32.   Irving Babow and Edward Howden, *A Civil Rights Inventory of San Francisco: Part I, Employment* (San Francisco: Council for Civic Unity, 1958), 21-29.

33.   U.S. Commission on Civil Rights, *The 50 States Reports* (Washington: GPO, 1961), 302-307.

34.   *New York Times*, May 20, 1948, 25:3.

35.   U.S. Congress, House, Committee on Education and Labor, Special Subcommittee on Labor, Hearings, *Equal Employment Opportunity*, 87 Cong., 1st and 2nd Sess., Oct. 23, 1961-Jan. 24, 1962, Appendix G, "Clerical Hiring by the Illinois Bell Telephone Company," Federation of Telephone Clerks of Illinois.

36.   *New York Times*, Feb. 5, 1952, 18:6.

37.   Donald Dewey, "Four Studies of Negro Employment in the Upper South," in National Planning Association, Committee of the South, *Selected Studies of Negro Employment in the South* (Washington: National Planning Association, 1955), 205-207; Langston T. Hawley, "Negro Employment in the Birmingham Metropolitan Area," in *ibid.*, 280-281.

38.   Paul H. Norgren and Samuel E. Hill, *Toward Fair Employment* (New York: Columbia University Press, 1964), 24-27.

39.   Marjorie Greene, "Fair Employment is Good Business at G. Fox of Hartford," *Opportunity*, XXVI (Apr., 1948), 58.

40.   *Women's Wear Daily*, Mar. 14, 1946, 54:1

41.   Gerhart Saenger and Emily Gilbert, "Customer Reactions to the Integration of Negro Sales Personnel," *International Journal of Attitude and Opinion Research*, IV (Spring, 1950), 57-76.

42.   Interview, Boston, June 23, 1950, AFSC, Community Relations Visits Book, 1950-1951.

43.   Robert O. Blood, Jr., *Northern Breakthrough* (Belmont, Cal.: Wadsworth Publishing Co., 1968), 7.

44.   Interview [Philadelphia], Jan. 15, 1946, Committee on Racial Equality, Committee on Fair Employment in Department Stores, AFSC, Race Relations File, 1946.

45.   Frank Loescher, memo: fair employment in department stores, May 3, 1946, AFSC, Race Relations File.

46.   Interview, Philadelphia, Oct. 15, 1946, AFSC, Interview Book.

47.   *New York Times*, Mar. 12, 1948, 48:1.

48.   Interview, Apr. 7, 1954, Chester Pa., AFSC, Philadelphia and Area Visits from 1954.

49.   In 1953 and 1954 Wilmington stores were still not serving Negroes in their dining rooms and cafeterias; interview, Wilmington, Nov. 4, 1953, AFSC, Letter Book, Community Relations, a-z; interview [Wilmington], Apr. 20, 1954, AFSC, Philadelphia Visits Book.

50.   Interview, Feb. 15, 1955, AFSC, Greensboro Visits Book, 1954-1957.

51.   Interview, May 25, 1950, AFSC, JOP, Chicago.

52.   Interview, May 1, 1950, AFSC, JOP, Chicago.

53.   Interview, May 17, 1950, AFSC, JOP, Chicago; interview, May 21, 1950, AFSC, JOP, Chicago.

54.   Drake and Cayton, *Black Metropolis*, 102.

55.   Interview, May 5, 1950, AFSC, JOP, Chicago; interview, Jan. 26, 1950, AFSC, JOP, Chicago.

56.   Interview, Jan. 31, 1953, AFSC, JOP, Chicago.

57.   Memo, May 10, 1951, AFSC, JOP, Chicago; "memo: material for the NAIRO conference," Oct. 20, 1952, AFSC, JOP, Chicago.

58.   Letter, July 1, 1950, AFSC, JOP, Chicago; summary version of this material can be found in Stephen Habbe, ed., *Company Experience with Negro Employment, Studies in Personnel Policy*, No. 201, Vol. I (New York: National Industrial Conference Board, 1966), 94.

59.   Interview, Feb. 23, 1955, AFSC, JOP, Chicago; interview, Nov. 3, 1950, AFSC, Employment on Merit (EOM), Chicago.

60.   Interview, Nov. 1, 1950, AFSC, JOP, Chicago; interview, Nov. 3, 1950, AFSC, JOP, Chicago.

61.   Interview, June 7, 1954, AFSC, JOP, Chicago; interview, Oct. 4, 1954, AFSC, JOP, Chicago; interview, Oct. 20, 1954, AFSC, JOP, Chicago.

62.   Interview, Jan. 24, 1951, AFSC, JOP, Chicago; interview, Nov. 10, 1950, AFSC, JOP, Chicago.

63.   "An Outline of the Job Opportunities Program of AFSC in Chicago as of November 15, 1950," AFSC, JOP, Chicago.

64.   Interview, Jan. 3, 1953, AFSC, EOM, Chicago.

65.   Interview, Sept. 13, 1950, AFSC, JOP, Chicago.

66.   Interview, Dec. 7, 1950, AFSC, JOP, Chicago.

67.   Interview, Apr. 28, 1950, AFSC, JOP, Chicago; interview May 4, 1950, AFSC, JOP, Chicago.

68.   Interview, May 23, 1950, AFSC, JOP, Chicago.

69.   Interview, April 24, 1952, AFSC, JOP, Chicago.

70.   Interview [fall, 1952], AFSC, JOP, Chicago; interview, Dec. 31, 1952, AFSC, JOP, Chicago; interview, Nov. 11, 1952, AFSC, JOP, Chicago.

71.   Interview, Feb. 24, 1953, AFSC, JOP, Chicago.

72.   "Progress on State Street," *Time*, LXII (Sept. 14, 1953), 25.

73.   Interview, June 4, 1952, AFSC, JOP, Chicago; interview, Dec. 19, 1955, AFSC, JOP, Chicago; President's Committee on Government Contracts, *Youth Training— Incentives Conference Proceedings* (Washington: GPO, 1957), remarks by Thomas H. Coulter, 44-49.

74.   Percy H. Williams, "Annual Report, Job Opportunities Program, draft copy." Mar., 1957, AFSC, JOP, Chicago.

Chapter 4

1.   Interview, Chicago, Dec. 20, 1955, American Friends Service Committee (AFSC) archives, Job Opportunities Program (JOP), Chicago.

2.   U.S. Congress, Senate, Subcommittee of the Committee on Labor and Public Welfare, Hearings, *Anti-discrimination in Employment: Hearings*, 80 Cong., 1st Sess., June 11-July 18, 1947, 604-606.

3.   Everett C. Hughes, "Race Relations in Industry," in William Foote Whyte, ed., *Industry and Society* (New York: McGraw Hill, 1946), 118.

4.   Dwight D. Vines, "The Impact of Title VII of the 1964 Civil Rights Law on Personnel Policies and Practices," (D.B.A. diss., University of Colorado, 1967), 161.

5.   U.S. Congress, House, Committee on Education and Labor, *Hearings, To Prohibit Discrimination in Employment*, 81 Cong., 1st Sess., May 10-26, 1949, testimony of J. D. Henderson, national managing director, American Association of Small Business in Opposition to HR 4453, 575.

6.   "Memo: Random Observations on Attempts to Obtain Photographs," June 6, 1962, AFSC, Employment on Merit Program (EOM), Atlanta.

7.   Interview, Nov. 3, 1953, AFSC, Indianapolis Visits Book, a-l.

8.   The "rank order" of discrimination which Myrdal discovered in the late 1930's remained virtually unchanged until at least 1960; Gunnar Myrdal, *An American Dilemma* (New York: Harper & Bros., 1944), 60-61; U.S. Commission on Civil Rights, *The 50 States Reports* (Washington: GPO, 1961), 83.

9.   Bernard Rosenberg and Penney Chapin, "Management and Minority Groups," in Aaron Antonovsky and Lewis L. Lorwin, eds., *Discrimination and Low Incomes* (New York: State of New York Interdepartmental Committee on Low Incomes, 1959), 185.

10.   Interview, Feb. 25, 1955, AFSC, JOP, Chicago.

11.   Interview, [early 1960's], AFSC, EOM, Atlanta.

12.   William E. Noland and E. Wight Bakke, *Workers Wanted* (New York: Harper Bros., 1949), 32; Irving Babow and Edward Howden, *A Civil Rights Inventory of San Francisco, Part I, Employment* (San Francisco: Council for Civic Unity, 1958), 107-108.

13.   Interview, Apr. 12, 1955, AFSC, Baton Rouge Visits, 1955.

14.   L. Wilson and H. Gilmore, "White Employers and Negro Workers," *American Sociological Review*, VIII (Dec., 1943) 701.

15.   Interview, Nov. 27, 1962, AFSC, EOM, Atlanta.

16.   Minnesota Governor, *The Negro Worker*, 30; interview, Apr., 1950, AFSC, JOP, Chicago; Frank T. Mohr, "Management Policies and Bi-racial Integration in Industry" (Master's thesis, University of Illinois, Urbana, 1954), 38.

17.   Vines, "The Impact of Title VII," 182-184, 224.

18.   For the war period see Robert C. Weaver, *Negro Labor: A National Problem* (New York: Harcourt, Brace & Co., 1946), 194.

19.   W. C. Leland, Jr., "We Believe in Employment on Merit, But—," *Minnesota Law Review*, XXXVII (March, 1953, 247); Babow and Howden, *A Civil Rights Inventory*, 98-99, 26-28; Frank F. Lee, *Negro and White in Connecticut Town* (New York: Bookman Associates, 1961), 89.

20.   Robert O. Blood, Jr., *Northern Breakthrough* (Belmont, Cal.: Wadsworth Publishing Co., 1968), 42-46.

21.   Interview, July 13, 1955, AFSC, Greensboro Visits, 1954-1957.

22.   Interview, Jan. 29, 1952, AFSC, JOP, Chicago.

23.   "Memo: Random Observations on Attempts to Obtain Photographs," June 6, 1962, AFSC, EOM, Atlanta.

24.   Vines, "The Impact of Title VII," 170.

25.   "Memo: re JOP," Indianapolis, May 16, 1952, AFSC, Race Relations File, 1952; Interview, High Point, N.C., Dec., 1955, Greensboro Visits Book, 1954-1957, j-z.

26.   Interview, Danville, N.C., Dec. 14, 1956, AFSC, Greensboro Visits Book, 1954-1957, a-m.

27.   L. M. Killian, "Effects of Southern White Workers on Race Relations," *American Sociological Review*, XXVI (June, 1952), 327-331; B. A. Reed, "Accommodation between Negro and White Employees in a West Coast Aircraft Industry," *Social Forces*, XXVI (Oct., 1947), 76-87; E. B. Palmore, "The Introduction of Negroes into White Departments," *Human Organization* (Spring, 1955), 27.

28.   Interview, Oct. 7, 1952, AFSC, Dallas Visits Book, m-z; Sara E. Southall, *Industry's Unfinished Business* (New York: Harper, 1950), 92-93.

29.   Interview, Oct. 29, 1953, AFSC, Dallas Visits Book, m-z.

30.   Interview, Feb. 7, 1954, AFSC, Dallas Visits Book, 1954-1956.

31.   Louis Ruchames, *Race, Jobs, and Politics* (New York: Columbia University Press, 1953), 40-41.

32.   Weaver, *Negro Labor*, 205.

33.   *Ibid.*, 201.

34.   Interview, Dec. 7, 1954, AFSC, JOP, Chicago; interview, Dec. 15, 1954, AFSC, JOP, Chicago; interview, Feb. 15, 1955, AFSC, JOP, Chicago; interview, Sept. 27, 1955, AFSC, JOP, Chicago.

35.   John S. Ellsworth, Jr., *Factory Folkways* (New Haven: Yale University Press, 1952), 204.

36.   Frank T. Mohr, "Management Policies and Biracial Integration in Industry" (Master's thesis, University of Illinois, 1954), 57-63.

37.   *Wall Street Journal*, Apr. 3, 1956, 1.

38.   "Memo to G. L. Bergen, 'Hypothetical Program'," Nov. 24, 1950, AFSC, American Section, Race Relations, 1950.

39.   Vines, "The Impact of Title VII," 93.

40.   Interview, Feb. 9, 1955, AFSC, Dallas Visits Book, 1954-1956.

41.   Interview, Mar. 10, 1953, AFSC, Indianapolis Visits Book, m-z; interview, Raleigh, N.C., Apr. 14, 1954, AFSC, Greensboro Visits Book, 1954, j-z.

42.   Langston T. Hawley, "Negro Employment in the Birmingham Metropolitan Area," in National Planning Association, Committee of the South, *Selected Studies of Negro Employment in the South* (Washington: National Planning Association, 1955), 271.

43. William H. Wesson, Jr., "Negro Employment Practices in the Chattanooga Area," in *ibid.*, 411.

44. Interview, March 10, 1954; July 24, 1957, AFSC, Greensboro Visits Book, 1954-1957, a-m.

45. Interview, Sept. 20, 1955, AFSC, JOP, Chicago.

46. Interview, Oct. 28, 1952, AFSC, Dallas Visits Book, m-z.

47. Interview, Apr. 10, 1953, AFSC, Dallas Visits Book, m-z.

48. Interview, Jan. 8, 1962, AFSC, EOM, Atlanta.

49. *RWDSU Record* [Retail, Wholesale and Department Store Union], June 2, 1963, 7:1.

50. *Ibid.*, April 6, 1964, 7:3.

51. For examples see Richard L. Rowan, "Negro Employment in Birmingham: Three Cases," in Arthur M. Ross and Herbert Hill, eds., *Employment, Race and Poverty* (New York: Harcourt, Brace & World, 1967), 318, 324, 331; Theodore W. Kheel, *Guide to Fair Employment Practices* (Englewood Cliffs, New Jersey: Prentice Hall, 1964), 85, 93-94; Stephen Habbe, ed., *Company Experience with Negro Employment, Studies in Personnel Policy*, No. 201, Vol. I, (New York: National Industrial Conference Board, 1966), 74-75, 116-117; *ibid.*, Vol. II, 106-107, 117.

52. Interview, Jan. 4, 1962, AFSC, EOM, Atlanta.

53. George F. Doriot, ed., *The Management of Racial Integration in Business* (New York: McGraw Hill, 1964), 77.

54. W. N. Rozelle, "How is the Negro Faring?", *Textile Industries*, CXXI (Mar., 1967), 80-81; Herbert R. Northrup, *The Negro in the Rubber Tire Industry* (Philadelphia: Industrial Research Unit, Department of Industry, Wharton School of Finance and Commerce, University of Pennsylvania, 1969), 118.

55. Interview, Dec. 31, 1952, AFSC, Greensboro Visits Book.

56. Interview, May 5, 1964, AFSC, EOM, Atlanta.

57. Gunnar Myrdal, *An American Dilemma* (New York: Harper & Bros., 1944), 60-61; U.S. Commission on Civil Rights, *The 50 States Reports*, 83.

58. Henry G. Stetler, *Minority Group Integration by Labor and Management* (Hartford: Connecticut Commission on Civil Rights, 1953), 25.

59. Mohr, "Management Policies," 66-67.

60. William L. Crump, "A Study of the Employment Problems of Negro Office Workers in Integrated and Segregated Work Programs with Implications for Business Education" (Ph.D. diss., Northwestern University, 1949), 208-209.

61. Rosenberg and Chapin, "Management," in Antonovsky, *Discrimination*, 166.

62. Interview, May 26, 1953, AFSC, Greensboro Visits Book; interview, Nov. 12, 1954, AFSC, Dallas Visits Book, 1954-1956.

63. Habbe, *Company Experience*, Vol. I, 49-50; *ibid.*, Vol. II, 112-113.

64. *Ibid.*, Vol. I, 50; "Integration in Industry; Special Report," *Factory*, CXXII (Dec., 1964), 50; interview, Aug. 24, 1964, AFSC, EOM, Atlanta; "Memo: Highlights, Augusta Trip," Dec. 12, 1963, AFSC, EOM, Atlanta.

Chapter 5

1. Seymour Spilerman, "The Distribution of Negro Males Among Industries in 1960" (Ph.D. diss., The Johns Hopkins University, 1968), 149.

2. *Ibid.*, 149-152.

3. Interview, Feb. 25, 1963, American Friends Service Committee (AFSC), Employment on Merit Program (EOM), Atlanta.

4. Roi Ottley, *New World A-Coming: Inside Black America* (Boston: Houghton Mifflin, 1943), 113-121.

5. Interview, June 5, 1953, AFSC, Greensboro Visits Book.

6. Interview, Sept. 26, 1955, AFSC, Job Opportunities Program (JOP), Chicago.

7. Interview, July 17, 1962, AFSC, EOM, Atlanta.

8.   See Chapter III, 60-61; P. H. Norgren, et al., *Employing the Negro in American Industry* (New York: Industrial Relations Counselors, Inc., 1964), 41-42; U.S. Commission on Civil Rights, District of Columbia Advisory Commission, *Report on Washington, D.C.: Employment* (Washington: GPO, July, 1963), 29.

9.   Interview, Oct. 28, 1955, AFSC, JOP, Chicago.

10.   D. J. Sullivan, "Why Change the Rules When You Hire Negro Salesmen?", *Sales Management,* LXXI (Nov. 10, 1953), 158-160.

11.   J. Robinson, "American Enterprise and the Racial Crisis," *Sales Management,* XCI (Aug. 16, 1963), 34; cf. *ibid.,* 37.

12.   Interview, Oct. 20, 1952, AFSC, JOP, Chicago.

13.   Interview, Columbia, S.C., n.d., AFSC, Greensboro Visits Book, 1954-1957.

14.   Interview, Aug. 7, 1954, AFSC, JOP, Chicago.

15.   Interview, Feb. 27, 1952, Atlanta, Ga., AFSC, Letter Book, Community Relations, a-z.

16.   Gerhart Saenger and Emily Gilbert, "Customer Reactions to the Integration of Negro Sales Personnel," *International Journal of Attitudes and Opinion Research,* IV (Spring, 1950), 57-76; Robert O. Blood, Jr., *Northern Breakthrough* (Belmont, Cal.: Wadsworth Publishing Co., 1968), 56-60.

17.   Interview, Aug. 31, 1962, AFSC, EOM, Atlanta.

18.   Interview, Jan. 6, 1962, AFSC, EOM, Atlanta; interview June 16, 1962, AFSC, EOM, Atlanta.

19.   "Symposium on Automation, Manpower and Merit," Apr. 2, 1964, AFSC, EOM, Atlanta.

20.   Interview, Mar. 14, 1963, AFSC, EOM, Atlanta.

21.   A. J. Vogel, "Negroes on the Sales Force: The Quiet Integration," *Sales Management,* XCIII (Oct. 16, 1964), 25-28; Stephen Habbe, ed., *Company Experience with Negro Employment, Studies in Personnel Policy,* No. 201, Vol. I (New York: National Industrial Conference Board, 1966), 110-113.

22.   Richard L. Rowan, *The Negro in the Steel Industry,* Report No. 3, *The Racial Policies of American Industry* (Philadelphia: Industrial Research Unit, Department of Industry, Wharton School of Finance and Commerce, University of Pennsylvania, 1968), 63.

23.   Governor's Advisory Commission on Industrial Race Relations, *Employment Practices in Pennsylvania* (Harrisburg, 1953), 23-26; Dwight D. Vines, "The Impact of Title VII of the 1964 Civil Rights Law on Personnel Policies and Practices" (D.B.A. diss., University of Colorado, 1967), 170.

24.   Interview, May 18, 1950, AFSC, JOP, Chicago.

25.   Interview, Mar. 13, 1952, AFSC, Letter Book, Community Relations, a-z.

26.   Interview, Feb. 4, 1953, AFSC, Indianapolis Visits Book, a-l.

27.   Interview, Sept. 15, 1953, AFSC, Columbus Visits Book, a-h.

28.   Norgren, *Employing the Negro,* 53-54.

29.   Major J. Jones, *The Negro and Employment Opportunities in the South: Chattanooga* (Atlanta: Southern Regional Council, 1961), 6-7; Langston T. Hawley, "Negro Employment in the Birmingham Metropolitan Area," in National Planning Association, Committee of the South, *Selected Studies of Negro Employment in the South* (Washington: National Planning Association, 1955), 282; Art Gallaher, Jr., *The Negro and Employment Opportunities in the South—Houston* (Atlanta, Ga.: Southern Regional Council, 1961), 22; Jack Gourlay, *The Negro Salaried Worker,* AMA Research Study, No. 70 (New York: The American Management Association, 1965), 14-15; Theodore W. Kheel, *Guide to Fair Employment* (Englewood Cliffs, N.J.: Prentice Hall, 1964), 73.

30.   Interview, Feb. 17, 1954, AFSC, Greensboro Visits Book, 1954-1957, j-z.

31.   Governor's Advisory Commission, *Employment in Pennsylvania,* appendix table no. 6, n.p.

32.   Interview, Dec. 8, 1952, AFSC, Indianapolis Visits, a-l.

33.   Norgren, *Employing the Negro,* 42-44.

34. U.S. Congress, Senate, Committee on Labor and Public Welfare, Subcommitte on Employment and Manpower, Hearings, *Equal Employment Opportunity,* 88 Cong., 1st Sess., July 24-Aug. 20, 1963, statement of Joseph Ross, president, Davidson Bros., Inc., Detroit, Mich., 315.

35. Interview, Dec. 18, 1953, AFSC, Indianapolis Visits, a-l.

36. Frank T. Mohr, "Management Policies and Biracial Integration in Industry" (Master's thesis, University of Illinois, Urbana, 1954), 38.

37. Interview, Sept. 24, 1953, AFSC, Philadelphia Visits Book.

38. Interview, Mar. 16, 1952, AFSC, JOP, Chicago.

39. *New York Times,* July 20, 1947, 2:2.

40. *Ibid.,* Sept. 18, 1963, 26:1.

41. *Ibid.,* Sept. 24, 1963, 32:3.

42. *Ibid.,* Oct. 1, 1963, 23:3.

43. For a full list of U.S. Steel's good deeds, see Blough's letter, *New York Times,* Nov. 7, 1963, 36:5; but for its shortcomings see "Steel Giants Face a Blast on Bias," *Business Week* (June. 11, 1966), 81; "Negroes Zero in on Steel Industry," *Business Week* (Dec. 10, 1966), 156; *Wall Street Journal,* June 23, 1966, 14; Habbe, *Company Experience,* Vol. II, 83-87.

44. *New York Times,* Oct. 25, 1963, 1:2.

45. *Ibid.,* Oct. 30, 1963, 1:7.

46. *Ibid.,* Nov. 7, 1963, 36:5; Oct. 31, 1963, 32:1; Nov. 1, 1963, 14:5.

47. J. P. Mitchell, "Business and Civil Rights," *Vital Speeches,* XXX (July 1, 1964), 549-551; L. Zimpel, "When Equality is Not Enough," *Christian Century,* LXXXII (Sept. 1, 1965), 1060.

48. "There Isn't Any Time," *Fortune,* LXX (July, 1964), 127-128.

49. Vera Rony, "Bogalusa: The Economics of Tragedy," *Dissent,* XIII (May-June, 1966), 234-237; *New York Times,* Jan. 17, 1965, 88:2.

50. Rony, *Dissent* (May-June, 1966), 234-239.

51. *Ibid.,* 241.

52. *Ibid.,* 242.

53. David G. Wood, "How Businessmen Can Fight Big Government and Win," *Harper's Magazine,* CCXXVII (Nov., 1963), 80.

54. Arthur B. Shostak, "Two Issues of Negro Advancement," in Herbert R. Northrup, ed., *The Negro and Employment Opportunities* (Ann Arbor: Bureau of Industrial Relations, Graduate School of Business Administration, University of Michigan, 1965) 322-324.

55. Elisha Gray, "If not Us, Who, If not Now, When?", a summary of remarks from an address to distributors of Whirlpool home appliances, Sept., 1967.

56. Habbe, *Company Experience,* Vol. I, 105.

57. "Truce in Chicago," *Business Week* (Sept. 3, 1966), 37-38.

58. Charles B. McCoy, "Business and the Community," address to the Governor's Conference on Business and Industry, Wilmington, Del., Apr. 4, 1968.

59. "The Committee Report: The President's Committee on Equal Employment Opportunities," No. 2, May, 1964, U.S. Government nondepository item, 1965-3232.

60. *The Racine Journal Times,* Oct. 10, 1967, 11A:4.

61. Interview, Feb. 17, 1955, AFSC, National Contact folder, 1954-_____.

62. See Chapter I.

63. Governor's Advisory Commission, *Employment Practices in Pennsylvania,* 21; Norgren, *Employing the Negro,* 158.

64. Interview, Dec. 5, 1951, AFSC, JOP, Chicago.

65. Interview, Mar. 25, 1953, AFSC, Columbus Visits Book, a-h.

66. National Association of Intergroup Relations Officials, Committee on Manpower Utilization, "NAIRO Reports on Employment" (1955), 18; Blood, *Northern Breakthrough;* Frank S. Loescher, "Techniques for Democratic Placement," *Occupations,* XXV (May, 1947), 539.

67.   Interview, Feb. 22, 1953, AFSC, Columbus Visits Book, a-h; Special Projects, "Merit Employment Survey, Durham, N.C., 1959," AFSC.

68.   Blood, *Northern Breakthrough*, 108-109.

69.   Interview, Oct. 30, 1951, AFSC, Indianapolis Visits, a-l.

70.   Interview, May 6, 1952, AFSC, Indianapolis Visits, a-l.

71.   Interview, Aug. 14, 1952, AFSC, JOP, Chicago.

72.   Interview, Sept. 3, 1952, AFSC, Indianapolis Visits, a-l.

73.   Interview, Oct. 2, 1952, AFSC, Indianapolis Visits, a-l; interview, Nov. 11, 1952, AFSC, Indianapolis Visits, m-z; interview, Dec. 3, 1952, AFSC, Indianapolis Visits, m-z.

74.   Interview, June 1, 1950, AFSC, JOP, Chicago.

75.   Interview, June 3, 1951, AFSC, JOP, Chicago; interview, Mar. 14, 1953, AFSC, JOP, Chicago; interview April 8, 1952, AFSC, JOP, Chicago.

76.   Interview, July 11, 1952, AFSC, JOP, Chicago.

77.   "Report of Status and Plans to be Submitted to Philadelphia" [1954], AFSC, JOP, Chicago; interview, Nov. 12, 1954, AFSC, JOP, Chicago; interview, Nov. 12, 1954, AFSC, JOP, Chicago.

78.   Letter, June 8, 1955, AFSC, JOP, Chicago; *Wall Street Journal*, Oct. 24, 1957, 14:2.

79.   Interview, Oct. 21, 1955, AFSC, JOP, Chicago.

80.   See Chapter IV.

81.   Interview, Jan. 12, 1956, AFSC, JOP, Chicago.

82.   Memo, Dec. 10, 1957, AFSC, JOP, Chicago.

83.   NAIRO, "1953 Commission Reports," 18.

84.   Interview, Waynesville, N.C., Oct. 27, 1955, AFSC, Greensboro Visits, 1954-1957, j-z; "Discriminatory Employers and Employment in Philadelphia: A Confidential Report," AFSC, American Section, Race Relations File, 1950.

85.   Taylor, "Remarks," U.S. nondepository item 1965-14978.

86.   Habbe, *Company Experience*, Vol. II, 51.

Chapter 6

1.   See Chapter II.

2.   Elaine Pollard, "Add-a-firm: An Illustrative Compilation," American Friends Service Committee (AFSC) archives, Race Relations File, 1948.

3.   Gunnar Myrdal, *An American Dilemma* (New York: Harper & Bros., 1944), 8-12.

4.   Malcolm H. Ross, *All Manner of Men* (New York: Reynal & Hitchcock, 1948), 41.

5.   Robert C. Weaver, *Negro Labor: A National Problem* (New York: Harcourt, Brace & Co., 1946), 206; "Solving Racial Problems in Your Plant," *Management Review*, XXXIV (May, 1945), 177.

6.   See Chapter II.

7.   B. A. Reed, "Accommodation Between Negro and White Employees in a West Coast Aircraft Industry, 1942-1944," *Social Forces*, XXVI (October, 1947), 77.

8.   William F. Rasche, "The Need in Milwaukee for Extending Employment of Negroes" (Milwaukee Employers' Association, 1946, mimeographed), 7.

9.   See Chapter II.

10.   Interview, n.p., April 28, 1952, AFSC, Race Relations File, 1952.

11.   Interview, n.p., May 18, 1950, AFSC, Community Relations Visits Book, 1950-1951.

12.   Stanley H. Smith, *Freedom to Work* (New York: Vantage Press, 1955), 143.

13.   A. Forster, "In Favor of FEPC," *Personnel Journal*, XXX (Jan. 1952), 302-303; Elmo Roper, "The Price Business Pays," in R. M. MacIver, ed., *Discrimination and National Welfare* (New York: Institute for Religious and Social Studies, 1949),

15-16; R. M. McKeon, "Color Bar in U.S. Industry," *America*, XC (March 6, 1954), 595; *New York Times*, June 16, 1956, 8:3; Joseph J. Morrow, "American Negroes— A Wasted Resource," *Harvard Business Review*, XXXV (Jan.-Feb., 1957), 65; F. S. Connell, "Letter to the Editor," *Harvard Business Review*, XXXVII (Jan.-Feb., 1959), 158.

14.   U.S. Commission on Civil Rights, Hearings, Jan. 25-28, 1960 (Washington: GPO, 1960), 403.

15.   Louis A. Ferman, *The Negro and Equal Employment Opportunities* (New York: Frederick A. Praeger, 1968), 64.

16.   Paul H. Norgren et al., *Employing the Negro in American Industry* (New York: Industrial Relations Counselors, Inc., 1964), 38-39.

17.   Robert O. Blood, Jr., *Northern Breakthrough* (Belmont, Cal.: Wadsworth Publishing Co., 1968), 50.

18.   Interview, Apr. 2, 1953, AFSC, Columbus Visits Book, a-h.

19.   Interview, Feb. 16, 1953, AFSC, Greensboro Visits Book.

20.   Interview, Mar. 19, 1956, AFSC, Greensboro Visits, 1954-1957, j-z.

21.   Stephen Habbe, ed., *Company Experience With Negro Employment: Studies in Personnel Policy*, No. 201, Vol. II, 37.

22.   Blood, *Northern Breakthrough*, 80, 94.

23.   U.S. Congress, House, Committee on Education and Labor, General Subcommittee on Labor, Hearings, *Equal Employment Opportunity*, 88 Cong., 1st Sess., Apr. 22-June 6, 1963, testimony of W. E. Pannill of Peoples Drug Stores, 342.

24.   Interview, Jan.-Feb., 1953, AFSC, JOP, Chicago.

25.   Letter, Dec. 13, 1962, AFSC, EOM, Atlanta.

26.   Memo, "Job Opportunities in the Chicago Area," Aug. 29, 1949, AFSC, Race Relations File, 1949.

27.   Interview, May 31, 1955, AFSC, JOP, Chicago.

28.   See Chapters II and III.

29.   Interview, Feb. 2, 1953, AFSC, Columbus Visits Book, a-h.

30.   Interview, Sept. 14, 1954, AFSC, Indianapolis Visits, a-l.

31.   Interview, May 18, 1953, AFSC, Columbus Visits Book, a-h.

32.   Interview, Oct. 28, 1952, AFSC, Columbus Visits Book, a-h.

33.   J. J. Morrow, "Employment on Merit: The Continuing Challenge to Business," *Management Review*, XLVI (Feb., 1957), 10.

34.   Interview, Aug. 5, 1952, AFSC, Indianapolis Visits, a-l.

35.   Interview, Nov. 3, 1955, AFSC, Dallas Visits, 1954-1956.

36.   Interview, Oct. 15, 1954, AFSC, Dallas Visits, 1954-1956.

37.   Interview, June 24, 1952, AFSC, Indianapolis Visits, a-l; interview, Mar. 4, 1953, AFSC, Indianapolis Visits, m-z; Bernard Rosenberg and Penney Chapin, "Management and Minority Groups," in Aaron Antonovsky and Lewis L. Lorwin, eds., *Discrimination and Low Incomes* (New York: State of New York Interdepartmental Committee on Low Incomes, 1959), 192; John J. Millia, "Comments to Rhode Island Council for Equal Employment Opportunity," April 29, 1965, mimeographed.

38.   Interview, Jan. 13, 1965, AFSC, Greensboro Visits, 1954-1957, a-m.

39.   Interview, Dec. 23, 1954, AFSC, JOP, Chicago.

40.   Interview, Boston, June 23, 1950, AFSC, Community Relations Visits Book, 1950-1951.

41.   Blood, *Northern Breakthrough*, 85.

42.   *New York Times*, Dec. 19, 1963, 49:2.

43.   Letter, Oct. 29, 1964, AFSC, EOM, Atlanta.

44.   Interview, Mar. 19, 1953, Dec. 15, 1953, AFSC, Greensboro Visits, 1954-1957, j-z; interview, Mar. 2, 1954, AFSC, Greensboro Visits, 1954-1957, j-z.

45.   C. A. Wood, "Putting Negroes on a Job Equality Basis; Pollack Manufacturing Co., Arlington, New Jersey," *Factory Management and Maintenance*, CIII (Oct., 1945), 131.

46. Jack Gourlay, *The Negro Salaried Worker* (New York: American Management Association, AMA Research Study No. 70, 1965), 49.

47. Interview, Sept. 15, 1955, AFSC, JOP, Chicago.

48. Interview, 1953, AFSC, Indianapolis Visits Book, m-z.

49. Interview, April 29, 1955, AFSC, JOP, Chicago.

50. Interview, Oct. 29, 1954, AFSC, JOP, Chicago; interview, May 15, 1963, AFSC, Community Relations Development, Houston, 1963.

51. Myrdal, *American Dilemma*, 1023.

52. *Ibid.*, 383.

53. Frank S. Loescher, "The Placement Service of the American Friends Service Committee," *Occupations*, XXV (Nov., 1946), 92-93.

54. Ralph A. Rose, "Remarks to National Conference of Social Work," Atlantic City, N.J., Apr. 25, 1950, AFSC.

55. Wood, *Factory Management and Maintenance* (Oct., 1945), 133.

56. Ross, *All Manner of Men*, 72-79; interview with Dwight R. G. Palmer, Short Hills, N.J., Dec. 20, 1967.

57. Ross, *All Manner of Men*, 302-303.

58. Interview with Dwight R. G. Palmer, Dec. 20, 1967.

59. Dwight R. G. Palmer, "Address to Canadian Council of Christians and Jews, Board of Directors Meeting," Toronto, Oct. 4, 1951.

60. *Ibid.*

61. *Ibid.*

62. Dwight R. G. Palmer, "Cyrus Fogg Brackett Lecture," Princeton University, Dec. 7, 1949.

63. "Labor and Management Fight Prejudice; Perth Amboy Plant of General Cable Corp.," *Factory Management and Maintenance*, CVII (Aug., 1949), 120-121; "Getting Rid of Prejudice; General Cable Corporation," *Business Week* (July 23, 1949), 72-73; "Fight on Intolerance Eases Management's Load," *Printer's Ink*, CCXXIX (July 29, 1949), 31; *New York Times*, July 14, 1949, 29:8.

64. Dwight R. G. Palmer, "Address to Canadian Council."

65. Rosenberg and Chapin, "Management," in Antonovsky, *Discrimination*, 194.

Chapter 7

1. See Chapter I.

2. John J. Millia, Personnel Director, Narragansett Electric Company, "Comments to Rhode Island Council for Equal Employment Opportunity Conference," n.p., April 29, 1965.

3. Robert Ozanne, *A Century of Labor-Management Relations at McCormick and International Harvester* (Madison, Wis.: University of Wisconsin Press, 1967), 183-184.

4. *Ibid.*, 186-188.

5. Interview, Apr. 11, 1950, American Friends Service Committee (AFSC) archives, Job Opportunities Program (JOP), Chicago.

6. Fowler McCormick, "Forward," in Sara Southall, *Industry's Unfinished Business* (New York: Harper, 1950) xi.

7. *New York Times*, July 20, 1947, 2:2.

8. "Through the Color Barrier," *Time*, LXIII (Mar. 22, 1954), 104.

9. Southall, *Industry's Unfinished Business*, 108.

10. *New York Times*, July 20, 1947, 2:2.

11. *Time*, (Mar. 22, 1954), 104.

12. *New York Times*, Nov. 16, 1951, 18:3.

13. Southall, *Industry's Unfinished Business*, 108.

14.   U.S. Congress, House, Committee on Labor, Hearings, *Discrimination and Full Utilization of Manpower Resources,* 82 Cong., 2nd Sess., Apr. 7-May 6, 1952, 93.

15.   *Ibid.,* 15.

16.   Harry C. Baker, "A Voluntary Approach to Equal Opportunity," in Herbert R. Northrup, ed., *The Negro and Employment Opportunities* (Ann Arbor: Bureau of Industrial Relations, Graduate School of Business Administration, University of Michigan, 1965), 119.

17.   Interview, Oct. 4, 1954, AFSC, JOP, Chicago; Governor's Commission on the Los Angeles Riots, *Testimony,* Vol. XII, testimony of H. C. McClellan, Los Angeles, Nov. 1, 1965, 38-9.

18.   Dale L. Hiestand, *Economic Growth and Employment Opportunities for Minorities* (New York: Columbia University Press, 1964), 117.

19.   Herbert R. Northrup, *The Negro in the Automobile Industry,* Report No. 1, *The Racial Policies of American Industry* (Philadelphia: Industrial Research Unit, Department of Industry, Wharton School of Finance and Commerce, University of Pennsylvania, 1968), 58-59.

20.   Robert C. Weaver, *Negro Labor, A National Problem* (New York: Harcourt, Brace & Co., 1946), table 2.

21.   L. Wilson and H. Gilmore, "White Employers and Negro Workers," *American Sociological Review,* VIII (Dec., 1943), 699.

22.   Langston T. Hawley, "Negro Employment in the Birmingham Metropolitan Area," in National Planning Association, Committee of the South, *Selected Studies of Negro Employment in the South* (Washington: National Planning Association, 1955), 267; T. C. McCormick and R. A. Hornseth, "Negro in Madison, Wisconsin," *American Sociological Review,* XII (Oct., 1947), 521, f.n. 4.

23.   Interview, Grand Prairie, Tex., Mar. 3, 1952, AFSC, Dallas Visits Book, a-l.

24.   Interview, Oct. 24, 1952, AFSC, Columbus Visits Book, a-h.

25.   "Hiring Minorities," *Modern Industry* (Jan. 15, 1952), 59.

26.   Interview, Mar. 13, 1953, AFSC, Philadelphia Visits Book.

27.   Arthur A. Chapin, "Address to Conference on Social Welfare," Minneapolis, May 16, 1961, U.S. Government nondepository item 1961-9392.

28.   W. N. Rozelle, "How is the Negro Faring?" *Textile Industries,* CXXXI (Mar., 1967), 81.

29.   "Quakers, Negroes and Jobs," (typewritten report [1951]), AFSC, JOP, Chicago.

30.   Interview, summer, 1952, AFSC, JOP, Chicago.

31.   Southall, *Industry's Unfinished Business,* 136.

32.   Interview, Nov. 19, 1953, AFSC, Letter Book, Community Relations, a-z.

33.   Thomas F. Hilbert, Jr., "An Industry Review," in National Association of Manufacturers, *A Tale of 22 Cities* (New York: NAM, 1964), 48.

34.   Millia, "Comments to Rhode Island Council," Apr. 29, 1965.

35.   Interview, New York City, Jan. 9, 1952, AFSC, Letter Book, Community Relations, a-z; interview, Nov. 5, 1952, AFSC, Letter Book, Community Relations, a-z.

36.   Elmo Roper, "The Price Business Pays," in R. M. McIver, ed., *Discrimination and National Welfare* (New York: Institute for Religious and Social Studies, 1949), 16-24.

37.   *New York Times,* Sept. 11, 1958, 23:1.

38.   *Ibid.,* Apr. 1, 1950, 17:8; "Equal Employment Opportunity: Company Policies and Experience," *Management Review,* LIII (Apr., 1964), 6; John D. Harper, "Remarks to Meeting of Officers of 62 Companies," White House, Jan. 16, 1964, U.S. Government nondepository item, 1965-3509; G. J. McManus, "How Industry Views Integration," *Iron Age,* CXCIII (Feb. 27, 1964), 45; J. J. Morrow, "Employment on Merit," *Management Review,* XLVI (Feb., 1957), 9; Joseph J. Morrow, "American Negroes—A Wasted Resource," *Harvard Business Review,* XXXV (Jan.-Feb., 1957), 65-66; Howard J. Samuels, "Industry's Stake in Erasing Poverty," *American Child,* XLVI (Mar., 1964), 19; C. W. V. Meares, "Is Equal Opportunity Good Business?", *Best's Insurance News (Life Edition)* LXCII (Sept., 1966), 66.

39. Roper, "The Price," 22; Morrow, *Management Review* (Feb., 1957), 8.

40. "The Equal Opportunity Employer" (Baltimore: Voluntary Council on Equal Opportunity, Apr., 1966, mimeographed), 3.

41. Interview, Apr. 30, 1962, AFSC, EOM, Atlanta.

42. Paul H. Norgren, et al., *Employing the Negro in American Industry* (New York: Industrial Relations Counselors, Inc., 1964), 37.

43. Interview, Boston, Sept. 8, 1953, AFSC, Letter Book, Community Relations, a-z.

44. Interview, New York City, Feb. 11, 1953, AFSC, Letter Book, Community Relations, a-z.

45. Paul H. Norgren and Samuel E. Hill, *Toward Fair Employment* (New York: Columbia University Press, 1964), 119.

46. Norgren, *Toward Fair Employment,* 118-130; U.S. Congress, House, Committee on Education and Labor, Special Subcommittee on Labor, *Equal Employment Opportunity,* 87 Cong., 1st and 2nd Sess., Oct. 23, 1961-Jan. 24, 1962, 491-494; Stanley H. Smith, *Freedom to Work* (New York: Vantage Press, 1955), 177-179; Robert O. Blood, Jr., *Northern Breakthrough* (Belmont, Cal.: Wadsworth Publishing Co., 1968), 102-107, 112-116.

47. Colorado, Indiana, and Wisconsin had nonenforcable laws. *A Brief Summary of State Laws Against Discrimination in Employment: Fair Employment Practice Acts* (Washington: GPO, 1964).

48. U.S. Commission on Civil Rights, *Report, 1961,* Book 3, *Employment* (Washington: GPO, 1961), 12-14.

49. Hodding Carter, "Eisenhower's Program for Economic Equality," *Reader's Digest,* LXIX (Sept., 1956), 74.

50. U.S. Commission on Civil Rights, *Report, 1961,* 57.

51. "Drive on Bias Moves Into New Spotlight," *Business Week* (Oct. 29, 1955), 162.

52. U.S. Commission on Civil Rights, *Report, 1961,* 58.

53. U.S. President's Commission on Government Contracts, *Pattern for Progress: Final Report to President Eisenhower* (Washington: GPO, 1960), 4-5; E. Kemler, "Nixon's FEPC," *Nation,* CLXXXI (Nov. 5, 1955), 375.

54. U.S. President's Commission on Government Contracts, *Pattern for Progress,* 5.

55. *Ibid.; New York Times,* Dec. 15, 1954, 23:3.

56. Kemler, *Nation* (Nov. 5, 1955), 375.

57. A. E. Adams, "How the President is Winning the War on Discrimination," *Factory Management,* CXIV (Jan., 1956), 105.

58. "Drive on Bias," *Business Week* (Oct. 29, 1955), 162.

59. Adams, *Factory Management* (Jan., 1956), 105.

60. President's Committee on Government Contracts, *Youth Training—Incentives Conference Proceedings* (Washington: GPO, April, 1957), 10; G. B. McKibbin, "Conference on Equal Job Opportunity," *Monthly Labor Review,* LXXIX (Jan., 1956), 31-33.

61. U.S. Commission on Civil Rights, *Report, 1961,* 60.

62. Norgren, *Toward Fair Employment,* 167.

63. "Drive on Bias," *Business Week* (Oct. 29, 1955), 162.

64. Interview, Nov. 14, 1955, AFSC, Dallas Visits, 1954-1956.

65. U.S. President's Commission on Government Contracts, *Five Years of Progress, 1953-1958* (Washington: GPO, 1958), 6-12 ibid., *Sixth Report, July 1, 1958-Sept. 30, 1959* (Washington: GPO, 1959), 10-15.

66. Interview, Nov. 4, 1955, AFSC, Dallas Visits Book, 1954-1956.

67. *Wall Street Journal,* Oct. 24, 1957, 1.

68. U.S. Commission on Civil Rights, *Report, 1961,* 60-63.

69. Ray Marshall, "Some Factors Influencing the Upgrading of Negroes in the

Southern Petroleum Refining Industry," *Social Forces,* XLII (Dec., 1963), 186-195; "Brighter Opportunities Dawning for the Negro Worker," *Chemical Week,* LXXXI (Aug. 24, 1957), 21; Carl B. King and Howard W. Risher, Jr., *The Negro in the Petroleum Industry,* Report No. 5, *The Racial Policies of American Industry* (Philadelphia: Industrial Research Unit, Department of Industry, Wharton School of Finance and Commerce, University of Pennsylvania, 1969), 39.

70.   U.S. President's Committee on Goverment Contracts, *Pattern for Progress,* 6.

71.   Norgren, *Toward Fair Employment,* 196; U.S. Commission on Civil Rights, *Report, 1961,* 65-66.

72.   U.S. Commission on Civil Rights, *The 50 States Reports* (Washington: GPO, 1961), 492.

73.   Adams, *Factory Management* (Jan., 1956), 105.

74.   U.S. Commission on Civil Rights, Hearings, Jan. 25-28, 1960 (Washington: GPO, 1960), 496-497.

75.   F. J. Haas and G. J. Fleming, "Personnel Practices and Wartime Changes," *Annals of the American Academy of Political and Social Science,* CCXLIV (Mar., 1946), 54-55.

76.   Frank T. Mohr, "Management Policies and Biracial Integration in Industry" (Master's thesis, University of Illinois, Urbana, 1954), 101.

77.   Interview, Aug. 5, 1952, AFSC, Dallas Visits Book, a-l.

78.   "Report, Eighth Annual Race Relations Institute," Fisk University, July 4-6, 1951, AFSC, JOP, Chicago.

79.   *New York Times,* Apr. 26, 1956, 26:2.

80.   *Ibid.*

81.   Bernard Rosenberg and Penney Chapin, "Management and Minority Groups," in Aaron Antonovsky and Lewis L. Lorwin, *Discrimination and Low Incomes* (New York, State of New York Interdepartment Committee on Low Incomes, 1959), 194.

82.   "Progress Toward Fair Employment Practices," *Monthly Labor Review,* LX (May,1945), 1005; Haas, *Annals of the American Academy,* 53.

83.   Henry G. Stetler, *Minority Group Integration by Labor and Management* (Hartford: Connecticut Commission on Civil Rights, 1953), 27.

84.   Anon. to G. L. Bergen, "Hypothetical Program," Nov. 24, 1950, AFSC, American Section, Race Relations, 1950.

85.   George F. Doriot, ed., *The Management of Racial Integration in Business* (New York: McGraw Hill, 1964), 16, 20; Theodore W. Kheel, *Guide to Fair Employment Practices* (Englewood Cliffs, N.J.: Prentice Hall, 1964), 16-17, 78; Norgren, *Employing the Negro,* 57-59.

86.   Caroline Bird, "More Room at the Top," *Management Review,* LII (March, 1963), 5-13.

87.   "One Company's Answer to the Negro Job Problem," *Business Management,* XXV (Feb., 1964), 44-45.

88.   T. Cox, "Counselor's Views on Changing Management Policies," *Public Relations Journal,* XIX (Nov., 1963), 9.

89.   National Association of Manufacturers, *Tale of 22 Cities,* 49; Hugh Hoffman, "A Management Perspective Toward Negro Economic Pressures," *Public Relations Quarterly,* VIII (Winter, 1964), 24; *Equal Opportunity in Industry* (n.p., National Conference of Christians and Jews, May, 1968).

Chapter 8

1.   N. D. Glenn, "White Gains From Negro Subordination," *Social Problems,* XIV (Fall, 1966), 172-173.

2.   *Ibid.,* 159-178; Norval D. Glenn, "Occupational Benefits to Whites From the Subordination of Negroes," *American Sociological Review,* XXVIII (June, 1963), 443-448; Alma F. Taeuber et al., "Occupational Assimilation and the Competitive Process," *American Journal of Sociology,* LXXII (Nov., 1966), 273-285; R. W.

Hodge and P. Hodge, "Occupational Assimilation as a Competitive Process," *American Journal of Sociology,* LXXI (Nov., 1965), 249-264; Robert W. Hodge and Patricia Hodge, "Comment," *American Journal of Sociology,* LXII (Nov., 1966), 286-289.

3. See Chapter IV.

4. Donald Dewey, "Negro Employment in Southern Industry," *Journal of Political Economy,* LX (Aug., 1952), 283.

5. Donald Dewey, "Southern Poverty and the Racial Division of Labor," *New South,* XVII (May, 1962), 3 ff.

6. Sara Southall, *Industry's Unfinished Business* (New York: Harper, 1950), 92.

7. See Chapter VII.

8. Interview, Oct. 14, 1961, American Friends Service Committee (AFSC) archives, Community Relations Department, Houston, 1961.

9. U.S. President's Committee on Equal Employment Opportunity, *Report to the President* (Washington: GPO, Nov. 1963), 10-13.

10. Theodore W. Kheel, *Guide to Fair Employment Practices* (Englewood Cliffs, N.J.; Prentice Hall, 1964), 98-100; U.S. President's Committee on Equal Employment Opportunity, *Report,* 10-11.

11. Carl B. King and Howard W. Risher, Jr., *The Negro in the Petroleum Industry,* Report No. 5, *The Racial Policies of American Industry* (Philadelphia: Industrial Research Unit, Department of Industry, Wharton School of Finance and Commerce, University of Pennsylvania, 1969), 51.

12. Interview, Oct. 11, 1955, AFSC, Baton Rouge Visits, 1955——.

13. Herbert R. Northrup, *The Negro in the Rubber Tire Industry,* Report No. 6, *The Racial Policies of American Industry* (Philadelphia: Industrial Research Unit, Department of Industry, Wharton School of Finance and Commerce, University of Pennsylvania, 1969), 51, 64.

14. P. H. Norgren et al., *Employing the Negro in American Industry* (New York: Industrial Relations Counselors, Inc., 1964), 42-44.

15. Irving Babow and Edward Howden, *A Civil Rights Inventory of San Francisco,* Part I, *Employment* (San Francisco: Council for Civic Unity, 1958), 93; Bernard Rosenberg and Penney Chapin, "Management and Minority Groups," in Aaron Antonovsky and Lewis L. Lorwin, eds., *Discrimination and Low Incomes* (New York: State of New York Interdepartmental Committee on Low Incomes, 1959), 180.

16. David P. Taylor, "Discrimination and Occupational Wage Differences in the Market for Unskilled Labor," *Industrial and Labor Relations Review,* XXI (Apr., 1968), 375-390.

17. Babow and Howden, *A Civil Rights Inventory,* 99.

18. *Ibid.,* 100.

19. Interview, Dec. 2, 1955, Job Opportunities Plan (JOP), Chicago.

20. Caroline Bird, "More Room at the Top," *Management Review,* LII (March, 1963), 14.

21. "Crashing Gates to Better Jobs," *Business Week* (June 22, 1963), 25.

22. J. Hope, "Minority Utilization Practices—Rational or Sentimental?" *Social Research,* XVIII (June, 1951), 166.

23. D. Smith, "Help Wanted, Negro," *Electronics,* XXXVII (Mar. 23, 1964), 96.

24. *Ibid.*

25. Donald Dewey, "Four Studies of Negro Employment in the Upper South," in National Planning Association, Committee of the South, *Selected Studies of Negro Employment in the South* (Washington: National Planning Association, 1955), 166.

26. Frank T. Mohr, "Management Policies and Biracial Integration in Industry" (Master's thesis, University of Illinois, Urbana, 1954), 78-79.

27. *Ibid.*

28.   Dwight D. Vines, "The Impact of Title VII of the 1964 Civil Rights Law on Personnel Policies and Practices" (D.B.A. diss., University of Colorado, 1967), 177.

29.   Fred Brunning, "Many Success Stories are Written," *Miami Herald Sunday Magazine* (July 30, 1967), 11.

30.   *New York Times,* July 15, 1948, 25:3; J. A. Thomas, "What About Fair Employment?", *Challenge Magazine* (Dec., 1953), 52-57.

31.   U.S. President's Commission on Government Contracts, *Five Years of Progress, 1953-1958* (Washington: GPO, 1958), 6-12.

32.   U.S. President's Committee on Equal Employment Opportunity, *Report,* 23.

33.   Hobart Taylor, "Address to Industrial Relations Research Association, Detroit Area Chapter," Nov. 7, 1963, U.S. Government nondepository item, 1964-1543.

34.   U.S. Commission on Civil Rights, District of Columbia Advisory Commission, *Report on Washington, D.C.: Employment* (Washington: GPO, July, 1963), 29.

35.   Dewey, *New South* (May, 1962), 10; Art Gallaher, Jr., *The Negro and Employment Opportunities in the South—Houston* (Atlanta: Southern Regional Council, 1961), 17-21; *New York Times,* July 12, 1963, 27:5.

36.   "The House Nigger," *News Front* (Nov., 1968), 21.

37.   Ulric Haynes, Jr., "Equal Job Opportunity: The Credibility Gap," *Harvard Business Review,* XLVI (May-June, 1968), 116.

38.   *New York Times,* June 26, 1968, 63:5.

39.   *News Front* (Nov., 1968), 21-23.

40.   "Jobs for Negroes—Is There a Real Shortage?", *U.S. News and World Report,* LV (Aug. 12, 1963), 29.

41.   John Hope, II, "Control Role of Intergroup Agencies in the Labor Market," *Journal of Intergroup Relations,* II (Spring, 1961), 132-142.

42.   "CPI Takes Lead in Antibias Drive," *Chemical Week,* LXXXIX (Oct. 21, 1961), 80.

43.   Letter, Jan. 18, 1962, AFSC, Employment on Merit Program (EOM), Atlanta.

44.   "AFSC, Atlanta Employment Program," AFSC, mimeographed report, March 25, 1964.

45.   *New York Times,* Sept. 2, 1962, 44:2.

46.   *New York Times,* June 21, 1964, 67:4.

47.   *New York Times,* Dec. 12, 1964, 19:3.

48.   Bettye K. Eidson, "Major Employers and Their Manpower Policies," in U.S. National Advisory Commission on Civil Disorders, *Supplemental Studies* (Washington: GPO, July, 1968), 122.

49.   Letter, Nov. 30, 1947, AFSC, Race Relations File, 1947; J. A. Thomas "The Negro Worker Lifts His Sights," *Opportunity,* XXIV (April, 1946), 55.

50.   Virgil B. Day, "Progress in Equal Employment Opportunity at General Electric," in Herbert R. Northrup, ed., *The Negro and Employment Opportunities* (Ann Arbor: Bureau of Industrial Relations, Graduate School of Business Administration, University of Michigan, 1965), 160.

51.   W. N. Rozelle, "Civil Rights, Kangaroo Style," *Textile Industries,* CXXXI (Mar., 1967), 78.

52.   "Jobs for Negroes," *U.S. News and World Report,* LV (Aug. 12, 1963), 29.

53.   "MVEEOC, Upgrading Seminar, March 19, 1968, A Resume," in the files of the Milwaukee Voluntary Equal Employment Opportunity Council, Milwaukee, Wisconsin.

54.   "Industrial Psychologist: Selection and Equal Employment Opportunity: Symposium," *Personnel Psychology,* XIX (Spring, 1966), 3.

55.   Interview, Jan, 29, 1964, AFSC, EOM, Atlanta.

56.   Interview, Feb. 1, 1962, AFSC, EOM, Atlanta.

57.   George Kennedy, "Task Force Opens New Avenue," *Miami Herald Sunday Magazine* (July 30, 1967), 17.

58.   J. C. Gourlay, *The Negro Salaried Worker* (New York: American Management Association, Research Study, No. 70, 1965), 64.

59.   Gallagher, *The Negro and Employment,* 22.

60.   Rosenberg and Chapin, "Management," in Antonovsky, *Discrimination,* 190.

61.   Harold Mayfield, "New Horizons for Negroes," *Chemical Engineering,* LXXI (Nov. 9, 1964), 242.

62.   Harold Mayfield, "Equal Employment Opportunity: Should Hiring Standards be Relaxed?", *Personnel,* XLI (Sept., 1964), 15.

63.   *Racine Journal Times,* Nov. 29, 1967, 4A.

64.   Mimeographed flyer, Committee for Employment Opportunity, Indianapolis, Indiana, n.d. [1967].

65.   *You Too Can Be A Winner* (Los Angeles: Merit Employment Council of Greater Los Angeles [c. 1965]).

66.   For examples of formal nondiscrimination policies frequently ignored by companies, see U.S. Congress, House, Committee on Education and Labor, *Hearings,* 81 Cong., 1st Sess., May 10-26, 1949, 571-574; Jack London and Richard Hammett, "Impact of Company Policy Upon Discrimination," *Sociology and Sociological Research,* XXXIX (Nov.-Dec., 1954), 88-91; Leon E. Lunden, "Antidiscrimination Provisions in Major Contracts," *Monthly Labor Review,* LXXXV 643-651; Max S. Wortman and Fred Luthans, "The Prevalence of Antidiscrimination Policies," *Business Perspectives,* II (Winter, 1966), 10-13.

Chapter 9

1.   U.S. Commission on Civil Rights, (usccr)*Report, 1961,* Book 3, Employment (Washington: GPO, 1961), 71-74.

2.   Michael I. Sovern, *Legal Restraints on Racial Discrimination in Employment* (New York: Twentieth Century Fund, 1966), 228.

3.   usccr, *Report, 1961,* 74-75.

4.   Sovern, *Legal Restraints,* 105.

5.   U.S. Congress, Senate, Committee on Labor and Public Welfare, Subcommittee on Employment and Manpower, Hearings, *Equal Employment Opportunity,* 88 Cong., 1st Sess., July 24-Aug. 20, 1963, testimony of W. Willard Wirtz, Secretary of Labor, 409-413.

6.   *Ibid.,* 410-411; *New York Times,* Apr. 18, 1962, 1:7.

7.   U.S. Congress, Senate, Committee on Labor and Public Welfare, *Equal Employment Opportunity,* July 24-Aug. 20, 1963, 410; *New York Times,* May 19, 1962, 27:1.

8.   U.S. Congress, Senate, Committee on Labor and Public Welfare, *Equal Employment Opportunity,* 1963, 411; *New York Times,* Apr. 18, 1962, 1:7; *ibid.,* May 3, 1962, 22:3.

9.   Sovern, *Legal Restraints,* 113.

10.   "Billion Dollar Prize Spurs Integration," *Business Week* (June 3, 1961), 23.

11.   *New York Times,* Feb. 7, 1962, 40:3; *ibid.,* July 27, 1962, 9:5; Theodore W. Kheel, *Guide to Fair Employment Practices* (Englewood Cliffs, N. J.: Prentice Hall, 1964), 25-26, 81.

12.   See limited claims of success in U.S. President's Committee on Equal Employment Opportunity, (pceeo), *Report to the President* (Washington: GPO, Nov. 26, 1963), 10-13.

13.   "The Negro Drive for Jobs," *Business Week* (Aug. 17, 1963), 55-56.

14.   *Ibid.*

15.   Herbert Hill, "Black Labor in the American Economy," in Patricia W. Romero, ed., *In Black America, 1968* (Washington: United Publishing Corp., 1969), 182-183.

16.   *New York Times,* June 21, 1961, 1:6.

17.   Interview, March 19, 1963, American Friends Service Committee (AFSC) archives, Employment on Merit Program (EOM), Atlanta.

18.   George F. Doriot, ed., *The Management of Racial Integration in Business* (New York: McGraw Hill, 1964), 7; D. Smith, "Help Wanted: Negro," *Electronics,* XXVII (Mar. 23, 1964), 95; Herbert R. Northrup, *The Negro in the Aerospace Industry,* Report No. 2, *The Racial Policies of American Industry* (Philadelphia: Industrial Research Unit, Department of Industry, Wharton School of Finance and Commerce, University of Pennsylvania, 1968), 76; "Integration in Industry; Special Report," *Factory,* CXXII (Dec., 1964), 51; "Finding Open Doors," *Chemical Week,* XCVI (Jan. 9, 1965), 64.

19.   *AFL-CIO News,* July 27, 1963, 4:1.

20.   U.S. Congress, House, Committee on Education and Labor, Special Subcommittee on Labor, Hearings, *Equal Employment Opportunity,* 87 Cong., 1st and 2nd Sess., Oct. 23, 1961-Jan. 24, 1962, testimony of E. Edgerton Hart, secretary, Illinois Manufacturers Association, Chicago, 114-117.

21.   *Wall Street Journal,* June 23, 1964, 16:1.

22.   "The Controversy Over the 'Equal Employment Opportunity' Provision of the Civil Rights Bill," *Congressional Digest,* XLIII (Mar., 1964), 83-95.

23.   *New York Times,* April 10, 1964, 1:6; *ibid.,* May 13, 1964, 22:1.

24.   For examples see, U.S. Congress, House, *Equal Employment,* 1961-1962, 92; U.S. Congress, Senate, *Equal Employment,* 1963, 315.

25.   Richard A. Enion and Halward L. Homan, "What are Some Industrial Relations Approaches to Integration?", *Personnel Administration,* XXVI (Nov.-Dec., 1963), 55.

26.   For discussion see Sovern, *Legal Restraints,* 61-102.

27.   *New York Times,* Feb. 5, 1965, 17:7.

28.   U.S. EEOC, *Second Annual Report* (Washington: GPO, 1968), 8-15; U.S. EEOC, *Third Annual Report* (Washington: GPO, 1969), 6.

29.   Neil R. Regimbal, "Bias Behind the Wheel," *Commercial Car Journal,* CXL (June, 1966), 114.

30.   U.S. EEOC, *Third Annual Report,* 9.

31.   U.S. EEOC, *Employment Patterns in the Drug Industry, 1966 Research Report, 1967-20* (Washington: GPO, Sept. 29, 1967); U.S. EEOC, *Hearings Before the USEEOC on Discrimination in White Collar Employment: New York,* Jan. 15-18, 1968 (Washington: GPO, 1968), 527-652.

32.   Stephen Habbe, ed., *Company Experience With Negro Employment, Studies in Personnel Policy,* No. 201, Vol. II (New York: National Industrial Conference Board, 1966), 21.

33.   "Hiring and Promotion Policies Under Fair Employment Practices Legislation," *Monthly Labor Review,* XC (Feb., 1967), 55-56.

34.   Interview, [1953], AFSC, Greensboro Visits Book; H. D. Bloch, "Discrimination Against the Negro in Employment in New York, 1920-1963," *American Journal of Economics and Sociology,* XXIV (Oct. 1965), 379.

35.   *Ibid.;* Roi Ottley, *New World A-Coming* (Boston: Houghton Mifflin, 1943), 113-121.

36.   Sanford Jay Rosen, "The Law and Racial Discrimination in Employment," in Arthur M. Ross and Herbert Hill, eds., *Employment, Race and Poverty* (New York: Harcourt, Brace & World, 1967), 502.

37.   Bloch, *American Journal of Economics and Sociology* (Oct., 1965), 380.

38.   S. I. Hayakawa, "Answering a Want Ad," *Common Ground,* III (1946), 91-92.

39.   August Meier, "Civil Rights Strategies for Negro Employment," in Ross and Hill, *Employment, Race,* 188-189.

40.   Helen Hill Miller, "Business Citizenship in the Deep South," *Business Horizons,* V (Spring, 1962), 62.

41.   Art Gallaher, Jr., *The Negro and Employment Opportunities in the South—Houston* (Atlanta: Southern Regional Council, 1961), 12.

42.   Vivian W. Henderson, "Economic Dimensions in Race Relations," in Jitsuichi Masuoka and Preston Valien, eds., *Race Relations: Problems and Theory* (Chapel Hill: University of North Carolina Press, 1961), 264.

43.   Miller, *Business Horizons* (Spring, 1962), 62.

44.   Henderson, "Economic Dimensions," in Masuoka, *Race Relations,* 264; Helen Hill Miller, "Private Business and Education in the South," *Harvard Business Review,* XXXVIII (July-Aug., 1960), 77-78.

45.   Miller, *Harvard Business Review* (July-Aug., 1960), 88.

46.   *Ibid.,* 81; Henderson, "Economic Dimensions," in Masuoka, *Race Relations,* 265; Miller, *Business Horizons* (Spring, 1962), 62-63.

47.   Miller, *Harvard Business Review* (July-Aug., 1960), 88.

48.   Henderson, "Economic Dimensions," in Masuoka, *Race Relations,* 265.

49.   Bob Smith, *They Closed Their Schools* (Chapel Hill: University of North Carolina Press, 1965), 178-179.

50.   Miller, *Harvard Business Review* (July-Aug., 1960), 87.

51.   Miller, *Business Horizons* (Spring, 1962), 63.

52.   William R. Carmack and Theodore Freedman, *Factors Affecting School Desegregation: Dallas, Texas, Field Reports on Desegregation in the South* (New York: Anti-Defamation League of B'nai B'rith, [1962]), 8-9.

53.   *Ibid.,* 12-15; Miller, *Business Horizons* (Spring, 1962), 64-65.

54.   Carmack, *Factors Affecting,* 9; *Wall Street Journal,* Nov. 24, 1961, 1; "New Business Ways in the South," *Business Week* (Aug. 5, 1961), 63.

55.   "Annual Report," Sept., 1960, Employment on Merit Program, High Point, North Carolina, AFSC, Community Relations Division, High Point, 1962.

56.   "Progress Report," EOM, Houston, April, 1961, AFSC, Community Relations Division, Houston, 1961.

57.   "Memo," Jan. 11, 1963, AFSC, EOM, Atlanta.

58.   Kheel, *Guide to Fair Employment,* 6.

59.   "The Negro Drive for Jobs," *Business Week* (Aug. 17, 1963), 56.

60.   "Jobs for Negroes—Is There a Real Shortage?", *U.S. News and World Report,* LV (Aug. 12, 1963), 31.

61.   *Ibid.,* 30-31; Habbe, *Company Experience,* Vol. I, 65-66.

62.   Gene Grove, "Making the System Work," *Tuesday Magazine* (July, 1967), 4; "Philadelphia Opportunities Industrialization Center: Its People, Performance, and Promise," (Philadelphia: OIC [1967]).

63.   "He Helps the Poor Help Themselves," *Nation's Business,* LV (July, 1967), 44.

64.   John Perry, "Business: Next Target for Integration?", *Harvard Business Review,* XLI (Mar.-Apr., 1963), 104-105.

65.   For examples see, "The Negro Drive for Jobs," *Business Week* (Aug. 17, 1963), 59-61; interview, July 13, 1962, AFSC, EOM, Atlanta; "Memo," Mar. 31, 1964, AFSC, EOM, Atlanta; Kheel, *Guide to Fair Employment,* 6-7; "They Make Opportunity Knock," *Chemical Week,* XCIII (Oct. 26, 1963), 75.

66.   "Detroit Feels Brunt of Negro Pressure," *Business Week* (June 29, 1963), 90-91.

67.   "Negroes Take Aim at GM," *Business Week* (Jul. 20, 1963), 32.

68.   "GM and the Negro," *Business Week* (Apr. 18, 1964), 36.

69.   *Racine Journal Times,* Oct. 2, 1967, 2A; 4; *ibid.,* Aug. 30, 1967, 10A.

70.   David A. Sawyer, "Fair Employment in the Nation's Capital: A Study of Progress and Dilemma," *Journal of Intergroup Relations,* IV (Winter, 1962-1963), 51-52.

71.   "The Negro Drive for Jobs," *Business Week* (Aug. 17, 1963), 52; H. D. Bloch, "Some Economic Effects of Discrimination in Employment," *American Journal*

of Economics and Sociology, XXV (Jan., 1966), 20-21: *New York Times,* Feb. 8, 1964, 11:1.

72.   "Pact Reached to Halt Negro Job Protests," *Electrical World,* CLX (Sept. 2, 1963), 60.

73.   *Wall Street Journal,* Jan. 18, 1964, 1:7.

74.   *San Francisco Examiner,* Feb. 25, 1964, 1:2; *ibid.,* Feb. 27, 1964, 1:1.

75.   *Ibid.,* Feb. 29, 1964, 1:5.

76.   *Ibid.,* Mar. 1, 1964, 1:3; *ibid.,* Mar. 6, 1964, 14:6.

77.   *Ibid.,* Mar. 7, 1964, 1:7.

78.   *Ibid.,* Mar. 8, 1964, 1:1.

79.   *Ibid.,* Mar. 10, 1964, 17:1.

80.   *Ibid.,* Mar. 15, 1964, 1:8.

81.   *Ibid.,* B:1.

82.   *Ibid.,* Apr. 7, 1964, 16:6.

83.   *Ibid.,* Apr. 12, 1964, 1:1.

84.   *Ibid.,* Apr.18, 1964, 7:3.

85.   *Ibid.,* Apr. 19, 1964, B:1.

86.   *Ibid.,* Mar. 16, 1964, 11:1.

87.   *Ibid.*

88.   James F. Langton, "What Should the Business Response Be to the Negro Revolution?", *Public Relations Journal,* XXI (June, 1965), 13.

89.   *San Francisco Examiner,* Mar. 16, 1964, 11:1.

90.   Habbe, *Company Experience,* Vol. I, 78-79.

91.   *San Francisco Examiner,* May 19, 1964, 1:3; *ibid.,* May 22, 1964, 14:2.

92.   *Ibid.,* May 23, 1964, 1:1; *ibid.,* May 24, 1964, 8:1; Langton, *Public Relations Journal* (June, 1965), 13-14.

93.   Habbe, *Company Experience,* Vol. I, 77.

94.   *San Francisco Examiner,* June 2, 1964, 1:1, 1:2; Langton, *Public Relations Journal* (June, 1965), 13-14.

95.   "There Isn't Any Time," *Fortune,* LXX (July, 1964), 128.

96.   *Wall Street Journal,* July 3, 1963, 1:6.

97.   *New York Times,* Jan. 11, 1965, 62:3.

98.   "After the Riots: A Survey," *Newsweek,* LXX (Aug. 21, 1967), 19; Daniel Patrick Moynihan, "Behind Los Angeles," *Reporter,* XXXIII (Sept. 9, 1965), 31.

99.   See Chapter VII.

100.   "Equal Employment Opportunity," *Management Review* (Apr., 1964), 7.

101.   James C. Worthy, *Big Business and Free Men* (New York: Harper, 1959), 186-187.

102.   Henry Ford II, "Remarks to Meeting of National Alliance of Businessmen," Toledo, Ohio, Mar. 26, 1968.

103.   W. P. Gullander, "Employment—A Step Toward Crime Prevention" (STEP, National Assoc. of Manufacturers).

104.   "Summer's Backlash: More Job Programs," *Business Week* (Oct. 21, 1967), 194; *Action Report* (Summer, 1968).

105.   *Wall Street Journal,* Mar. 5, 1968, 18:4; *Business and the Urban Crisis* (McGraw Hill Special Report [1968]), 3.

106.   *Wall Street Journal,* Mar. 5, 1968, 18:4.

107.   Henry Ford II, "Remarks to Buffalo Area Chamber of Commerce," May 16, 1968.

108.   William H. Smith, Executive Vice President, Federated Employers of the Bay Area, to Steven M. Gelber, April 25, 1968.

109.   *Dealing the Negro In (Business Week,* Special Report [May, 1968]).

Chapter 10

1.   For example, see Jack Dawson, "ODC," *Buffalo Magazine* (Oct., 1966), 35.

2.   Metropolitan Dade County Community Relations Board, *Equal Employment News* (Aug., 1967), 1.

3.   *New York Times,* Sept. 3, 1967, III, 1:1.

4.   "Why Race Riots Strike 'Nice' Northern City," *Business Week* (Aug. 1, 1964), 24.

5.   Governor's Commission on the Los Angeles Riots, *Selected Interviews and Other Documents,* Vol. 15, No. 21, interview with Dr. Walter Cooper, Rochester, N.Y., Nov. 18, 1965, 3-6.

6.   *Ibid.*

7.   "Company Sponsored Training," (STEP, National Assoc. of Manufacturers, n.d.); *New York Times,* Jan. 8, 1968, 91:1.

8.   "Fight That Swirls Around Eastman Kodak," *Business Week* (Apr. 29, 1967), 38.

9.   *Ibid.,* 39.

10.   William S. Vaughn, "Equal Employment Opportunity—Eastman Kodak Company's Positive Program," remarks to annual meeting, Apr. 25, 1967.

11.   *Business Week* (Apr. 29, 1967), 40.

12.   Vaughn, "Equal Employment."

13.   *Rochester Times Union,* Mar. 11, 1967 (clipping); *ibid.,* April 12, 1967 (clipping); Vaughn, "Equal Employment"; National Citizen's Committee for Community Relations and the Community Relations Service of the U.S. Department of Justice, *Putting the Hard-Core Unemployed into Jobs: A Report of the Business-Civic Leadership Conference on Employment Problems, June 5-7, 1967, Chicago, Illinois,* Part II, *Case Studies* (Washington: GPO, 1968), 56.

14.   Rochester Jobs, Inc. (RJI), "Working Principles" [April, 1967].

15.   *Ibid.*

16.   *Ibid.;* *Rochester Times Union,* Apr. 12, 1967 (clipping).

17.   Vaughn, "Equal Employment."

18.   *Rochester Times Union,* Apr. 12, 1967 (clipping).

19.   National Citizen's Committee, *Putting the Hard-Core,* 57.

20.   *Rochester Times Union,* June 13, 1967 (clipping); "Rochester Jobs to Recruit in Inner City Neighborhoods," News Release, RJI, Sept. 14, 1967; *Rochester Democrat and Chronicle,* Sept. 27, 1967 (clipping).

21.   *Ibid.,* Dec. 4, 1967 (clipping); RJI, "Activity Report, Dec. 31, 1967."

22.   *Rochester Times Union,* Nov. 9, 1967 (clipping); RJI, "Activity Report, Dec. 31, 1967."

23.   RJI, "Advancement Through Clerical Training"; RJI, "Activity Report, Dec. 31, 1967."

24.   *New York Times,* Jan. 8, 1968, 91:1.

25.   Lockheed Plans for Progress will be fully discussed in Chapter XII.

26.   Whitney M. Young, Jr., "Should There Be Compensation for Negroes?", *New York Times Magazine* (Oct. 6, 1963), 43.

27.   "Integration in Industry; Special Report," *Factory,* CXXII (Dec., 1964), 54.

28.   See Chapter IX.

29.   Charles E. Silberman, "The Businessman and the Negro," *Fortune,* LXVIII (Sept., 1963), 191.

30.   Luther H. Hodges, "Address to National Urban League," New York, Nov. 19, 1963, U.S. Government nondepository item, 1964-224.

31.   U.S. Equal Employment Opportunity Commission, *Equal Employment Opportunity is Good Business* (Washington: GPO, 1966).

32.   "Affirmative Action: Assuring the Right to Equal Job Opportunity" (State of Michigan Civil Rights Commission, June, 1967); Alfonso J. Cervantes, "To

Prevent a Chain of Super-Watts," *Harvard Business Review,* XLV (Sept.-Oct., 1967), 60.

33.   U.S. Congress, House, Committee on Labor, Hearings, *Discrimination and Full Utilization of Manpower Resources,* 82 Cong., 2nd Sess., April 7–May 6, 1952, 83.

34.   Paul H. Norgren et al., *Employing the Negro in American Industry* (New York: Industrial Relations Counselors, 1964), 56.

35.   "Will Negroes Really Get More Jobs Under New Law?", *U.S. News and World Report,* LIX (July 19, 1965), 83.

36.   Lawrence F. Mihlon, "Industrial Discrimination—The Skeleton in Everyone's Closet," *Factory,* LXX (April, 1962), 85.

37.   Jack Gourlay, *The Negro Salaried Worker* (New York: American Management Association, Study No. 70, 1965), 64.

38.   George A. Spater, "Breaking the Bias Barrier," *Management Review,* LIII (Apr., 1964), 22.

39.   U.S. Congress, Senate, Committee on Labor and Public Welfare, Subcommittee on Employment and Manpower, Hearings, *Equal Employment Opportunity,* 88 Cong., 1st Sess., July 24-Aug. 20, 1963, 208-209.

40.   "How Integration is Working Out in Industry," *Management Review,* XLV (July, 1956), 548-549.

41.   National Association of Intergroup Relations Officials, "1953 Commission Reports: Manpower Education" (Toledo, Ohio: NAIRO, 1953, mimeographed), 22-23; Joseph J. Morrow, "Integrating the Negro Worker into Factories and Offices," address to the Personnel Association of Stamford-Greenwich Manufacturers' Council, Oct. 27, 1947, AFSC, interviews.

42.   Joseph J. Morrow, "American Negroes—A Wasted Resource," *Harvard Business Review,* XXXV (Jan.-Feb., 1957), 65 ff.

43.   "One Company's Answer to Negro Job Problem," *Business Management,* XXV (Feb., 1964), 42-43.

44.   James P. Mitchell, "Business and Civil Rights," *Vital Speeches,* XXX (July 1, 1964), 551.

45.   Governor's Commission on the Los Angeles Riots, *Testimony,* Vol. 12, H. C. McClellan, Los Angeles, Cal., Nov. 1, 1965, 20.

46.   *Ibid.*

47.   Harold S. Mayfield, "Seeks Preferred Treatment for Negroes but Warns of Being Unfair to Existing Personnel," *National Underwriter (Life Edition),* LXX (Oct. 22, 1966), 22-23.

48.   See for examples, Irving Babow and Edward Howden, *A Civil Rights Inventory of San Francisco,* Part I, *Employment* (San Francisco: Council for Civic Unity, 1958); Ray Marshall, "Prospects For Equal Employment, Conflicting Portents," *Monthly Labor Review,* LXXXVIII (June, 1965), 651; John J. Puma, "Improving Negro Employment in Boston," *Industrial Management Review,* VIII (Fall, 1966), 41.

49.   Dwight D. Vines, "The Impact of Title VII of the 1964 Civil Rights Law on Personnel Policies and Practices," (D.B.A. diss., University of Colorado, 1967), 173.

50.   Norgren, *Employing the Negro,* 64.

51.   "Industry Rushes for Negro Grads," *Business Week* (Apr. 25, 1964), 78.

52.   Theodore W. Kheel, *Guide to Fair Employment Practices* (Englewood Cliffs, N.J.: Prentice Hall, 1964), 111–114: Louis A. Ferman, *The Negro and Equal Employment Opportunities* (New York: Frederick A. Praeger, 1968), 21–2.

53.   George F. Doriot, ed., *The Management of Racial Integration in Business* (New York: McGraw Hill, 1964), 45.

54.   "Hiring and Promotion Policies Under Fair Employment Practices Legislation," *Monthly Labor Review,* XC (Feb., 1967), 54; *Wall Street Journal,* Sept. 14, 1965, 1:5.

55.   Carl E. Haugen, "Short Term Financing," in Eli Ginzberg, ed., *Business Leadership and the Negro Crisis* (New York: McGraw Hill, 1968), 101.

56. For an early example, see *New York Times,* Nov. 2, 1963, 12:7; *ibid.,* Nov. 15, 1965, 27:3.

57. *Wall Street Journal,* Aug. 4, 1964, 1:4; MVEEOC Bulletin, Feb., 1965.

58. Employer's Council for Merit Employment and Office of the Mayor, *The Houston Summer Job Fair of 1967* (Houston: Humble Oil and Refining Co., 1967).

59. Voluntary groups will be discussed in Chapter XI.

60. "More Jobs For Negroes," *Nation's Business,* LV (Sept., 1967), 574–577; *New York Times,* Aug. 11, 1967, 35:5; *ibid.,* Aug. 26, 1967, 23:3; Mayor's Council on Youth Opportunity, "Operation Job Alert" (Oklahoma City: [1967]); Businessmen's Interracial Committee on Community Affairs, "Inner City High School Graduates Get Jobs" (Cleveland: Sept., 1967); Omaha Equal Opportunity Committee, "The Omaha Equal Opportunity Committee, 1963–1966" (Omaha: 1966); Marvin F. Oberg, chairman, Advisory Council, Omaha Equal Opportunity Committee, to Steven M. Gelber, April 10, 1968.

61. *New York Times,* Nov. 8, 1968, 1:7.

62. National Citizen's Committee, *Putting the Hard-Core,* 11–15; *New York Times,* Jan. 22, 1968, 23:1.

63. Gertrude Samuels, "Help Wanted: The Hard-Core Unemployed," *The New York Times Magazine* (Jan. 28, 1968), 27.

64. *Ibid.*

65. *New York Times,* Oct. 31, 1968, 20:1; in the absence of continued riots Ford closed down its inner-city recruiting posts by the summer of 1970, *ibid.,* July 23, 1970, 18:1.

66. W. N. Rozelle, "How Is the Negro Faring?", *Textile Industries,* CXXXI (Mar., 1967), 84.

67. G. J. McManus, "How Industry Views Integration," *Iron Age,* CXCII (Feb. 27, 1964), 45.

68. National Citizen's Committee, *Putting the Hard-Core,* 29.

69. William L. Crump, "A Study of the Employment Problems of Negro Office Workers in Integrated and Segregated Work Programs with Implications for Business Education" (Ph.D. diss., Northwestern University, 1949), 53.

70. Doriot, *The Management,* 74; Ferman, *The Negro,* 55–56, 60.

71. Memo, Aug. 17, 1964, AFSC, EOM, Atlanta.

72. C. E. Yount, "Anti-Discrimination in Industry," *Conference Board Management Record,* VII (Oct., 1945), 288.

73. William H. Reynolds, *Experience of Los Angeles Employers with Minority Group Employees: Report to Management No. 16* (Los Angeles: Graduate School of Business Administration, University of Southern California, Mar., 1967), 21. Eleven percent used a different cut-off for blacks but the survey does not say if it was higher or lower.

74. Ray Marshall, "Some Factors Influencing the Upgrading of Negroes in the Southern Petroleum Refining Industry," *Social Forces,* XLII (Dec., 1963), 191.

75. L. Holcomb, "Civil Rights and You: Equal Employment Opportunity Problems," *Textile Industries,* CXXX (May, 1966), 143.

76. For discussions of the Motorola case, see *New York Times,* Nov. 20, 1964, 19:1; *ibid.,* Nov. 22, 1964, IV, 9:1; H. C. Lockwood, "Testing Minority Applicants for Employment," *Personnel Journal,* XLIV (July-Aug., 1965), 356.

77. Vines, "The Impact of Title VII," 109.

78. U.S. EEOC, *Guidelines on Employment Testing Procedures* (Washington: GPO, Aug. 24, 1966).

79. Vines, "The Impact of Title VII," 108–109.

80. Ferman, *The Negro,* 48; George Strauss, "How Management Views its Race Relations Responsibilities," in Arthur M. Ross and Herbert Hill, eds., *Employment, Race, and Poverty* (New York: Harcourt, Brace & World, 1967), 285; U.S. EEOC, *Hearings Before the USEEOC on Discrimination in White Collar Employment: New York, New York, Jan. 15–18, 1968* (Washington: GPO, 1968), testimony of Stanley A. Rasch, Bache and Co., 120–121.

81.   National Citizen's Committee, *Putting the Hard-Core,* 20–21.

82.   *Ibid.*

83.   H. Mayfield, "Equal Employment Opportunity: Should Hiring Standards be Relaxed?", *Personnel,* XLI (Sept., 1964), 14.

84.   Vines, "The Impact of Title VII," 110; Lockwood, *Personnel Journal* (July-Aug., 1965), 356–360; Voluntary Council on Equal Opportunity, *The Equal Opportunity Employer* (Baltimore: Apr., 1966), 8–9.

85.   *New York Times,* Apr. 27, 1965, 44:5.

86.   Malcolm Ross, "Should the U.S. Permanently Ban Racial and Religious Discrimination in Jobs?", *Modern Industry* (April 5, 1945), 121.

87.   Interview, June 13, 1950, AFSC, JOP, Chicago.

88.   Crump, "A Study of the Employment Problems of Negro Office Workers," 159; Robert O. Blood, Jr., *Northern Breakthrough* (Belmont, Cal.: Wadsworth Publishing Co., 1968), 21–22.

89.   Babow and Howden, *A Civil Rights Inventory,* 138; Norgren, *Employing the Negro,* 82.

90.   Stephen Habbe, ed., *Company Experience With Negro Employment, Studies in Personnel Policy,* No. 201, Vol. I (New York: National Industrial Conference Board, 1966), 72.

91.   Howard Lockwood, "Progress in Plans for Progress for Negro Managers," in *The Selection and Training of Negroes for Managerial Positions, Proceedings of the Executive Study Conference, Nov. 10–11, 1964* (Princeton, N.J.; Educational Testing Service, 1965), 651.

92.   Ray Marshall, "Prospects for Equal Employment, Conflicting Portents," *Monthly Labor Review,* LXXXVIII (June, 1965), 651.

93.   Richard L. Rowan, *The Negro in the Steel Industry,* Report No. 3, *The Racial Policies of American Industry* (Philadelphia: Industrial Research Unit, Department of Industry, Wharton School of Finance and Commerce, University of Pennsylvania, 1968), 108.

94.   Vines, "The Impact of Title VII," 89.

95.   Habbe, *Company Experience,* Vol. I, 83.

96.   Richard A. Enion and Halward L. Homan, "What Are Some Industrial Relations Approaches to Integration?", *Personnel Administration,* XXVI (Nov.-Dec., 1963), 56; L. Zimpel, "When Equality is Not Enough," *Christian Century,* LXXXII (Sept. 1, 1965), 1062–1063.

97.   "Preferential Hiring for Negroes: A Debate," *American Child,* XLV (Nov., 1963), 22.

98.   See Chapter VIII.

99.   W. Caples, "Managers Must Help Integration Succeed," *Iron Age,* CXCVIII (Sept., 1966), 71.

100.   Virgil C. Martin, "Utilizing the Dropout," in Herbert R. Northrup, *The Negro and Employment Opportunity* (Ann Arbor: Bureau of Industrial Relations, Graduate School of Business Administration, University of Michigan, 1965), 338.

101.   *Ibid.,* 341.

102.   *Ibid.,* 331–341; Governor's Commission on the Los Angeles Riots, *Selected Interviews and Other Documents,* No. 34, Employment program for high school dropouts run by the Chicago Board of Education and Carson, Pirie, Scott and Co., interview with Fred W. England, corporate vice president and Mrs. Virginia Mason, personnel representative, Chicago, Illinois, Nov. 19, 1965, 3–4.

103.   Virgil B. Day, "Progress in Equal Employment Opportunity at General Electric," in Northrup, *The Negro,* 160.

104.   *New York Times,* Jan. 23, 1968, 21:2.

105.   One such program in Charlotte, N.C., included both blacks and whites as early as 1951, interview, Feb. 23, 1955, AFSC, Greensboro Visits, 1954–1957, a-m.

106.   [Plans for Progress] "Fact Sheet, Plans for Progress Vocational Guidance Institutes" [1967], mimeographed.

107. Hugh L. Gordon, Lockheed Georgia Co., "Remarks to National Conference, Leaders of Local Voluntary EEO Councils, Tulsa, Okla., May 8-9, 1968," mimeographed.

108. Theo Volsky, *A Summary Evaluation: Vocational Guidance Institutes,* 1966 (Washington: Plans for Progress [1967]).

109. President's Committee on Equal Employment Opportunity, *Report to the President* (Washington: GPO, Nov. 26, 1963), 112.

110. NAB will be discussed more fully in Chapter XII.

111. Doriot, *The Management,* 69.

112. "Company Sponsored Training," (STEP, National Assoc. of Manufacturers).

113. President's Committee on Equal Employment Opportunity, *Eastern Region,* comments of Malcolm Anderson; C. W. V. Meares, *Bests Insurance News (Life Edition)* (Sept., 1966), 70.

Chapter 11

1. See Chapter III.

2. Ray Marshall, "Prospects for Equal Employment, Conflicting Portents," *Monthly Labor Review,* LXXXVIII (June, 1965), 650.

3. "The Dimensions of the Problem," in *Community Action Kit* (STEP, National Assoc. of Manufacturers, n.d.).

4. "NAM Tracks Down Solutions to Employment Woes," *Steel Magazine* (Sept. 18, 1967), 97.

5. Erwin D. Canham, ed., *The Disadvantaged Poor: Education and Employment, Task Force on Economic Growth and Opportunity,* Third Report (Washington: Chamber of Commerce of the U.S.A., 1966), 107.

6. *Ibid.,* 104.

7. New York Chamber of Commerce, Committee on Law Reform, *Racial Tensions in New York State* (New York: 1963), 36-37, cited in Richard L. Rowan, "A Survey of Employer Association Activities in the Civil Rights Movement," in Herbert R. Northrup, ed., *The Negro and Employment Opportunities* (Ann Arbor: Bureau of Industrial Relations, Graduate School of Business Administration, University of Michigan, 1965), 214.

8. Letter, Nov. 6, 1963, files of the Milwaukee Voluntary Equal Employment Opportunity Council (MVEEOC), Milwaukee, Wisconsin.

9. W. J. McGowan, "An Employer Viewpoint on Equal Employment Opportunity," remarks before the Governor's Conference on Human Rights, Madison, Wis., Sept. 23, 1963, MVEEOC.

10. Robert A. Burns, "Equal Employment Opportunity Program—Milwaukee, Wisconsin," Nov. 27, 1963, MVEEOC.

11. *Ibid.*

12. *Ibid.*

13. McGowan, "An Employer Viewpoint."

14. "Milwaukee Employers' Voluntary Plan for Equal Employment Opportunity, Adopted Dec. 16, 1963," MVEEOC.

15. *Ibid.*

16. Elmer L. Winter, "Remarks to MVEEOC Seminar," Feb. 26, 1964, 3–4, MVEEOC.

17. Peter G. Scotese, "Equal Employment Opportunity, Why You Need It, Why It Needs You," remarks to MVEEOC seminar, Feb. 26, 1964, 1–5, MVEEOC.

18. Letter, Mar. 11, 1964, MVEEOC.

19. Letter, April 30, 1964, MVEEOC.

20. Letter, May 21, 1964, MVEEOC.

21. *MVEEOC Bulletin* (June 3, 1964).

22. "MVEEOC Six Months Report," Aug. 3, 1964, MVEEOC.

23. Memorandum, Aug. 3, 1964, MVEEOC.

24.   *Ibid.*
25.   "To members of advisory committee," Mar. 16, 1964, MVEEOC.
26.   Minutes of advisory committee meeting, Mar. 30, 1964, MVEEOC.
27.   Memorandum, Aug. 3, 1964, MVEEOC.
28.   "Memorandum of Meeting of Principals and Guidance Counselors and Advisory Committee," Jan. 21, 1965, MVEEOC.
29.   Letter, May 25, 1965, MVEEOC.
30.   Letter, Dec. 6, 1965, MVEEOC; letter, Dec. 8, 1965, MVEEOC.
31.   "Self Development" (STEP, National Assoc. of Manufacturers, n.d.).
32.   Minutes of the advisory committee meeting, Sept. 21, 1965, MVEEOC.
33.   *MVEEOC Bulletin* (Oct. 19, 1964).
34.   "How to Get a Job—MVEEOC Project Outline" [Nov., 1965], MVEEOC; *MVEEOC Bulletin* (June, 1965).
35.   *Ibid.*
36.   Elmer L. Winter, "A Challenge to the Businessmen of Milwaukee," speech to the Greater Milwaukee Committee, Oct. 11, 1965, MVEEOC; *MVEEOC Bulletin* (Nov., 1965).
37.   Minutes of advisory committee meeting, Dec. 21, 1965, MVEEOC.
38.   Minutes of MVEEOC meeting with leaders of minority groups at Northtown Development Center, Sept. 25, 1965, MVEEOC.
39.   Walter Jones, "Straight Facts," *Milwaukee Star*, Jan. 15, 1966 (clipping).
40.   *Milwaukee Sentinel*, Jan. 21, 1966 (clipping).
41.   *MVEEOC Bulletin* (Feb., 1966).
42.   Letter, Feb. 1, 1966, MVEEOC.
43.   "An Affirmative Program for MVEEOC Members to Implement Minority Group Employment" [Feb. 1, 1966], MVEEOC.
44.   Elmer Winter to members of MVEEOC, Feb. 1, 1966, MVEEOC.
45.   Memorandum to all member companies on the Youth Opportunity Board, 1967 summer program, July 21, 1967, MVEEOC.
46.   Charles W. Garrison, "A Community Project With an Open Door Employment Policy," in Northrup, *The Negro*, 302.
47.   *Ibid.*
48.   Garrison, "A Community," in Northrup, *The Negro*, 304.
49.   *Ibid.*
50.   National Citizens' Committee for Community Relations and the Community Relations Service of the U.S. Department of Justice, *Putting the Hard-Core Unemployed into Jobs: A Report of the Business-Civic Leadership Conference on Employment Problems, June 5–7, 1967, Chicago, Illinois*, Part II, *Case Studies* (Washington: GPO, 1968), 72; Charles W. Garrison, "A New Approach to Greater Employment of Negroes," *Newark Commerce* (Fall, 1966), 17.
48.   Garrison, "A Community," in Northrup, *The Negro*, 304.
49.   *Ibid.*
50.   National Citizens' Committee, *Putting the Hard-Core*, 73.
51.   *New York Times*, Sept. 21, 1963, 8:6.
52.   Garrison, *Newark Commerce* (Fall, 1966), 41.
53.   National Citizens' Committee, *Putting the Hard-Core*, 74.
54.   *New York Times*, Aug. 16, 1964, 78:2.
55.   National Citizens' Committee, *Putting the Hard-Core*, 74; Garrison, "A Community," in Northrup, *The Negro*, 306.
56.   Garrison, *Newark Commerce* (Fall, 1966), 41.
57.   National Citizens' Committee, *Putting the Hard-Core*, 63–64; *The Chattanooga Times*, Sept. 10, 1967, reprinted in *AHAC Newsletter*, n.d.
58.   "Fact Sheet, Association of Huntsville Area Companies," n.d., mimeo.; also see National Citizens' Committee, *Putting the Hard-Core*, 63–71.

59.   *1967 Association of Huntsville Area Companies Report* (Huntsville: 1968), 4.

60.   "AHAC Objectives," n.d., mimeo.

61.   "Plans for Progress, A Report, Jan. 1966-Aug., 1967," (Washington: PfP, 1967); "Voluntary Merit Employment Councils," n.d., n.p. [May, 1968], mimeographed.

62.   "Suggested Constitution and Bylaws of the (city or town) Community Resources Development Council," AHAC.

63.   This wording, with minor variations, can be found in the statements of objectives of at least half a dozen councils.

64.   George Schermer, *Employers Guide to Equal Opportunity* (Washington: The Potomac Institute, 1966), 59.

65.   *Wall Street Journal,* July 13, 1967, 1:1.

66.   *Ibid.*

67.   Rowan, "A Survey," in Northrup, *The Negro,* 214; Schermer, *Employer's Guide,* 61.

68.   "Chicago Starts Moving on Equal Job Question," *Business Week* (May 30, 1964), 22.

69.   "What's the Chicago Merit Employment Committee Trying to Do?" (Chicago Assoc. of Commerce and Industry, n.d.), pamphlet.

70.   *Ibid.*

71.   John D. deButts, "Merit Employment is Good Business," *Commerce* (Aug., 1965), reprint.

72.   T. H. Coulter, "Eye on Chicagoland," *Commerce* (Apri., 1966), reprint.

73.   "Tulsa Conference," mimeographed summary, National Conference of Local Voluntary Councils on Equal Employment Opportunity, Tulsa, Okla., May 9–10, 1968.

74.   The GCPFPC was a separate organization from the much more active Businessmen's Interracial Committee.

75.   Greater Cleveland Plans for Progress Council, "Greater Cleveland Plans for Progress Council, September, 1965-September, 1967."

76.   National Citizens' Committee, *Putting the Hard-Core,* 39–44.

77.   For discussions of Cleveland activities, see Lawrence L. Evert, "How Cleveland is Building Interracial Understanding; Tips and Tactics," *PR Reporter,* III (Sept. 1965), n.p.; *Report of the Businessmen's Interracial Committee on Community Affairs for the Year 1966* (Cleveland: BICCA, Jan., 1967); *Report for 1967 of the Businessmen's Interracial Committee on Community Affairs* (Cleveland: BICCA, Jan., 1968).

78.   National Citizens' Committee, *Putting the Hard-Core,* 25-26.

79.   Jack Hulbrud and Karl R. Kunze, *The First Annual Report of the Los Angeles Merit Employment Committee* (Los Angeles: North American Aviation, Nov., 1966).

80.   *Ibid.*

81.   "New Drive to Fulfill These Rights," *Business Week* (May 28, 1966), 40; for other estimates see Institute of Government and Public Affairs, UCLA, *Economic Background—The Los Angeles Riot* (Los Angeles: 1967), 4; William H. Reynolds, *Experience of Los Angeles Employers With Minority Group Employees: Report to Management, No. 16* (Los Angeles: Graduate School of Business Administration, University of Southern Cal., Mar., 1967), 2.

Chapter 12

1.   Kenosha Employer's Voluntary Equal Opportunity Council, "General Statement" [June, 1965], mimeographed.

2.   Sara Southall, *Industry's Unfinished Business* (New York: Harper, 1950), 148.

3.   G. J. McManus, "How Industry Views Integration," *Iron Age,* CXCIII (Feb. 27, 1964), 44.

4.   Stephen Habbe, ed., *Company Experience With Negro Employment, Studies*

in Personnel Policy, No. 201, Vol. II (New York: National Industrial Conference Board, 1966), 22.

5.   Robert C. Weaver, *Negro Labor, A National Problem* (New York: Harcourt, Brace & Co., 1946), 196-198.

6.   E. G. Mattison, "Integrating the Work Force in Southern Industry," in Herbert R. Northrup, *The Negro and Employment Opportunities* (Ann Arbor: Bureau of Industrial Relations, Graduate School of Business Administration, University of Michigan, 1965), 147-148.

7.   *Wall Street Journal,* Oct. 24, 1957, 1.

8.   U.S. Commission on Civil Rights, *Report, 1961,* Book 3, *Employment* (Washington: GPO, 1961), 68; Habbe, *Company Experience,* Vol. II, 23.

9.   U.S. Commission on Civil Rights, *Report, 1961,* 77-78; Michael I. Sovern, *Legal Restraints on Racial Discrimination in Employment* (New York: Twentieth Century Fund, 1966), 109; "Billion Dollar Prize Spurs Integration," *Business Week* (June 3, 1961), 23.

10.   *New York Times,* Apr. 8, 1961, 1:1.

11.   U.S. Commission on Civil Rights, *Report, 1961,* 77.

12.   *New York Times,* Apr. 8, 1961, 1:1.

13.   Howard Lockwood, "Progress in Plans for Progress for Negro Managers," in *Selection and Training of Negroes for Managerial Positions, Proceedings of the Executive Conference, Nov. 10-11, 1964* (Princeton: Educational Testing Service, 1965), 2.

14.   George F. Doriot, ed., *The Management of Racial Integration in Business* (New York: McGraw-Hill, 1964), 104.

15.   *New York Times,* June 18, 1961, 1:2.

16.   Doriot, *The Management,* 104-106.

17.   *New York Times,* Feb. 8, 1962, 20:2.

18.   *Ibid.*

19.   Herbert Hill, "Black Labor in the American Economy," in Patricia W. Romero, ed., *In Black America, 1968* (Washington: United Publishing Corp., 1969), 183.

20.   *New York Times,* June 18, 1962, 17:5.

21.   Sovern, *Legal Restraints,* 117; for a "model" Plan for Progress see, Habbe, *Company Experience,* Vol. I, 136-138.

22.   Doriot, *The Management,* 101.

23.   H. W. Wittenborn, "A Company Case History," AMA Midwinter Personnel Conterence, Feb. 14, 1964, mimeo; partially reprinted in "Equal Employment Opportunity; Company Experience; Symposium," *Management Review,* LIII (Apr., 1964), 16-20.

24.   Lockwood, "Progress," in *The Selection,* 4.

25.   Doriot, *The Management,* 18.

26.   Richard L. Rowan, *"The Negro in the Steel Industry,* Report No. 3, *The Racial Policies of American Industry* (Philadelphia: Industrial Research Unit, Department of Industry, Wharton School of Finance and Commerce, University of Pennsylvania, 1968), 90.

27.   Dwight D. Vines, "The Impact of Title VII of the 1964 Civil Rights Law on Personnel Policies and Practices" (D.B.A. diss., University of Colorado, 1967), 241.

28.   William S. Vaughn, "Equal Employment Opportunity—Eastman Kodak Company's Positive Program," Remarks of the chairman of the board to Annual Meeting, Apr. 25, 1967.

29.   *New York Times,* Feb. 8, 1962, 20:2.

30.   *Ibid.,* Apr. 6, 1962, 23:1

31.   *Ibid.*

32.   *Ibid.,* July 4, 1962, 9:4.

33. Southern Regional Council, "Plans for Progress: Atlanta Survey—Special Report" (Atlanta: Jan., 1963, mimeo.), 2.

34. *New York Times,* Aug. 19, 1962, 1:4.

35. Theodore W. Kheel, *Guide to Fair Employment Practices* (Englewood Cliffs, N.J.: Prentice Hall, 1964), 110-111.

36. President's Committee on Equal Employment Opportunity, *Report to the President* (Washington: GPO, Nov. 26, 1963), 116.

37. Southern Regional Council, "Plans for Progress," 8; *Wall Street Journal,* Nov. 9, 1966, 1:6.

38. Southern Regional Council, "Plans for Progress," 9-11.

39. *Ibid.,* 11.

40. *New York Times,* Apr. 17, 1963, 21:1.

41. Lockwood, "Progress," in *The Selection,* 14.

42. Herbert R. Northrup, *The Negro in the Automobile Industry,* Report No. 1, *The Racial Policies of American Industry* (Philadelphia: Industrial Research Unit, Department of Industry, Wharton School of Finance and Commerce, University of Pennsylvania, 1968), 1-62.

43. *New York Times,* Dec. 3, 1964, 55:1.

44. Arjay Miller, "Comments at Acceptance of Award Presented by the Detroit Round Table of Catholics, Jews and Protestants," Detroit, Dec. 12, 1965, 5, 7-8.

45. *New York Times,* Aug. 28, 1967, 26:3.

46. Joseph L. Hudson, Jr., "The Problems are Here, They are Real and they are Urgent," clipping from unknown magazine, Nov. 1, 1967.

47. *New York Times,* Aug. 28, 1967, 26:3.

48. *Hudson,* "The Problems."

49. *Ibid.*

50. *New York Times,* Oct. 27, 1967, 1:2; *ibid.,* Nov. 10, 1967, 38:3; *ibid.,* Jan. 11, 1968, 49:7.

51. Northrup, *The Negro in the Automobile Industry,* 61-62.

52. *New York Times,* Dec. 20, 1967, 32:3.

53. *New York Times,* Jan. 9, 1968, 22:4.

54. *Ibid.,* Apr. 19, 1968, 47:1.

55. *Ibid.*

56. *Wall Street Journal,* Apr. 26, 1966, 1:5.

57. William G. Caples, "The Challenge of Hope," address to National Conference of Christians and Jews, Cornell Seminar, Oct. 29, 1967, mimeo.

58. *New York Times,* Jan. 24, 1968, 1:3, 24:1.

59. *Ibid.,* Oct. 3, 1967, 1:1; *ibid.,* Oct. 4, 1967, 32:1.

60. *Ibid.,* 42:2.

61. "What Business Can Do For the Cities," *Fortune,* LXXVII (Jan., 1968), 128.

62. U.S. National Advisory Commission on Civil Disorders, *Report* (New York: Bantam Books, 1968), 559-560.

63. *Ibid.,* 561.

64. *Ibid.,* 565-567.

65. *New York Times,* Jan. 24, 1968, 24.

66. *Ibid.;* R. A. Tetu, "Plans for Progress Conference, N.A.B. Presentation," 1968, mimeo.

67. "Tulsa Conference, Summary of Proceedings," National Conference of Local Voluntary Councils on Equal Employment Opportunity, Tulsa, Okla., May 9-10, 1968, mimeo.

68. National Alliance of Businessmen, "A New Partnership," (Washington: [1968]).

69. *New York Times,* Feb. 3, 1968, 19:2.

70.   *Ibid.,* Feb. 3, 1969, 20:1.

71.   *Ibid.,* Oct. 27, 1969, 1:6; *ibid.,* Dec. 26, 1970, 1:4.

72.   *Ibid.,* June 27, 1968, 41:2; "Employing the Unemployables," *U.S. News and World Report* (Aug. 12, 1968), 49-53.

73.   *New York Times,* Feb. 3, 1968, 19:2.

74.   National Alliance of Businessmen, Miami Metropolitan Office, "Miami Business and Industry Leaders Seek Work for 9,000 Hard-Core Jobless," press release, n.d.

75.   Roscoe Drummond, *Racine Journal Times,* Jan. 13, 1968, 10:4.

76.   *New York Times,* April 11, 1970, 62:3; *ibid.,* Dec. 26, 1970, 1:4; *San Francisco Sunday Examiner and Chronicle,* July 19, 1970, 10:3.

77.   *New York Times,* Oct. 27, 1969, 1:6.

78.   William A. Gillett, employee relations advisor, Humble Oil Co., "Comments," National Conference of Voluntary Councils on Equal Employment Opportunity, Tulsa, Okla., May 9, 1968.

79.   *New York Times,* Mar. 25, 1969, 44:1; *ibid.,* Dec. 26, 1970, 1:4; *ibid.,* Feb. 3, 1969, 20:1; Sar A. Levitan et al., *Economic Opportunity in the Ghetto: The Partnership of Government and Business* (Baltimore: The Johns Hopkins Press, 1970), 28-35.

80.   *New York Times,* Feb. 25, 1968, 1:1; *ibid.,* Mar. 25, 1969, 44:1.

81.   Emergency Convocation: The Urban Coalition, "Statement of Principles, Goals and Commitments," Washington, Aug. 24, 1967, mimeo; *New York Times,* Aug. 25, 1967, 1:1.

82.   Emergency Convocation, "Statement of Principles."

83.   *Ibid.*

84.   *New York Times,* Jan. 31, 1968, 2:6.

85.   *Wall Street Journal,* Apr. 17, 1968, 50:3.

86.   *New York Times,* Dec. 5, 1968, 50:3.

87.   *Ibid.,* July 2, 1968, 15:1; *ibid.,* Feb. 14, 1968, 1:4.

88.   Emergency Convocation, "Statement of Principles."

89.   *Wall Street Journal,* April 17, 1968, 1:6.

90.   *New York Times,* Oct. 11, 1967, 1:1.

Bibliography

The following brief bibliography contains only the most useful books and articles dealing with main themes of this book. I have not included difficult to find material, such as privately printed speeches, company reports, etc. Where such material was used it is, of course, contained in the notes. This study depended heavily on published sources, and it would be a monumental task to include even a fair sampling of the more than 1,700 books and articles I used in gathering data. Even the notes in this volume do not contain exhaustive documentation. For every source included in the notes, many more making the same point were deleted. Scholars interested in pursuing additional sources should consult my dissertation, University Microfilms No. 72-22.091.

The archives of the American Friends Service Committee at Haverford College contain thousands of personal interviews conducted by AFSC field workers, who were usually businessmen themselves, during the years after World War II. While the interviews provide fascinating stories and illustrations of the difficulty in getting businessmen to integrate employment, they contribute to, but do not change, conclusions that can be drawn from published materials.

Books

Babow, Irving and Edward Howden, *A Civil Rights Inventory of San Francisco* (San Francisco: Council for Civic Unity, 1958).

Becker, Gary S., *The Economics of Discrimination* (Chicago: University of Chicago Press, 1957).

Blalock, Hubert M., Jr., *Toward a Theory of Minority-Group Relations* (N.Y., Capricorn Books, 1967).

Blood, Robert O., Jr., *Northern Breakthrough* (Belmont, Calif.: Wadsworth Publishing Co., 1968).

Bowen, Howard R., *Social Responsibilities of the Businessman* (New York: Harper & Bros., 1953).

Business and the Urban Crisis (McGraw-Hill, Special Report, 1968).

Canham, Erwin D., ed., *The Disadvantaged Poor: Education and Employment Task Force on Economic Growth and Opportunity, Third Report* (Washington, D.C.: Chamber of Commerce of the United States of America, 1966).

Carmack, William R. and Theodore Freedman, *Factors Affecting School Desegregation: Dallas, Texas, Field Reports on Desegregation in the South* (N.Y.: Anti-Defamation League of B'nai B'rith, 1962).

Cohn, Jules, *The Conscience of the Corporation: Business and Urban Affairs, 1967-1970* (Baltimore: The Johns Hopkins Press, 1971).

Cornuelle, Richard C., *Reclaiming the American Dream* (New York, Random House, 1965).

Doriot, George F., ed., *The Management of Racial Integration in Business* (New York: McGraw-Hill, 1964).

Eells, Richard, *The Meaning of Modern Business* (N.Y., Columbia University Press, 1960).

Eidson, Bettye K., "Major Employers and Their Manpower Policies," in U.S. National Advisory Commission on Civil Disorders, *Supplemental Studies* (Washington, G.P.O., July, 1968).

Garfinkel, Herbert, *When Negroes March* (New York: Free Press, 1959).

Gourlay, Jack C., *The Negro Salaried Worker* (American Management Association Research Study, No. 70., N.Y.: A.M.A., 1965).

Habbe, Stephen, ed., *Company Experience With Negro Employment: Studies in Personnel Policy*, No. 201, 2 vol. (New York: National Industrial Conference Board, 1966).

Heald, Morrell. "Management's Responsibility to Society: The Growth of an Idea," in Greenwood, William T., ed. *Issues in Business and Society: Readings and Cases* (Boston: Houghton Mifflin, 1964).

Heald, Morrell, *The Social Responsibility of Business: Company and Community, 1900-1960* (Cleveland: The Press of Case Western Reserve University, 1970).

Henderson, Vivian W., "Economic Dimensions in Race Relations," in Jitsuichi Masuoka and Preston Valien, eds., *Race Relations: Problems and Theory* (Chapel Hill: University of North Carolina Press, 1961).

Hill, Herbert, "Black Labor in the American Economy," in Patricia W. Romero, ed. *In Black America, 1968: The Year of Awakening* (Washington, D.C.: United Publishing Corp., 1969).

Jones, Major J., *The Negro and Employment Opportunities in the South: Chattanooga* (Atlanta: Southern Regional Council, 1961).

Kesselman, Louis C., *The Social Politics of FEPC: A Study in Reform Pressure Movements* (Chapel Hill: The University of North Carolina Press, 1948).

Kheel, Theodore W., *Guide to Fair Employment Practices* (Englewood Cliffs, N.J.: Prentice Hall, 1964).

Levitan, Sar. A., Garth L. Mangum and Robert Taggart III, *Economic Opportunity in the Ghetto: The Partnership of Government and Business* (Baltimore: The Johns Hopkins Press, 1970).

Merton, Robert K., "Discrimination and the American Creed," in R. M. MacIver, ed. *Discrimination and National Welfare* (New York: Institute for Religious and Social Studies, 1949).

Mohr, Frank T., "Management Policies and Bi-racial Integration in Industry" (Master Thesis, Urbana, Ill.: University of Illinois, 1954).

Myrdal, Gunnar, *An American Dilemma: The Negro Problem and Modern Democracy* (New York: Harper & Bros., 1944).

National Association of Manufacturers, *A Tale of 22 Cities* (New York, NAM, 1964).

National Citizens' Committee for Community Relations and the Community Relations Service of the U.S. Department of Justice, *Putting the Hard-Core Unemployed into Jobs: A Report of the Business-Civic Leadership Conference on Employment Problems, June 5-7, 1967, Chicago, Ill.*, Part II, *Case Studies* (Washington, D.C., G.P.O., 1968).

National Conference of Christians and Jews, *Merit Employment is Good Business* (N.C.C.J., 1967).

National Planning Association, Committee of the South, *Selected Studies of Negro Employment in the South* (Washington, D.C.: National Planning Association, 1955).

Noland, E. William and E. Wight Bakke, *Workers Wanted: A Study of Employer Hiring Policies, Preferences and Practices* (New York: Harper Bros., 1949).

Norgren, Paul H., Albert N. Webster, Roger D. Borgeson and Maud B. Patten, *Employing the Negro in American Industry: A Study of Management Practices,* Industrial Relations Monograph No. 17, (New York: Industrial Relations Counselors, Inc., 1959).

Northrup, Herbert R., ed., *The Negro and Employment Opportunity: Problems and Practices* (Ann Arbor: Bureau of Industrial Relations, Graduate School of Business Administration, University of Michigan, 1965).

Ozanne, Robert, *A Century of Labor-Management Relations at McCormick and International Harvester* (Madison, Wis.: University of Wisconsin Press, 1967).

The Racial Policies of American Industry (Philadelphia: Industrial Research Unit, Department of Industry, Wharton School of Finance and Commerce, University of Pennsylvania), see individual volumes in series.

Roper, Elmo, "The Price Business Pays," in R. M. MacIver, ed., *Discrimination and National Welfare* (New York: Institute for Religious and Social Studies, 1949).

Rosenberg, Bernard and Penney Chapin, "Management and Minority Groups," in Aaron Antonovsky and Lewis L. Lorwin, eds., *Discrimination and Low Incomes* (New York: State of New York Interdepartmental Committee on Low Incomes, 1959).

Ross, Arthur M. and Herbert Hill, eds., *Employment, Race and Poverty* (New York: Harcourt, Brace & World, 1967).

Ruchames, Louis, *Race, Jobs, and Politics: The Story of FEPC* (New York: Columbia University Press, 1953).

Smith, Bob, *They Closed Their Schools* (Chapel Hill: University of North Carolina Press, 1965).

Southall, Sara E., *Industry's Unfinished Business* (N.Y.: Harper, 1950).

Sovern, Michael I., *Legal Restraints on Racial Discrimination in Employment* (N.Y.: Twentieth Century Fund, 1966).

Spilerman, Seymour, "The Distribution of Negro Males Among Industries in 1960" (Baltimore: Ph.D. Dissertation, The Johns Hopkins University, 1968).

Sutton, Francis X., Seymour E. Harris, Carl Kaysen, and James Tobin, *The American Business Creed* (Cambridge, Mass.: Harvard University Press, 1956).

Vines, Dwight Delbert, "The Impact of Title VII of the 1964 Civil Rights Law on Personnel Policies and Practices" (D.B.A. Dissertation, University of Colorado, 1967).

Wachtel, Dawn, *The Negro and Discrimination in Employment* (Ann Arbor: Institute of Industrial and Labor Relations, University of Michigan-Wayne State University, 1965).

Weaver, Robert C., *Negro Labor: A National Problem* (New York: Harcourt, Brace & Co., 1946).

Periodical Articles

"Attack on Bias," *Business Week* (April 30, 1949), 106-108.

Bambrick, J. J. and Harold Stieflitz, "Negro Hiring: Some Case Studies," *Conference Board Management Record* (Dec., 1949), 520.

Batchelder, A., "Decline in the Relative Income of Negro Men," *Quarterly Journal of Economics* (Nov., 1964), 525-548.

Bird, Caroline, "More Room at the Top," *Management Review* (March, 1963), 4-16.

Blalock, H. M., Jr., "Occupational Discrimination: Some Theoretical Propositions," *Social Problems* (Winter, 1962), 240-247.

Blicksilver, Jack, "Special Responsibilities of Businessmen, Parts I-II," *Atlanta Economic Review* (March-April, 1966), 3-5.

Bloch, Herman D., "Discrimination Against the Negro in Employment in New York, 1920-1963," *American Journal of Economics & Sociology*, Oct., 1965), 361-82.

Bloch, Herman D., "Recognition of Discrimination—A Solution," *Journal of Social Psychology* (Nov., 1958), 291-295.

Bullock, Paul, "Combating Discrimination in Employment," *California Management Review* (Summer, 1961), 18-32.

Campbell, T., "Using Fairness and Firmness to Avoid Civil Rights Pains," *Iron Age* (Nov. 18, 1965), 54-56.

Caples, W., "Managers Must Help Integration Succeed", *Iron Age* (Sept. 1, 1966), 71.

Carter, Hodding, "Eisenhower's Program for Economic Equality," *Reader's Digest* (Sept., 1956), 74-78.

Cox, T, "Counselor's Views on Changing Management Policies," *Public Relations Journal* (Nov., 1963), 8-9.

Davis, J., "Negro Employment: A Progress Report," *Fortune* (July, 1952), 102-3ff.

Davis, Keith, "Understanding the Social Responsibility Puzzle," *Business Horizons* (Winter, 1967), 45-50.

Elwert, Bert E., "A New Look at the Soulful Corporation," *Business and Economic Dimensions* (Nov., 1967), 1-6.

Enion, Richard A. & Halward L. Homan, "What are some Industrial Relations Approaches to Integration?", *Personnel Administration* (Nov.-Dec., 1963), 55-57.

"Equal Employment Opportunity: Company Policies and Experience; Symposium," *Management Review* (April, 1964), 4-23.

"Fight That Swirls Around Eastman Kodak," *Business Week* (April 29, 1967), 38-41.

Finely, Grace J., "Business Defines its Social Responsibilities," *Conference Board Record* (Nov., 1967), 9-12.

Forster, A., "In favor of FEPC," *Personnel Journal* (Jan., 1952), 298-303.

Frederick, William C., "The Growing Concern Over Business Responsibility," *California Management Review* (Summer, 1960), 54-61.

"Getting Rid of Prejudice," *Business Week* (July 23, 1949), 72-3.

Glenn, Norval D., "Occupational Benefits to Whites From the Subordination of Negroes," *American Sociological Review* (June, 1963), 443-448.

Glenn, Norval D., "White Gains from Negro Subordination," *Social Problems* (Fall, 1966), 159-178.

Grove, Gene, "Making the System Work," *Tuesday Magazine* (July 15, 1967).

Haynes, Ulric, Jr., "Equal Job Opportunity: The Credibility Gap," *Harvard Business Review* (May-June, 1968), 113-120.

"He Helps the Poor Help Themselves," *Nation's Business* (July, 1967), 42-9.

Hilkert, Robert N., "The Responsibility of Business and Industry for Social Welfare in Today's World," *Federal Reserve Bank of Philadelphia Business Review* (July, 1966), 3-9.

Hodge, R. W. and P. Hodge, "Occupational Assimilation as a Competitive Process," *American Journal of Sociology* (Nov., 1965), 249-264.

Hope, J. "Minority Utilization Practices—Rational or Sentimental?", *Social Research* (June, 1951), 152-170.

"The House Nigger," *News Front* (Nov., 1968).

"Industry Rushes for Negro Grads," *Business Week* (April 25, 1964), 78-80 ff.

"It's Good Business," *Business Week* (March 31, 1951), 38-40.

Johnson, Harold L., "An Evaluation of the Social Responsibility of Businessman Concept," *Atlanta Economic Review* (April, 1957), 1-5.

Johnson, Mead et al. "Consultation: Are Profits and Social Responsibility Compatible?", *Business Horizons* (Summer, 1959), 54-64.

"Labor and Management Fight Prejudice," *Factory Management and Maintenance* (Aug., 1949), 120-121.

Langton, James F., "What Should the Business Response be to the Negro Revolution?", *Public Relations Journal* (June, 1965), 12-17.

Levitt, Theodore, "The Dangers of Social Responsibility," *Harvard Business Review* (Sept.-Oct., 1958), 41-50.

McKersie, Robert B., "The Civil Rights Movement and Employment," *Industrial Relations* (May, 1964) 1-22.

McKersie, Robert B., "The Civil Rights Revolution and the Businessman," *Business Topics* (Summer, 1965), 23-31.

McManus, G. J., "How Industry Views Integration," *Iron Age* (Feb. 27, 1964), 44-45.

Mayfield, H., "Equal Employment Opportunity; Should Hiring Standards Be Relaxed?" *Personnel* (Sept., 1964), 8-17.

Mayfield, H. S., "Seeks Preferred Treatment for Negroes," *National Underwriter (Life ed.)* (Oct. 22, 1966), 21-24.

Miller, G. W., "Equal Policies and Experience," *Management Review* (April, 1964). 4-23.

Miller, Helen Hill, "Business Citizenship in the Deep South," *Business Horizons* (Spring, 1962), 61-1.

Miller, Helen Hill, "Private Business and Education in the South," *Harvard Business Review* (July-Aug., 1960), 75-88.

"More Jobs for Negroes," *Nation's Business* (Sept., 1967), 574-577.

Morrow, Joseph J., "American Negroes—a Wasted Resource," *Harvard Business Review* (Jan., Feb., 1957), 65-74.

"NAM Tracks Down Solutions to Employment Woes," *Steel Magazine* (Sept. 18, 1967).

"The Negro Drive for Jobs," *Business Week* (Aug. 17, 1963), 52-4 ff.

"One Company's Answer to Negro Job Problem," *Business Management* (Feb., 1964), 42-45.

Palmer, Dwight, "The General Cable Corporation," *Modern Industry* (Jan. 15, 1952), 144.

"Preferential Hiring for Negroes: A Debate," *American Child* (Nov., 1963), 1-23.

"Progress on State Street," *Time* (Sept. 14, 1953), 25.

Richberg, Donald R., "Fair Employment Practices Scheme," *Public Utilities Fortnightly* (April 22, 1948), 540-4.

Ross, Malcom, O. Clark Fisher, "Should the U.S. Permanently Ban Racial and Religious Discrimination in Jobs?", *Modern Industry* (April 5, 1945).

Rozelle, W. N., "How is the Negro Faring?", *Textile Industries* (March, 1967), 80-84.

Samuels, Gertrude, "Help Wanted: The Hard-Core Unemployed," *N. Y. Times Magazine* (Jan. 28, 1968), 27 ff.

Silberman, Charles E., "The Businessman and the Negro," *Fortune* (Sept., 1963), 96-9 ff.

Taeuber, Alma F., Karl E. Taeuber and Glen G. Cain, "Occupational Assimilation and the Competitive Process," *American Journal of Sociology* (Nov., 1966), 273-89.

Taylor, David P., "Discrimination and Occupational Wage Differences in the Market for Unskilled Labor," *Industrial and Labor Relations Review* (April, 1968), 375-90.

Walton, Clarence C., "The Changing Face of a Business Corporation's Responsibilities," *Economic and Business Bulletin* (Sept., 1964), 4-14.

"What the Kodak Fracas Means," *Business Week* (May 6, 1967), 192.

"Why Race Riots Strike 'Nice' Northern City," *Business Week* (Aug. 1, 1964), 24.

Wood, David G., "How Businessmen Can Fight Big Government—and Win," *Harper's Magazine* (Nov., 1963), 77-81.

Wright, Nathan, Jr., "Economics of Race," *American Journal of Economics & Sociology* (Jan., 1967), 1-12.

Young, Whitney M., Jr. and K. Haselden, "Should There Be Compensation for Negroes," *New York Times Magazine* (Oct. 6, 1963), 43 ff.

Government Documents

[California] Governor's Commission on the Los Angeles Riots, *Testimony,* Vol. 12, "H. C. McClellan," Los Angeles, Calif., Nov. 1, 1965.

[California] Governor's Commission on the Los Angeles Riots, *Selected Interviews and Other Documents #99,* "Opportunities Industrialization Center" (Phila.?), Nov. 18, 1965.

U. S. Commission on Civil Rights, *The 50 States Reports: submitted to the Commission on Civil Rights by the State Advisory Committees, 1961* (Washington, GPO, 1961).

U. S. Commission on Civil Rights, *Report, 1961: Book 3, Employment* (Washington, G.P.O., 1961).

U. S. Congress, House, Committee on Education and Labor, Hearings, *To Prohibit Discrimination in Employment,* 81 Cong., 1 Sess., May 10-26, 1949.

U. S. Congress, Senate, Committee on Labor and Public Welfare, Subcommittee on Civil Rights, hearings, *Anti-discrimination in Employment,* 83 Cong., 2 Sess., Feb. 23-Mar. 3, 1954.

U. S. Congress, Senate, Committee on Labor and Public Welfare, Subcommittee on Labor and Labor Management Relations, *Discrimination and Full Utilization of Manpower Resources,* 82 Cong., 2 Sess., April 7-May 6, 1952.

U. S. Congress, Senate, Committee on Labor and Public Welfare, Subcommittee on Employment and Manpower, *Equal Employment Opportunity,* 88 Cong., 1 Sess., July 24-Aug. 20, 1963.

U. S. Department of Labor, Bureau of Labor Statistics, *The Negroes in the United States: Their Economic and Social Situation,* Bulletin No. 1511 (Washington, G.P.O., June, 1966).

U. S. Equal Employment Opportunity Commission, *Document and Reference Text: An Index to Minority Group Employment Information* (Ann Arbor, Michigan: Research Division, Institute of Labor and Industrial Relations, University of Michigan—Wayne State University, 1967).

U. S. Equal Employment Opportunity Commission, *Hearings Before the U.S.E.E.O.C. on Discrimination in White Collar Employment: N.Y., N.Y., Jan. 15-18, 1968* (Washington, G.P.O., 1968-b).

U. S. National Advisory Commission on Civil Disorders, *Report,* Appendix H, "Report to the Commission by the Advisory Panel on Private Enterprise, Jan. 29, 1968" (New York: Bantam Books, 1968).

U. S. President's Commission on Government Contracts, *Pattern for Progress: Final Report to President Eisenhower* (Washington, G.P.O., 1960).

U. S. President's Commission on Government Contracts, *Youth Training-Incentives Conference Proceedings* (Washington, G.P.O., April, 1957).

Index